"By drawing on the parables, Kevin Hargaden helps us see that in fact Jesus does have some quite straightforward judgments about wealth and its dangers. He combines that analysis with a stunning knowledge of recent economic understanding that gives him an insightful account of the recent crisis in the Irish economy. This is a book that has been begging to be written and now Kevin Hargaden has done it—no mean feat."

—STANLEY HAUERWAS, author of *The Character of Virtue: Letters to a Godson* (2018)

"Kevin Hargaden has produced a timely, thoughtful, and provocative work of theological ethics. His critique of neoliberalism is highly original and persuasive. His analysis of the ways in which economic values are embedded in cultural practices is brilliant, allowing the reader to understand why neoliberalism persists, despite all of its woes. A deeply challenging but rewarding read."

—LINDA HOGAN, Professor of Ecumenics, Trinity College Dublin

"Hargaden's study is as engaging as it is unsettling precisely because he invites us to consider the theological depth and scope of our 'money troubles.' Working creatively at the intersection of ethics, theology, and economics, Hargaden suggests how attending to the new world attested in Jesus' parables can break open the seeming inevitability of our current economic regimes and animate a worshipful Christian freedom amidst wealth's captivity."

—PHILIP G. ZIEGLER, University of Aberdeen

"We live in an age when it seems we can never have enough, for there is always more to desire and obtain. Kevin ͮ ͮ   ͺ ͺ ͺ ͺ ͺ fantastic opportunity . . . to reflect anew on what Hargaden skillfully brings together co Karl Barth's theology, and a beautiful creatively reimagining what it means t(

GW00570243

—JANA M. BENNETT, University of Dɛ

"Kevin Hargaden is an exciting and prophetic young Irish theological voice, crying out in contemporary idiom and from the heart of the Reformed tradition. His biblical and theological analysis of the problem of wealth is both erudite and provocative . . . which challenges us to resist the hegemony of neoliberalism over our imaginations, and find sources of resistance in the parables of Jesus, theology, and worship."

—GERRY O'HANLON, SJ, theologian, author, and former Provincial of the Irish Jesuits

THEOLOGICAL ETHICS IN A NEOLIBERAL AGE

THEOPOLITICAL VISIONS

SERIES EDITORS:

Thomas Heilke
D. Stephen Long
and Debra Dean Murphy

Theopolitical Visions seeks to open up new vistas on public life, hosting fresh conversations between theology and political theory. This series assembles writers who wish to revive theopolitical imagination for the sake of our common good.

Theopolitical Visions hopes to re-source modern imaginations with those ancient traditions in which political theorists were often also theologians. Whether it was Jeremiah's prophetic vision of exiles "seeking the peace of the city," Plato's illuminations on piety and the civic virtues in the Republic, St. Paul's call to "a common life worthy of the Gospel," St. Augustine's beatific vision of the City of God, or the gothic heights of medieval political theology, much of Western thought has found it necessary to think theologically about politics, and to think politically about theology. This series is founded in the hope that the renewal of such mutual illumination might make a genuine contribution to the peace of our cities.

FORTHCOMING VOLUMES:

David Deane
The Matter of the Spirit: How Soteriology Shapes the Moral Life

THEOLOGICAL ETHICS

in a

NEOLIBERAL AGE

Confronting the Christian Problem with Wealth

KEVIN HARGADEN

FOREWORD BY
WILLIAM T. CAVANAUGH

 CASCADE *Books* • Eugene, Oregon

THEOLOGICAL ETHICS IN A NEOLIBERAL AGE
Confronting the Christian Problem with Wealth

Theopolitical Visions 24

Cascade Books
An Imprint of Wipf and Stock Publishers
199 W. 8th Ave., Suite 3
Eugene, OR 97401

www.wipfandstock.com

PAPERBACK ISBN: 978-1-5326-5500-5
HARDCOVER ISBN: 978-1-5326-5501-2
EBOOK ISBN: 978-1-5326-5502-9

Cataloguing-in-Publication data:

Names: Hargaden, Kevin, author.

Title: Theological ethics in a neoliberal age : confronting the Christian problem with wealth / Kevin Hargaden.

Description: Eugene, OR: Cascade Books, 2018 | Series: Theopolitical Visions 24 | Includes bibliographical references and index.

Identifiers: ISBN 978-1-5326-5500-5 (paperback) | ISBN 978-1-5326-5501-2 (hardcover) | ISBN 978-1-5326-5502-9 (ebook)

Subjects: LCSH: Political theology. |Neoliberalism. | Finance—Ireland.

Classification: BT83 .59 H40 2018 (print) | BT83 .59 (ebook)

All Scripture quotations, unless noted otherwise, are from the New International Version (UK) Bible.

Notice about the use of the Eavan Boland poem with credit to Carcanet for usage in the United Kingdom and the Republic of Ireland, WW Norton for the rest of the world.

Manufactured in the U.S.A.   10/29/18

This book is dedicated with love and gratitude
to Claire Catherine Hargaden, without whom,
in every sense, it could not exist.

Contents

Foreword

AT THE SAME TIME that economics extends its reach into nearly every field of human endeavor, experts from those fields outside of economics who comment on economic matters are told to butt out. Econometrics are peddled as a way to rationalize church-growth strategies, but when Pope Francis critiques the ideology of the "free" market, he is met with admonitions to mind his own business, which is supposedly the area of life cordoned off into "religion." We are repeatedly told that he lacks the requisite expertise, even though he sometimes seems like the only public figure who has something true and sensible to say about economics.

Kevin Hargaden, like Pope Francis, does not worship a god who is only the lord of religion. This book is a call to worship the God of life, all life, the life that happens Monday through Friday, not just the bit that takes place for an hour or so on Sunday morning. That hour is crucial, the focal point of our encounter with the living God, the hour during which we would strap on crash helmets if we really appreciated what was going on, to paraphrase Annie Dillard. But precisely because we are called together during that hour to worship the living God, to encounter the reality that stands at the heart of creation and holds all creation in being, we cannot abandon that creation to other gods. The God of Abraham, Isaac, and Jacob is the God of production, trade, and consumption, which is why the Bible has something to say about harvests and taxes, feasting and fasting. Those who find the details of the Torah puzzling, with its endless instructions for planting trees and sewing garments and cutting hair, should not miss the main point: our God is the God of the material, not merely the spiritual. If religion seems irrelevant to one's life, it is because religion has been defined too narrowly.

The point of all this is not to divinize economics but to humanize it; if God is God, then money is not. Using concrete examples from the Celtic Tiger—the roaring Irish economy based on speculation, which came crashing to earth in 2008—Kevin Hargaden shows how neoliberal economics can become totalizing, taking on divine pretensions. The island of saints and scholars became a land of buyers and sellers, and neoliberal capitalism became a kind of new, idolatrous religion, replete with its own myths, rites, and disciplines. Hargaden deftly shows how neoliberalism created a new sense of the self, in which people were encouraged to think of themselves as repositories of human capital developing their marketable skills. Debt created a future without any foreseeable rupture, a future without forgiveness and redemption. With a genuine Irish flair for storytelling, Hargaden shows us not only the economic but also the spiritual and human toll that the new religion extracted from his fellow citizens.

To deflate the pretensions of neoliberal economics, Hargaden turns not to some alternative grand revolutionary scheme to remake the world from the top down but to the parables of Jesus, which often touch on matters of economy. Jesus did not advocate burning down the current system and starting over; he was too radical to offer an alternative system or plan to solve all the world's injustices, as soon as all the right people are killed or coerced. As Hargaden puts it, revelation comes before revolution; Jesus' parables give people a sense for how to live into the coming kingdom of God through their everyday actions. The revolution that is the kingdom of God does not succeed by coercion. It requires not grand gestures of overhauling the system, but rather the attentiveness of ordinary people to the new things that God is doing in our midst. Jesus' parables reorient the listener to question the status quo and to attempt more faithful ways of living, building up a new society within the shell of the old.

Jesus' parables are both universal and adapted to the context in which he lived. What kind of parables would Jesus tell today? Combining a rich theological imagination with a firm grasp of property speculation and debt structuring and tax policy, Hargaden finds the equivalents of the rich young man, the hard master, the unfaithful steward and more in contemporary Ireland. Rooting his analysis in one particular context allows Hargaden to put flesh and blood on the bones of theory; the reader's attention is held and imagination is kindled by concrete stories of what went wrong in Ireland, in a way that abstract analysis of neoliberalism alone could never do. But the story Hargaden tells, like neoliberalism itself, is universal, extending well beyond Ireland to every part of the globe. Lest we think it can't happen here, it already has happened and is happening here, though perhaps not as abruptly or dramatically as in Ireland. We might think that the economic crisis of 2008 is now safely behind us, but even if another crash is not imminent, the underlying problems remain. For what went wrong in Ireland is not just the crash but the boom that preceded the crash. This is what makes Hargaden's book so challenging for us in the rich world. The problem is not just poverty, but wealth, especially the kind of pursuit of wealth that destroys community, turns basic human needs like housing and food into commodities, abandons the common good to private interests, favors owners over workers, turns from care of neighbor to a cosmopolitanism of capital, distorts the human person into a marketable product, and finally turns away from the worship of God to idolatry.

The only thing that will defy this idolatry is worship of the true God. Although Hargaden points toward a multitude of resistances from fresh cooperative ways of engaging in production and trade to Distributism to "micro-aggressions against Mammon," the root of any resistance goes back to that hour or so on Sunday morning when communities come together to worship God. Worship, in Hargaden's wonderful phrase, is the "engine-room of reality," the place where God comes to meet us and we become oriented toward the way things really are, shaped into a different kind of social body than the one the powers that be would discipline us into. Hargaden helpfully extends my work on the Eucharist to emphasize preaching (something we Catholics are not exactly known for). Preaching is not about talking to each other or talking to God, but about the Word of God breaking into our world and reorienting us toward the kingdom. It is here that we face the truth that all we have is through grace and that grace is all we have. This liberation from the illusion of our self-sufficiency is the beginning of a "liberation theology for the rich."

This is a brilliant and faithful book, and a wonderful read. We are told that theology is otherworldly and economics is concrete, but Hargaden shows that in fact neoliberalism encourages abstraction from the real world, and God calls us back to earth, to attend not to metrics but to the actual joys and sufferings of people. This book illustrates what worshipping an incarnate God looks like.

WILLIAM T. CAVANAUGH

DePaul University

Acknowledgements

This book began life as a PhD thesis at the University of Aberdeen. The first people to acknowledge, therefore, are my supervisors, Brian Brock and Stanley Hauerwas, who shared their wisdom, encouragement, and friendship in a way that has profoundly shaped me. I thank God for their friendship. The wider faculty at Aberdeen, especially Mike Mawson, Mike Laffin, Phil Ziegler, Tom Greggs, and John Swinton were a tremendous encouragement to me. Lisa Evans cannot go unmentioned, since she probably answered more of my dumb questions than everyone else combined.

My fellow students at Aberdeen played a central role in the forming of this argument. I shall forever owe Taido Chino, Declan Kelly, Joey Lear, DJ Konz, Matt Burdette, David Lilley, Allen Calhoun, Andrew Errington, Emily Hill, Ben Paulus, Amy Erickson, Wilson Tan, Joy Allan, and many other friends—most notably Alison, Mer, Hannah, Ruth, and Stephanie—a pint in Six Degrees North and in some instances even a purple Snack bar.

My research in Aberdeen was funded by the National University of Ireland who kindly made me one of their Travelling Students and the Kirby Laing Institute for Christian Ethics who made me one of their Transforming Business award holders.

I discovered my love of theology in the church, and so with joy I note the role that the congregations at Maynooth and Lucan have played in my life. In Aberdeen, the ministry of Isaac Poobalan was a balm and back in Dublin, I rely on the wise counsel of Richard Houston. There are many, many, many friends who helped me in diverse ways over the years as I researched and wrote this book. With Cian and Meaigs Synnott and Andrew Stribblehill at the top of that list, I express my gratitude.

These words are written in the lovely office provided to me by the Jesuit Centre for Faith and Justice. I never anticipated becoming a Christian, never mind a theologian. But it is strangely fitting that this evangelical Presbyterian has been welcomed with such warmth by the Society of Jesus in Ireland. I am grateful especially for the support of my colleagues, most notably John Guiney, SJ.

The extended Hargaden clan have been typically low-key in their enthusiasm for this project, and as a Hargaden, I appreciate that approach. From Iarlaith dismissing any doctor who can't help a sick tummy to Eamonn and Bríd's constant affectionate encouragement, I thank my parents, my siblings, my nieces and nephews.

I've never been to Eugene, Oregon, but I hope to one day visit and express in person my thanks to the good folk at Wipf and Stock for taking this project on, especially Calvin Jaffarian and Rodney Clapp. I am grateful to Róisín Nic Cóil, Amy Laura Hall, and Martina Madden for their insight as I finalized this text.

Finally, reader, let me tell you about this girl I met twenty years ago. She was sharp and funny and her voice reflected her character, speaking with confidence and clarity and a profound gentleness driven by a love of justice. She introduced me to grace. She argued me into seeing the importance of theology. She left the city she loved and moved near the Arctic Circle and put her vocation on hold to let me think these things through. Most of the good ideas are hers. If you notice a lovely turn of phrase, I probably robbed it from her. Claire remains the reader I most desperately want to impress. Repaying my debt to her is the greatest pleasure a man could have.

As I write these final paragraphs, we are expecting the imminent birth of our first child. The hope of meeting him has been warming me through the months of finishing this project. I hope he reads and enjoys this book some time in the future, but more, my hope is that he will know and enjoy the God who stitched him together with an abundant love, which means he need never listen to the voices of the false gods that whisper that he has to take care of himself because there is not enough to go around.

Réamhrá

BEALACH ISTEACH

In Irish, *réamhrá* is the word for preamble. Quite literally it means a pre-talk. It suggests a pronouncement is about to begin. It heralds important speech. Who knows whether this introduction meets this lofty standard and rises above the throat-clearing that passes for most of our theology, but what we seek here is *bealach isteach*, an entrance point, an opening, a means of access. The problem of wealth is complex and we need a way inside, a path to get beyond issues so intricate that we often feel blocked from thinking about them. The purpose of this book is to consider the ethical difficulties that wealth poses to followers of Jesus. In his extensive engagement with concepts around money, profit, and wealth, Jesus appears (at best) ambivalent to the holding of riches. This puts Western Christians, who typically enjoy a material standard of life the like of which is unequalled in human history, in a precarious position.

This problem is, regrettably, not amenable to a simple solution. Jesus can say to one person that they should sell everything and give it to the poor, but Peter seems to keep his fishing boats. If taken crudely, Jesus's radical generosity can be construed as a form of altruistic trickle-down economics whereby the rich give to the poor, making them slightly less poor, before they give on down the pyramid to those below them, *ad infinitum*. Jesus's complex teaching here is clearly not a poverty alleviation scheme. Something deeper is at work at the level of our basic and fundamental desires and convictions. Jesus draws this out when he declares that we cannot love both God and Mammon. Wealth is depicted as a master, or a lord, or an idol whose quiet power can surreptitiously claim our allegiance.[1] When Jesus's

---

1. For the purposes of this book, we will work with a minimal definition of wealth as "the abundance of material possessions." This brief definition, informed by the biblical usage of the term, is intentionally blunt. It seeks to press the concept as something

XV

parables subvert the idea of prudent financial management and when his teaching advocates for apparently self-defeating economic practices, the conclusion must be drawn that Jesus is pursuing something other than fiscal sobriety amongst his followers.

Thus, the oft-quoted words of Paul in 1 Timothy, that it is the *love* of money that is the root of evil, is not a loophole that liberates the conscience of the rich Christian. Rather, it is an acceleration of our complication. Under the surface of the destructive effects of wealth, or the corrosive consequences of capitalism, there lies an idolatrous commitment to a force and a power that is not God, which in Jesus's teaching is presented as anti-God. To help unravel what it means to be wealthy Christians in the West, we must find a way to examine the weave that Mammon snakes around us in our daily lives. We need *a way inside* the hold that wealth has on us.

This book, then, intends to be a constructive work of Christian ethics that presents a theological analysis of wealth, and by reference to the parables, charts an alternative approach to being rich and following Jesus. It takes as its subject matter the recent economic history of the Republic of Ireland. I began thinking about these problems when members of the church I was pastoring shared their own struggles with reconciling their wealth with their faith. During the Celtic Tiger their salaries kept rising and the troubling words of Jesus about money persisted, largely avoided in ecclesial speech. With the crash in 2008 this problem did not go away. Although economic hardship was widespread and often severe, relative and objective wealth remained a lived reality.

Ireland is an interesting microcosm in which to consider neoliberal capitalism. An island nation, the economic vitality of which relies on open trading, Ireland has been one of the most remarkable beneficiaries of the form of capitalism that has emerged in the last quarter of the twentieth century, and since 2008, one of its most striking victims.[2] The insights gathered by considering a peripheral island on the Atlantic edge of Europe can be scaled to other Western settings because of the common assumptions and

---

that implicates us individually. It is not ignorant of the ways in which wealth functions non-materially (in, for example, cultural capital) because such entitlements are almost always associated with a prior material wealth. Martin, "Wealth," 1371.

2. This work concerns itself centrally with capitalism. A word on the usage is in order. On the one hand, the deployment of capitalism and associated synonyms is meant here in its broadest possible sense; an economic system that "involves the investment of money to make more money." Fulcher, *Capitalism: A Very Short Introduction*, 18. But the specific usage relates to how that very general definition is applied to Ireland. In this essay the instantiation of capitalism in Ireland is often referred to as "neoliberalism." Thus, when "neoliberalism" is encountered, it is specifically alluding to the real, existing economic system in Ireland. Ganti, "Neoliberalism," 93.

practices at play through capitalism. The universal begins with the parochial, and so the relatively tangential dramas of boom and bust that afflicted Ireland nonetheless have relevance for other places and other peoples, at the very least as a cautionary tale.[3]

Ireland won its independence in 1922 after a prolonged battle with British forces and a relatively brief civil war. The island was partitioned into two regions. Northern Ireland was made up of six of the nine counties that constituted the ancient province of Ulster. It continued to be part of the United Kingdom. The remaining twenty-six counties were brought together under a Dublin-based government that functioned as a dominion of the British Empire.[4]

Recovering from the Civil War and establishing the structures that would sustain independence was the central concern of the early years of the *Dáil* (the Irish parliament) and no major shift in economic policies was envisioned or attempted. In the words of the economist Cormac Ó'Gráda, the first government "made virtues of continuity and caution."[5] The economic policy flowed out of the triumphant political nationalism of the era.[6] Self-sufficiency was the goal. Internal industrial development would be fostered by agricultural exports. Patrick Hogan, the Minister for Agriculture, is reported as describing the economic policy as one of "helping the farmer who helped himself and letting the rest go to the devil."[7] Neutrality in World War II was of a piece with Irish economic

---

3. Karl Barth, whose work will be decisive in this book, implemented a method that broadly followed the same trajectory. "It is not the general which comes first but the particular. The general does not exist without this particular and cannot therefore be prior to the particular. . . . Thus we cannot move from the general to the particular, but only in the opposite direction—from this particular to the general." Barth, *Church Dogmatics II/1*, 602. In the Irish context, one thinks here of the poetry of Pádraig O'Túama, which explicitly takes up Robert Frost's contention that "in order to be universal, poetry must be parochial." Ó'Túama, *Sorry for Your Troubles*, 64.

4. A strategically gradual process of distancing led, eventually, to Ireland declaring itself a Republic in 1937.

5. Ó'Gráda, *A Rocky Road*, 4.

6. The cultural revival that played such a decisive role in the independence movement was driven by an aesthetic opposition to industrialized modernity. Keating and Desmond summarize the particular influence of these figures with a quote from the writer Sean O'Casey: "Ireland never was, never will be . . . furnace-burned . . . Commercialism is far from her shores . . . she, in her language, national dramatic revival, has turned her back upon Mammon." Keating and Desmond, *Culture and Capitalism in Contemporary Ireland*, 185.

7. Haughton, "Historical Background," 26.

isolationism; by the time war broke out in Europe, Ireland had over 2,000 protective trade measures in place.[8]

This policy changed decisively in the late 1950s. In the face of a stagnant economy, rampant unemployment, and massive emigration, a concerted shift to a more open, export-led trading economy was initiated. Ireland reformed its education system, opened its markets, actively courted foreign investment, tailored tax law to encourage commerce, and set itself on a trajectory to join the emerging European Economic Community.[9]

After years of modest growth, these measures seemed to yield a dramatic harvest in the mid-1990s. In one year alone, 1994, the Irish economy grew by almost a tenth, 50,000 people were added to the work force, and unemployment plummeted.[10] The growth continued and continued. The development came to be known as the "Celtic Tiger."[11] Clinch, Convery, and Walsh capture the national feeling of felicity when, writing in 2000, they compare the Celtic Tiger to "receiving an unexpected but welcome baby."[12] This surprise matured into a tentative expectation that things could stay this way forever. We can see this as early as 2004, when Tom Garvin comments on how "in the current literature, despite the spectacular growth of the 1990s, an underlying disquiet seems to resurface from time to time, as though these good times could not last."[13] That the disquiet was only occasional represents a phenomenal transformation in Irish self-understanding.

Yet these times were indeed coming to an end. The global economy twice went into recession at the turn of the millennium, first with the dotcom crash and then in the aftermath of the September 2001 attacks in America. During this period, Ireland's growth was sustained. However, the underlying economic activity had shifted towards property speculation. All the data remained positive through the subsequent years—the government returned surpluses, there was full employment (which, in one of the many confusing aspects of capitalism, still means that there is some unemployment), wages were rising, investment was flooding in—but it was all largely driven by the buying and selling of buildings. Warnings of a global financial panic were sounded in 2007 but went unheeded in Ireland.[14] When the

8. O'Hearn, *Inside the Celtic Tiger*, 36.

9. This transition is captured in an essay by T. K. Whitaker, a prominent civil servant seen as one of the critical architects of the wider policy shift. Whitaker, "From Protection to Free Trade—The Irish Experience."

10. Kirby, *Celtic Tiger in Collapse*, 33.

11. Gardiner, "The Irish Economy."

12. Clinch, Convery, and Walsh, *After the Celtic Tiger*, 24.

13. Garvin, *Preventing the Future*, 153.

14. Donovan and Murphy, *The Fall of the Celtic Tiger*, 171–72.

New York-based investment bank Lehmann Brothers went bankrupt in September 2008, the consequences in Ireland were swift. Within weeks, all six Irish banks were drained of liquidity and were quickly approaching the point of insolvency. The Irish government stepped in with a blanket bank guarantee, assuming that the roaring Tiger had the muscle to fight its way out of a tight spot.[15] Their assumption was wrong.

The bank guarantee was to cost many billions more than the Irish State's annual budget. The construction industry stalled as the property bubble burst. Tax-takes dwindled. Unemployment rose. The country went into a steep depression, adopted austerity economics, and yet still, two years later, in autumn 2010, it needed to call for a bailout from the International Monetary Fund and the European Union.[16] That process lasted four years. Now, a decade on from the collapse, many of Ireland's economic metrics have recovered, but the scars of austerity abound.

The wealth that was accumulated so rapidly through the boom remains relevant in the aftermath. Ireland is still firmly a first-world country, with standards of living comparable to other Western countries. While that wealth is spread with an injurious inequality and while the years of austerity have disproportionately afflicted the impoverished, the sick, the disabled, the young, and the old, the political imagination that gave rise to the Celtic Tiger, still holds sway.[17] The shattering experience of the 2008 crash has not prompted a re-examination of the desires and policies that brought the crash to bear. Instead, Ireland is as consumed with the pursuit of wealth in its bust as it was in its boom. The need for a theological analysis is as pertinent as ever.

The Path of the Argument

The course of this theological analysis will run as follows: In chapter 1, we will situate our study of wealth in terms of the concrete arrangements that generate it. Ireland's political and economic commitments lie firmly within the domain of what has come to be known as neoliberal capitalism. The goal in this chapter is to get under the surface of political rhetoric about free markets and globalization, to consider the ways in which economic values are embedded in cultural practices. Only when this is established can

15. Cooper, *Who Really Runs Ireland*, 319–26.

16. The bailout was orchestrated between the International Monetary Fund, the European Commission and the European Central Bank. This three-fold partnership is most commonly referred to, in both academic and popular discourse, as "the Troika."

17. Staunton, "The Distribution of Wealth in Ireland."

we properly identify the ways in which neoliberal capitalism might pose a theological problem for Christians.

In chapter 2, we turn to the parables of Jesus and consider them as apocalyptic narratives that announce and describe the kingdom of God. With the help of Karl Barth's exegesis, we will begin to see the ways in which in the parables mark out the uncommon sense of the kingdom. In an age when neoliberalism appears to be hegemonic, the parables point to the reality that all time is God's, and no human system or construct can vie with the lordship of Jesus. This will be established by paying close attention to how Barth reads the three parables of Matthew 25. There we find Jesus as an "insistent Lord" who subverts even our standard ideas of revolutionary fervor.

Thus, the parables shatter the totalized accounts of neoliberal capitalism. They direct us to another world that is coming and is already here in the kingdom of Jesus. With that in mind, we will return in chapter 3 to the business of real, existing capitalism, but this time we will re-describe the recent economic history of Ireland, which has been alluded to above, through three narratives. These homemade parables will seek to sketch an accurate account of the crash and its aftermath without recourse to the political rhetoric of economic vocabulary. Bypassing the abstractions and obfuscations that so often are used to describe the economy allows us to see the ways in which economic reality impinges on the lives of ordinary people. Theologically, of course, revelation always involves a hiddenness and vice versa, so obfuscation in and of itself is not the issue. Parables stand distinct as a genre, in part, based on their contents, which tease and allude towards a conclusion without stating it. There is a particular form of obfuscation that is presented as if it is transparent because it is objective that is here being interrogated. The abstraction of econometric language obscures while posing as if it has laid things out clearly. Key ethical questions will arise that would be hidden if we were content to settle on the statistical snapshots that usually drive such analyses.

The stage will then be set for the decisively constructive chapter, which will propose worship as a response to the problem of wealth. In the normal course of things, it is in worship that the parables are encountered as God's word. Worship becomes the site from which a response to wealth can be generated. If Christians in the West come to see the wealth they inherit as a result of neoliberal capitalism as problematic, there are two obvious modes of response. The first approach is to seek to reform the system that is identified as unjust. The second is to seek to withdraw from the corrupt dynamics and craft communities of difference based around some alternative economic logic. Both of these approaches are called into question, and in their place what is proposed is an embrace of worship as a reparative counter-formation that opposes the vagaries of neoliberal capitalism without committing to the conceit that we can evade it. This approach builds on the work of various theologians of worship, most notably William Cavanaugh, to articulate praise as a politically potent mode of resistance. Worship will give rise to action in the public sphere, but that action will be sufficiently different from place to place and time to time as to render any general predictions meaningless. The book closes with a brief afterword on lament as the appropriate mode for worship in the face of our wealth.

It may be appropriate at this juncture to forewarn the reader that the structure of this argument may be a little unusual. We are familiar with books that proceed in a linear format, constructed as straightforward Hellenistic syllogisms, where certain readings are established, building one atop another, until a conclusion can be drawn. This book is chiastic in nature. Chiasm is a term that has been "used loosely to refer to all types of literary structures, particularly those with some inversion of themes" and such an approach is adopted here.[18] There is a structural parallelism at play such that chapter one's diagnosis of neoliberalism is mirrored in chapter 3's retelling of the Irish financial crash, and chapter 2's exploration of the apocalyptic vision offered by the parables is echoed in chapter 4's proposal that worship is the location of Christian counter-formation in the face of neoliberalism's pervasive influence. The allusion to biblical rhetorical formats may not be the most illuminating available. Another way to consider the structure of this argument is as a simple two-step dance. With the left foot we begin by considering neoliberalism. Our right foot then responds by introducing Barth's interpretation of the parables. With our stance established, we can pivot gracefully with our left foot towards a close examination of neoliberalism in a specific locale (Ireland) and our right foot brings the movement to a close by broadening out from the parables to the wider potential for worship to constitute a response to Mammon's temptations.[19]

Time plays a critical role throughout the argument. Whether we turn to the accounts of physicists who consider time as "myriad quantum states separated by tiny gaps" that only feel to us a continuous flow,[20] or to technologists who assure us that our networks and gadgets will continue to ratchet

---

18. Bailey, *Poet & Peasant and Through Peasant Eyes*, 48, 47–49. See also: Bailey and Vander Broek, eds., *Literary Forms in the New Testament - A Handbook*, 49–54 and McBride, "Esther Passes: Chiasm, Lex Talio, and Money in the Book of Esther," 212.

19. It is important to note that this dance analogy is purely theoretical. The author's elegance on the dance-floor is as far removed from "finesse" as someone stumbling over a curb they have not noticed. It is hoped his arguments are somewhat less likely to step on the toes of his collaborators.

20. Gribbon, *The Time Illusion*, 43.

up the intensity of our experience of time until "we are bumping against a speed limit" defined by how fast our neurons fire,[21] or our bosses who operate off the assumption that time is money,[22] the common understanding of time is that it is speed and it is empty. It can be sliced into smaller sections, regulated and moderated. This understanding of time is contested throughout this argument. The apparent age of neoliberalism in which we live needs nothing more than the author's cheap Casio to keep time. In the kingdom of God, time need not be grasped. In the in-between time in which we live, we must retrain our attention so that the abundance that the Christian tradition claims can be found in creation applies to time as well as to space. If the argument is structurally similar to a dance, kingdom time is the rhythm we seek to keep up with.

Stanley Hauerwas has argued that "we are required to believe by the Gospel that being wealthy is a disability for anyone who desires to be a Christian."[23] Articulating this project as a work of disability theology may be taking things too far, but the basic assumption with which we begin our work is that wealth weakens our vision. The rich man lived his life with Lazarus at his gate and he never paid his neighbour any heed. We, likewise, comfortable in our luxuries, are too distracted by the maintenance of our convenience to perceive reality as it truly is. There is no intrinsic worth in poverty, but there is an inherent risk in wealth. When we take for granted the things we receive by the contingent fact of being born where we were born, when we were born, we are habituated into a way of life that is already opposed to the basic claim the gospel makes about our existence: that it is grace all the way down.

This theology of wealth might aspire to be a liberation theology for the rich, searching for a way out of our captivity to Mammon. It might aim at being a disability theology for those who are convinced they are self-sufficient, pointing them towards their deep reliance on the toil and sweat and labor of others. But what it must be, fundamentally, is an argument about God. Jesus was a homeless itinerant[24] who relied on the charity of women to survive.[25] He told us to model our economic life on the birds of the air.[26] We are told to resist selfish ambition, to concern ourselves with the interests of others,

---

21. Gleick, *Faster*, 100.
22. Duhigg, *Smarter Faster Better*.
23. Hauerwas, *The State of the University*, 47.
24. Luke 9:58.
25. Luke 8:3.
26. Matthew 6:26–27.

because to do so is to be like Jesus, who emptied himself in true humility.[27] The riches of friendship with God are beyond the dreams of Leo Messi, Bill Gates, or King Midas. All the gold, stock options, and crypto-currency you can get your hands on pale in comparison to the treasure at your disposal when called out to worship with the people of God. This apparently trite, easily dismissed claim demands justification. The argument outlined here is an attempt to put flesh and bones on this basic doctrinal commitment. There is no sacrifice that could be asked of us on our path of discipleship that comes close to the generosity God shows us in every passing moment of our lives.

27. Phil 2:3–11.

CHAPTER 1

We're All Neoliberal Now

The Time as it is on the Clock

INTRODUCTION

The Irish economy catastrophically collapsed in 2008. Effects of the global financial crisis arrived like a tsunami, sweeping away decades of consistent economic growth. The Irish population struggled to keep up with the news reports detailing an opaque world that was alien to many; discussions about credit default swaps and margin calls were unfamiliar territory, even if they were intrinsic components of the financial machinery that had produced prosperity.

Shock and confusion held sway during those weeks at the end of September 2008. As the details slowly emerged, it became obvious that widespread corruption and collusion was conducted at the highest levels of Irish financial institutions.[1] Yet cases were not promptly brought to trial. It took eight years to prosecute any senior bankers.[2] Assembling an explanation for how things went so wrong—the factors that led to the financial crash in the United States, the details of how Irish banks sourced liquidity, the particular political arrangements that shaped a culture of lax regulation—was so complicated that it was understandable if some sought for particular culprits, or even scapegoats.

For that reason, in the midst of the nadir of the crisis in October 2012, widespread dismay followed when it was announced that a prosecution was being prepared against two fishermen in the southern town of Kilmore Quay. On October 3 of that year, Jimmy Byrne, the captain of a fishing vessel

---

1. David Murphy and Martina Devlin, two prominent Irish journalists, offer an account of one such revelation involving the failed Anglo Irish Bank based on their contemporaneous reporting in their book, *Banksters*, 135–63.

2. Mac Cormaic, "Anglo Trial."

called *Saltees Crest*, which was owned by Seamus O'Flaherty, alerted locals and authorities that he was coming into harbor with a haul of monkfish for which he had no EU quota. Instead of dumping the fish, dead, into shallow waters, as regulations decreed, he intended to give the fish away for free. A crowd met the trawler as it docked and the crew placed 3,000 kilograms of fish, worth over €10,000, in 130 boxes on the pier wall for collection by anyone who cared to take some home.[3] A member of *an Garda Síochána* (the Irish police force) was also present and a report was prepared for the Sea Fisheries Protection Authority who arrived the following day to carry out a full inspection. They quickly condemned the actions of the crew and had a file prepared for the Director of Public Prosecutions.

Mr. Byrne accounted for his actions in an article in the *Irish Times* on October 5, saying:

> Four hundred thousand people are unemployed and people are ashamed to admit they don't have enough money to feed themselves. Children are going to school without breakfast or coming home to no dinner while we are encouraged by the Government to throw these fish back into the sea. I personally know people who are going hungry—this is why I had to take a stand.[4]

This case is profoundly complicated. On the surface, it appears to be an example of the kind of serious regulatory enforcement that Irish people wished had been applied to the banks, and yet in this instance it was met with an outcry.[5] The rationale for the regulations is environmental; the preservation of a sustainable fish stock in European seas is something that few people disagree with in principle. The specific crime is financial; the distribution of thousands of euros worth of a resource to which the fishing crew had no rights. The justification for the action is tied expressly with the larger issue of economic austerity facing Ireland. Yet in substance, the protest is part of a particular debate about national sovereignty, the ways in which the EU is seen to adversely restrict Irish industry, and the sense that Ireland as a minnow on the global stage is exploited by larger powers.[6] As economic

3. Furlong, "No Catch as Fish given Away Free."

4. McMahon, "Skipper Defends Giving Away Free Fish."

5. Moloney, "Fisherman Fight EU Dumping Disgrace."

6. This is made clear in an interview that the two men gave in the Irish Republican (in the Irish sense of the word) newspaper *An Phoblacht*. There, the protest is explicitly articulated as being "triggered by widespread anger over the EU's Common Fisheries Policy. In EU law, Ireland is part of the North Atlantic Area VII fishing zone, which is 75 percent Irish water. Despite this, Irish fishermen are only entitled to catch 7.6 percent of the monkfish quota here; France gets 55 percent, the Netherlands 22 percent, Britain 14 percent, and Spain 7 percent." Moloney, "Fisherman Fight EU Dumping Disgrace."

decisions about Ireland were in the hands of administrators of the EU/IMF bailout, these fishermen were staging a protest they said was about hunger, which regulators declared to be an environmental crime, and which was at base a gesture of discontent against what they saw as the infringement of their liberty by these large, distant, anonymous bodies that were exerting control on Irish life through an intricate web.

The protest at Kilmore Quay can be read from a range of perspectives and that those different narratives stack one on top of the other indicates how a certain understanding of economy now has a totalized grasp on our imaginations. Whether the dispute is about hunger, or creation care, or political authority, it will invariably crystallize in the public discourse in economic terms.

Even though the causes of the economic crash may not have been well understood throughout Irish society, the effects were felt everywhere. The case of the free monkfish is just one example of how the consequences of the end of the Celtic Tiger worked their way out in a Byzantine array of legal maneuvers, populist outrage, financial sanctions, and political intrigue. Thinking hard about wealth in Ireland requires more than a straightforward engagement with economic statistics. The statistics, after all, are not the real thing. The statistics point, however crudely or accurately, to the real business of fishermen and police officers meeting at a remote dock on a cold October night to squabble about boxes of fish. The dawn light of Kilmore Quay is a good place to start asking questions about economic ethics. The age in which free fish prompts active policing is an interesting one, doubly so when the absence of regulation of capital had such tragic consequences.

The argument unfolded in this book is a serious engagement with the economic age in which we live. In this chapter we begin to describe the complex ways in which the practices of the marketplace, the regulation of the state, and the academic study of economics interact in a particular place to generate something we call "the economy." We will turn to the writings of Karl Polanyi, a twentieth-century theorist, to articulate a description of the complicated mix of economic, political, and philosophical forces that are at work in the case of complimentary monkfish, as well as in the larger economic sphere. That dynamic, it will be argued, is best described as "neoliberalism"; a nexus of factors that shape and discipline society in such a way as to make it possible for giving away for free things caught in the sea to be considered a crime.

Thus, to live in Ireland in the contemporary era (and to live in many other places beside) is to live as neoliberal subjects. Framing our conversation in this way allows us to understand the entangled local factors in the light of a broader dialogue. Cultural theorists, economists, philosophers, and others will be drawn upon to ground this description in a meaningful sense. Only with such parameters in place can the argument move on to its conclusion. Neoliberalism represents a theological problem for Christians because those who live under its reign are encouraged to share a vision for our common life that is unavoidably idolatrous. As neoliberal subjects, we are trained in a rationality that seeks to apply the methods of economics to all aspects of life.

From this perspective, neoliberalism can perhaps best be viewed as "a particular school of ethics, one which provides a powerful and compelling description of human life."[7] Gary Becker is often cited as a key figure in the rise of this totalized perspective.[8] Indeed, Michel Foucault engages with him at length in his famous lectures on neoliberalism.[9] What matters is not so much the influence of solitary figures, but the ways in which those ideas diffuse through society and function at a popular level[10] and a policy level, transforming every ethical issue into an opportunity to imagine *homo oeconomicus* at work.[11]

At the end of this chapter, then, an argument will have been made that the age we live in appears to be the age of neoliberalism. We are all neoliberal subjects; there is no alternative. Society increasingly serves the market, which is a dramatic inversion of the preceding historical settlement. If prosperity arises from the machinations of the economy, only by naming that economic age can we consider the theological implications and imagine the theological responses possible for Christians who find themselves wealthy.

The prosecution of the fishermen has not, thus far, been advanced. The effects of the economic crash linger still, both in the hardship of the poor and in the growing wealth of the rich. "How now shall we live?" is a question that first requires knowing what "now" means.

---

7. This is from Kathryn Blanchard's book, which deserves a wide readership. Blanchard, *The Protestant Ethic or the Spirit of Capitalism*, 162.

8. Chiappori and Levitt, "An Examination of the Influence of Theory and Individual Theorists on Empirical Research in Microeconomics."

9. Foucault, *The Birth of Biopolitics*; see especially 218–33.

10. *Freakonomics* is the best known of such works. It includes the somewhat contentious claim that the legalization of abortion in the USA triggered, "a generation later, the greatest crime drop in recorded history." Levitt and Dubner, *Freakonomics*, 6. Others include: Frank, *The Economic Naturalist*; Harford, *The Undercover Economist*.

11. For example, the widespread experimentation in the creation of "tradable property in environmental services" as a means of addressing climate change. Robertson, "Discovering Price in All the Wrong Places," 503.

Polanyi's Insight: Locating the Economy

Historians sometimes chart the moment when Boris Yeltsin lost his faith in communism to an unscheduled stop, while on an official visit to the USA in 1989, at a grocery store in Clear Lake, Texas. On his way from a NASA research center to the airport, the Russian leader did what many visitors to foreign lands do: he checked out the food for sale. He had his driver visit a supermarket to look around. Jeffrey Kripal reports that Yeltsin and his entourage "were flabbergasted by a profusion of carefully arranged and beautifully lit fruits, vegetables, meats, cheeses, frozen entrees, and canned goods too numerous to count."[12] Yeltsin and his delegation knew that the Soviet citizen could never dream of such excess and returned home shaken and dispirited.

Capitalism generates this baffling diversity of goods that seek to satisfy consumer desire. It is important to note on these pages that this applies to theological publishing as much as to breakfast cereal. Log on to your preferred global trading behemoth's website or visit your local independent bookseller and you will encounter a huge range of texts that engage with poverty, wealth, and the history of the church's interaction with those concepts. Every product in the marketplace requires a "Unique Selling Point" and the initial feature that makes this book worth the paper it is written on, or the kilobytes it consumes, is that it represents a theological account that names the complex of cultural, political, and financial factors that make up "the economy" and that together exert neoliberalism's totalized influence on all matters. One of the leading theological voices in this conversation, D. Stephen Long, has written about the need for such an approach. He argues that the market tempts us to reduce "everything which is good, true and beautiful to a formal value based on usefulness and substitutability, flattening all hierarchies to formal equivalences."[13] This temptation towards totalizing our view of the world in line with the market means that often our theological considerations of wealth have assumed commitments to methodological angles that truncate and foreshorten the problem of wealth.[14] The most

---

12. Kripal, *Esalen*, 396–97.

13. Long, *Divine Economy*, 262.

14. "Capitalist markets always have the potential as well to become the organizing center of human life—a potential realized all over the world today—and in that capacity, by virtue of forming one particular way of life among others, invite normative evaluation. The market constitutes a certain manner of living that displaces and uproots others, often through a great deal of social disruption and cultural and normative disorientation of what preceded it. Why, one must ask, should one live this way rather than the way people did before the coming of a market in which impersonal exchanges become the key to economic well-being and everything that makes for human profit

pressing theological problem is finding a way beyond that logic, which trains us to forget the value of everything that cannot be priced.[15]

While scholars have operated for some time recognizing that the distinctive mode of political capitalism in which we live is best described as neoliberal,[16] there remains insufficient attention to how that plays out in how lives are lived in any concrete, particular expression of that order.[17] The dispersal of fish as a complicated, polyvalent protest is one such concrete, particular expression. The political decisions that amount to an intensified commitment to the logic of neoliberalism—in the form of austerity politics—is the narrative in which this argument is located. The story we are telling is the story in which we believe neoliberalism is the path to wealth, and we refuse to conceive of a world where we are not wealthy. Thus, our attention is focused on a certain place and time: Ireland, at the end of the economic boom known as the Celtic Tiger. By localizing the problem of wealth, and asking what Jesus's words mean for the people who live in that place after that crisis, this argument will cast fresh light on the wider question of how a Christian can follow Jesus in an age of Mammon.

An essential challenge for any theological treatment of wealth must be how to describe the economic terrain in question. For the purposes of this book, the terms of that investigation will be set by Karl Polanyi's classic text on the interaction of politics and economics, *The Great Transformation*.[18] Published originally in 1944, Polanyi's work is notable because of its focus on the ideas that drive economic developments. In this sense, Polanyi's work sits askew to economic accounts. Unlike, for example, John Maynard Keynes and Friedrich Hayek, who both, in different ways, set out to take the science of economics as a given and to present ways to move forward from there,[19] Polanyi's interest lies in charting how the political

has its price?" Tanner, "Is Capitalism a Belief System?," 618–19.

15. To remix the famous quip Oscar Wilde put in the mouth of Lord Darlington in Lady Windermere's Fan, that a cynic was "a man who knows the price of everything and the value of nothing." Wilde, *Lady Windermere's Fan*, 55.

16. For example, Daniel Bell describes the neoliberal "mutation" of liberal politics that began to take effect in the 1960s and 1970s which "aggressively advances the extension of economic reason into every fiber and cell of human life." Bell, *The Economy of Desire*, 76.

17. It should be noted that Kathryn Tanner's Gifford Lectures address the tangential issue of financialization of the economy, which is related but importantly different from what I pursue in this book. The lectures are due to be published in 2019 under the title *Christianity and the New Spirit of Capitalism*.

18. Polanyi, *The Great Transformation*.

19. That Polanyi resists grounding his treatment within the economists' guild means that *The Great Transformation* offers a flexibility ideally suited to our present purposes.

commitment to certain economic ideas became conceivable. It is this concern for how ideas work that makes *The Great Transformation* an ideal dialogue partner as we consider wealth from a theological perspective. To imagine that a theological consideration of "wealth" is a conversation straightforwardly about "economics" is both to terminate the exploration much too soon and to grant a reading of what economics is meant to do that economics itself cannot sustain.[20]

Considering the historical development of the idea of the market Polanyi's thesis "is that the idea of a self-adjusting market implied a stark utopia."[21] Etymologically, a utopia is a no-place. Polanyi seeks to identify the consequences of this unrealizable philosophical dream in the political and historical domain. As such, he turns to real places—famously to Speenhamland in Berkshire, where a prototypical social security net was established as early as 1795 in response to economic crisis—to both explain the way things are and to remind the reader that things could have turned out differently.[22]

This illumination of contingency is the great achievement of Polanyi's book. Drawing on historical and anthropological research, Polanyi contends that a society's economy is not driven by an invisible market force, but by communal concerns. In practically all cases, "man's economy, as a rule, is submerged in his social relationships."[23] The value that a person places on a good is rarely determined primarily by the market, but by their personal ends. This inversion of economic thinking, which argues that use-value has

---

Hayek explicitly takes the expertise of the trained economist as essential for entering into discussion of such topics. He depicted his *The Road to Serfdom* as a vocational work he was duty-bound to write because of the "alarming" prevalence of "amateurs and cranks" engaged in the political conversation around the economy at the end of the Second World War. Hayek, *The Road to Serfdom*, vii. Likewise, Keynes begins his most influential work declaring it to be written for experts, opining that the "superstructure" of economic thinking was not to be meddled with, since it had been "erected with great care for logical consistency." Keynes, *The General Theory of Employment, Interest and Money*, vi. The utility of Polanyi is thus that he offers us the critical distance from economic science required for serious theological analysis. As an aside, a valuable theological study could be made comparing and contrasting the different visions of the human and the common good on display in these three figures, although it is obviously outside the remit of our present purposes.

20. Introducing the conversation around the Arrow/Debreu model of a competitive economy, Ormerod et al. argue: "Contemporary mainstream economics holds that the market is simply about wealth creation, while any concern for the distribution of wealth pertains to the political realm." Ormerod, Oslington, and Koning, "The Development of Catholic Social Teaching on Economics," 410.

21. Polanyi, *The Great Transformation*, 3.

22. Polanyi, *The Great Transformation*, 82.

23. Polanyi, *The Great Transformation*, 48.

anthropological priority over exchange-value, is central to Polanyi's argument. Thus, Adam Smith's butcher, brewer, and baker, engaging in truck and barter, is not some primordial state of nature, but the expression of an institutional structure prevalent in a certain part of northern Britain around the year 1776.[24] And structuring economic activity overwhelmingly around a market is an institutional arrangement which "has been present at no time except our own, and even then it was only partially present."[25]

This historical innovation, implemented by the ascendant laissez-faire capitalism of nineteenth-century England, is an inversion of how previous societies understood economy. Now "instead of economy being embedded in social relations, social relations are embedded in the economic system."[26] The imaginative leap that allowed this new historical situation to come into being was the creation of the "fictitious commodities": labor, land, and money.[27] The market economy can only subjugate the wider societal activities to the apparently self-regulating mechanism once these three factors, which are not themselves generated for the purposes of resale, are treated as if they can be traded at will. A fundamental problem, for Polanyi, is that:

> Labor, land, and money are obviously *not* commodities; the postulate that anything that is bought and sold must have been produced for sale is emphatically untrue in regard to them. In other words, according to the empirical definition of a commodity, they are not commodities.[28]

The central insight that Polanyi is making here is to expose how what he terms the "market economy" is an intrinsically imaginative achievement.[29] At least since Polanyi's time, the easy rhetoric around "the markets" is that they are naturally occurring states of being. Examples abound where this is evidentially not the case.[30] Anthropological and historical observation demonstrates that "individual acts of barter or exchange—this is the

---

24. Smith, *An Inquiry into the Nature and Causes of the Wealth of Nations*, 27.

25. Polanyi, *The Great Transformation*, 37–38.

26. Polanyi, *The Great Transformation*, 60.

27. Polanyi, *The Great Transformation*, 71–80.

28. Polanyi, *The Great Transformation*, 75.

29. Polanyi is much more insightful here than so many contemporary Christians who, in the words of Brian Brock, "have assumed that globalization is a benign process of the extension of the power and reach of 'free markets' which in the end benefits all whom touches." Polanyi teaches us not to assume that institutional structures that appear total are therefore natural. Brock, "Globalisation, Eden and the Myth of Original Markets," 415.

30. This is a central component of David Graeber's argument. Graeber, *Debt*, 21–72.

bare fact—do not, as a rule, lead to the establishment of markets in societies where other principles of behaviour prevail."[31] For the market to emerge requires certain technologies (money, for example[32]) and for the market economy to emerge requires certain shared imaginative commitments (the three fictional commodities, for example).[33]

Objections can be raised about the detail of Polanyi's arguments,[34] but what has been called his "conceptual armature" stands nonetheless.[35] Fred Block and Margaret Somers place this theme which we have been pursuing—"that the free market celebrated by economists and political libertarians has never—and cannot ever—actually exist"—at the heart of this conceptual armature.[36] Polanyi demonstrates that the typical social arrangement embeds economic activity alongside the other concerns and activities of societies. Market economies represent an attempt to dis-embed economic activities from the warp and woof of a community's life. This can only be achieved through the philosophical reworking of what land or labor or money represent; a reconfiguration that must operate at the political level to subordinate other concerns to profit. Yet this is a quixotic quest since, as Block and Somers argue, "functioning market societies *must* maintain some threshold level of embeddedness or else risk social and economic disaster."[37] Polanyi notes that even the fiercest advocates of market economies had to

31. Polanyi, *The Great Transformation*, 64.

32. Braudel, *The Structures of Everyday Life*, 436–78.

33. Hodgson, "Conceptualizing Capitalism," 48. The rule of law is another critical requirement, often overlooked. It is axiomatic in the definition of neoliberalism that follows that the activity that makes up the economy is always a political event as well as an economic one. Such an account of capitalism is not uncommon. Geoffrey Hodgson, a central figure in the emerging "Institutional Economics" field, argues that institutions are the defining characteristic of capitalism. Placing institutions at the center "provides us with a clear, historically specific definition of this mode of production and highlights some of its generic features. The crucial role of the state is highlighted, along with an explanation of why capitalism can never be a 100 per cent market system." See also: Hodgson, *Conceptualizing Capitalism*.

34. Polanyi had argued that the Speenhamland poor-relief initiative was a desperate attempt to counterbalance negative effects of the embryonic laissez faire capitalism of the day, and that it was self-defeating. Jeffry Glaper's reconsideration of the initiative concludes that "in terms of direct input, and isolating Speenhamland as a wage-supplementation program, the evidence seems clear that Speenhamland did not produce the negative effect attributed to it." But it should also be noted that whatever errors might be found in Polanyi's interpretation of events, "this does not, however, blunt the potency of the general argument presented by Polanyi and relevance for our time." Glaper, "The Speenhamland Scales," 61–62.

35. Block and Somers, *The Power of Market Fundamentalism*, 8–11.

36. Block and Somers, *The Power of Market Fundamentalism*, 9.

37. Block and Somers, *The Power of Market Fundamentalism*, 93.

furnish the "state with the new powers, programs and instruments required for the establishment of laissez-faire."[38]

Polanyi's work alerts us to the reality that any project that attempts to position society as servant of the economy is a project that seeks the impossible. This, it should be noted, is not an argument against any particular school of economics, but rather a general stance in relation to the political rhetoric concerned with economy. The "free market" is a term loaded with disguised political significance. It appears to be the object of study by economists in a cold and objective fashion. Polanyi shows us three things: The way in which the idea of the free market falls under the domain of political ideology,[39] that it is subject to historical contingency,[40] and that it persists as a social institution that demands critical consideration.[41] Theological analysis is uniquely placed to engage in such a demythologization project.

NAMING THAT LOCATION: NEOLIBERALISM

Theology is not alone in critically considering the economy after Polanyi. There is a thriving market in such analyses, so to speak. Human geographers,[42] political scientists,[43] architects[44] and even graphic novelists,[45] among many others, have sought to map the territory of contemporary capitalism. A consistent narrative has emerged that describes the particular form of capitalism that prevails in the west as "neoliberalism."[46]

---

38. Polanyi, *The Great Transformation*, 147.

39. Polanyi, *The Great Transformation*, 31.

40. Polanyi, *The Great Transformation*, 31–32.

41. Polanyi, *The Great Transformation*, 267.

42. Harvey, *A Brief History of Neoliberalism*.

43. Brown, *Undoing the Demos*.

44. Spencer, *The Architecture of Neoliberalism*.

45. Cunningham, *The Age of Selfishness*.

46. Holding his contrarian position, Kean Birch is a useful companion here. He outlines four distinct ways of approaching neoliberalism: as a form of governmentality after the fashion described by Foucault, as a moral project as advocated by figures like Hayek, as a political project, as can be found in the work of David Harvey, and as an ongoing process, as exhibited in the work of Adam Tickell. Birch's insistence that neoliberal policy has never aligned with neoliberal theory harmonizes with what Polanyi predicted. The proposition we call neoliberalism "is always evolving, becoming something new, something different." The dazzling, bewildering proliferation of choice functions even on the level of definitions. Neoliberalism becomes, like that consumer gadget that will finally, totally satisfy our desires, ever just out of reach. Birch, *We Have Never Been Neoliberal*, 12–15, 43.

In a predictably ironic twist, the study of a capitalism that gains political momentum by promising ever-expanding choices generates an ever-expanding range of perspectives from which it can be critiqued. It can seem that there are as many definitions of neoliberalism as there are apps for your cell phone. Yet it can be defined minimally as a movement that centers politics around the idea that "optimal outcomes will be achieved if the demand and supply for goods and services are allowed to adjust to each other through the price mechanism."[47] It is not, therefore, simply a set of economic theories[48] or policy proposals.[49] Behind the commitment to deregulate, liberalize, and privatize lies an understanding of society that entails a certain kind of politics.[50] In one of the most significant early treatments of neoliberalism, Michel Foucault sought to excavate this political aspect of the dynamic. Neoliberalism utilizes the tools of economic science to advance a particular approach to governmentality. While the older liberalism was concerned with organising governance to shape a public square that granted maximum liberty for trade and exchange, the *neo*liberalism that Foucault considered seeks to organize governance so as to shape the private citizen for maximum productivity. The old liberalism generated a "supermarket society" but the new liberalism results in an "enterprise society" where the citizen becomes the "man of enterprise and production."[51] Taken in this light, neoliberalism becomes a political project to extend a philosophical vision about what makes us human into every area of society. In his protest against this movement, Fredric Jameson argues that "'the market is in human nature' is the proposition that cannot be allowed to stand unchallenged."[52] Under neoliberalism, the primal myth of capitalism—that all societies begin in barter and then evolve through truck and trade to

---

47. Crouch, *The Strange Non-Death of Neoliberalism*, 17.

48. Although it is closely bound up with particular concepts, for example the efficient market hypothesis. Quiggin, *Zombie Economics*, 35–36.

49. Although it is commonly associated with particular proposals such as DLP packages, which Lambin describes as "(a) Deregulation of the economy; (b) Liberalization of trade and industry; and (c) Privatization of state-owned enterprises," before adding, "DLP policy has triggered the process of commodification, which has progressively changed the nature of a market economy into a market society." Lambin, *Rethinking the Market Economy*, 264.

50. Mirowski talks of a "neoliberal thought collective," positioning the phenomenon as far more a political movement than an economic philosophy. His thirteen-part definition defies footnote quotation but is an excellent place to start if further reading is desired. Mirowski, *Never Let a Serious Crisis Go to Waste*, 27–67.

51. Foucault, *The Birth of Biopolitics*, 147.

52. Jameson, *Postmodernism, Or the Cultural Logic of Late Capitalism*, 263.

become, in maturity, fully developed globalized economies—becomes the story that determines all societies' stories.

It is important to note that Jameson's dissent comes as part of an argument about the politics and policies of the left-leaning parties in the Western world, which he characterizes as a "surrender" to the neoliberal agenda.[53] Thus, when neoliberalism is described as a political agenda, this is not a claim being made on the same political register as electoral politics. Neoliberalism is not a "right-wing" policy package. The British Labour party of Tony Blair and Gordon Brown, which held power from 1997 to 2010, was notionally left-leaning and yet enthusiastically embraced the deregulation of the economy,[54] the liberalization of labor law,[55] and the privatization of state-controlled services.[56] The Labour Party's historic socialism was no barrier to their contemporary adoption of neoliberalism.[57] Thus, along with being much more than a set of economic convictions, neoliberalism's political nature stretches beyond traditional left/right binaries. The political movement representing neoliberalism is not isolated to one or other partisan position but has achieved broad support across the mainstream political processes of Western democracies. This applies to Ireland, where the two dominant parties, *Fine Gael* and *Fianna Fáil*, have both pursued neoliberal agendas, and both were joined by coalition partners in government in the form of Labour and the Greens. Together, the historic socialist movement, the contemporary environmental movement, and the two center-right parties that emerged from the Irish Civil War, fill in practically the entirety of the Irish political spectrum, and they each fall in different ways under a neoliberal heading.

53. Jameson, *Postmodernism, Or the Cultural Logic of Late Capitalism*, 263.

54. For example, the deregulation of energy markets. Harker and Price, "Introducing Competition and Deregulating the British Domestic Energy Markets," 4.

55. Jessop, "From Thatcherism to New Labour," 151.

56. The historic political party of the British trade union movement, Labour's embrace of neoliberalism is perhaps best captured in its enthusiastic implemented of 'PFI' schemes where services previously considered public goods were encouraged to raise capital on the market, thus serving as a stealth privatization without the requirement for a thoroughgoing public or parliamentary debate. Such schemes were deployed widely, partially privatizing the construction of schools, the running of the London Underground, and most contentiously, the National Health Service. The story of how the NHS "which established health care as a right, has been progressively dismantled and privatized by successive governments" is told expertly in a Blair-era book by the senior medic, Allyson Pollock, *NHS Plc*.

57. "New Labour has largely followed in the tracks of the neo-liberal regime shift it inherited, as can be seen by examining the main elements of neo-liberalism as pursued in the Thatcher–Major years." Jessop, "New Labour or The Normalization of Neo-Liberalism?," 283.

It is important to note the relevance of debt in these discussions. While these public-private partnerships and privatizations were justified as inherently efficient, because they marketized what had been previously controlled by the State, the political justification for many of these innovations was the rising public debt that hung over after the 1970s oil crisis. Neoliberalism was positioned as a barrier to rampant profligacy. The increasing role that the financial sector played in economic life brought with it sources of credit that undergirded consumer spending. When financialized capitalism shuddered to a halt in 2008, that licensed a new round of austerity regimes across the globe.[58] Private investment risks became public debt-burdens expressed in cuts against the marginalized.[59] The crisis of 2008 stabilized into a widespread politics of austerity.[60] Christian theology has a vested interest in examining such social arrangements, since they function in opposition to grace. There are profound dogmatic reasons why we should expose to scrutiny political speech about efficiency and productivity.

Due to the volume of ink spilled over it, the term *neoliberalism* can often be read as a vague bogeyman, a rhetorical device meant to allude to anything and everything a writer disagrees with. It is explicitly a catch-all term that conceptually draws together a range of different analyses into a cohesive reading of a social situation.[61] The claim being made here requires a more fine-grained analysis, since any theological consideration of the wealth made possible by our markets requires a thorough description of those markets, embedded in the particularities of time and place, politics and culture.

Hence, while neoliberalism is associated with an economic agenda and it is a way to describe a political platform that has had widespread support across Western democracies in the last generation, it is also important

58. Thomas Palley has an excellent description, from an American perspective, of the role of the financial sector in the 2008 crash. Palley, *From Financial Crisis to Stagnation*, 58–66.

59. Streeck, "The Politics of Public Debt," 158–59. These were generally accompanied among other things by weak economic growth, rising unemployment, increasing inequality, growing tax resistance, and declining political participation. Following an initial period of fiscal consolidation in the 1990s, public debt took an unprecedented leap in response to the Great Recession. Renewed consolidation efforts, under the pressure of "financial markets," point to a general decline in state expenditure, particularly discretionary and investment expenditure, and of extensive retrenchment and privatization of state functions.

60. Mariana Mazzucato's defense of government value offers an important postmortem of this period. "Even though the crisis was caused by a combination of high private debt and reckless financial-sector behavior, the extraordinary policy conclusion was that governments were to blame." Mazzucato, *The Value of Everything*, 233.

61. Payne, *The Consumer, Credit and Neoliberalism*, 1–20.

to consider neoliberalism as a philosophy and as an ideological commitment that can orient both the shapes of economic policy and political positions. The term dates to an economic conference organized in 1938, attended by many thinkers who would go on to form the influential Mont Pélerin Society in 1947.[62] This body of economists, philosophers, and public intellectuals gathered around the theories of Friedrich von Hayek and influenced the distinctive intellectual trajectory of the Chicago School of Economics.[63] The philosophical movement that developed among these thinkers sought to make capitalist competition the "organizing principle of almost everything."[64] It began exerting its influence in the social sphere in the 1970s, first in South America, then in the UK and the USA with the elections of Thatcher and Reagan, and after the fall of the Soviet Union in 1989 it rose to an almost hegemonic status.[65]

If Polanyi teaches us that it is crucial that we describe the contingent details of economic embeddedness, then neoliberalism names our location. It refers to the reorientation of economies so that while the social democratic rhetoric of social mobility persists,[66] the flow of wealth is structured so as to increasingly serve the elite.[67] The same transformation operates on the private level of the individual, forging an entrepreneurship of the self so that the human exists "being for himself his own capital, being for himself his own producer, being for himself the source of [his] earning."[68] It shapes how we think. Wendy Brown describes it as "a peculiar form of reason that configures all aspects of existence in economic terms."[69] We

62. Mirowski and Plehwe, eds., *The Road from Mont Pèlerin*, 13.

63. This story is succinctly told in Van Horn and Mirowski, "Neoliberalism and Chicago," 200–5.

64. Graeber, *Debt*, 376.

65. Quinn Slobodian's account of the origins of the neoliberal era is quickly becoming the definitive account of how the movement arose. Slobodian, *Globalists*.

66. Most people now believe they are middle class, even as wages stagnate. So Estache and Leipziger begin their book, *Stuck in the Middle*, with the sentence: "It is well established that many more people consider themselves to be part of the middle class than actual income data would substantiate." Thomas Palley offers a sober account of how widespread economic stagnation will be a lingering consequence of the 2008 crash. Espache and Leipziger, eds., *Stuck in the Middle*, vii; Palley, *From Financial Crisis to Stagnation*, see especially chapter 1; Sullivan, Warren, and Westbrook, *The Fragile Middle Class*, 18–21.

67. As Duménil and Lévy describe it, neoliberalism's reorientation serves "the benefit of the highest income brackets, capitalist owners, and the upper fractions of management." Duménil and Lévy, *The Crisis of Neoliberalism*, 8.

68. Foucault, *The Birth of Biopolitics*, 226.

69. For Brown, neoliberalism is much more than an economic methodology or a legislative agenda. In fact, "neoliberal economic policy could be paused or reversed

are forced to see that the dynamic goes beyond commodifying healthcare or transforming public transport for profit. Rather, by the articulation of an anthropology and a sociology understood through the vocabulary and practices of production and consumption, neoliberalism aspires to a deep-level revolution of a person's understanding of themselves, their community, and their society. The neoliberal subject is the *homo oeconomicus* of classical capitalism converted, so that they come to understand themselves in the terms of their utility to the market. It influences what we value. David Harvey maintains that neoliberalism is:

> in the first instance a theory of political economic practices that proposes that human well-being can best be advanced by liberating individual entrepreneurial freedoms and skills within an institutional framework characterized by strong private property rights, free markets, and free trade.[70]

It primes us to organize the world in terms of the price-setting market, going so far as to imagine even nonmarket activities in terms of competition. This then shapes what we do. Drawing together the complex ways in which the economy, politics, and social mores are brought together under this term, William Davies argues that neoliberalism is "the disenchantment of politics by economics."[71] What we think and how we value is bound up in how we act and neoliberalism constrains our personal and political action within a rationale driven by the idea of competition and efficiency.

This talk of neoliberalism as a diffuse system of rationality that has connections to academic economics but is not academic economics, has policy ramifications but never successfully dominates policy, that ideologically promulgates the triumph of markets but seems to always be accompanied by a massive expansion in bureaucracy, leaves many unsettled.[72] I once found myself cornered over dinner by three economists who insisted that since no one ever adopts the label "neoliberal" for themselves, any academic discourse based around the term was bound to veer off into pejorative anecdote. I failed to convince them with my argument that while it may be

---

while the deleterious effects of neoliberal reason on democracy continued apace unless replaced with another order of political and social reason." It spills out of textbooks and over tax codes to make a home in our imaginations and our affections. Brown, *Undoing the Demos*, 201–202.

70. Harvey, *A Brief History of Neoliberalism*, 2.

71. Davies, *The Limits of Neoliberalism*, xiv.

72. Of course, if we think about what it might mean to think about something as complex as the role of markets in our societies, we would expect just this kind of intricacy. "When our purpose is to make a moral evaluation of this economic institution, we must attend to the moral ecology of markets." Finn, *The Moral Ecology of Markets*, 144.

true that barely anyone declares themselves neoliberal,[73] "nobody describes themselves as 'C1 lower-middle class'" either, and yet that category still allows election strategists to think clearly about how to campaign.[74]

As Wendy Brown positions it, "the norms and principles of neoliberal rationality do not dictate precise economic policy, but rather set out novel ways of conceiving and relating state, society, economy, and subject."[75] In so doing, it also inaugurates "a new 'economization' of heretofore noneconomic spheres and endeavors."[76] Brown focuses on how neoliberalism's economization can be traced in government, law, and education. Under neoliberal influence, the language of "governance" has become ascendant and as a consequence of this focus on process over goal, "public life is reduced to problem solving and program implementation."[77] In the legal sphere, decisions such as the infamous verdict of the United States of America's Supreme Court in the case of *Citizens United*, mean that the political terrain is being reshaped into the form of a market.[78] *Homo politicus* must operate as *homo oeconomicus*, since it is now a matter of statute that "individuals, corporations, and other associations are all operating to enhance their competitive positioning and capital value."[79] For Brown, the influence of neoliberalism on higher education surfaces when we consider how difficult it can be to describe something as a public good without an evident instrumental pay-off.[80] Universities willingly participate in bureaucratized ranking systems that are often tied to government funding. Now they are sometimes even run on a for-profit basis. They are starved of funding, meaning that it is inconceivable that they would resist such alterations to their historic functioning. Neoliberalism's nexus of forces "exert enormous pressures on colleges and universities and especially on liberal arts curriculums to abandon all aims and ends other than making students 'shovel ready' when they graduate."[81] The higher good of an educated

---

73. The Adam Smith Institute, a prominent English think-tank, has sought to wholeheartedly embrace the term and popularize it as a movement. Pirie, "The Neoliberal Mind." It can be argued that Milton Friedman was happy for the term to be applied to his position. Friedman, "Neo-Liberalism and Its Prospects," 93.

74. Davies, *The Limits of Neoliberalism*, xiii.

75. Brown, *Undoing the Demos*, 50.

76. Brown, *Undoing the Demos*, 50.

77. Brown, *Undoing the Demos*, 127.

78. Kennedy, *Citizens United v. Federal Election Commission*.

79. Brown, *Undoing the Demos*, 155.

80. Brown, *Undoing the Demos*, 176.

81. Brown, *Undoing the Demos*, 192.

public is dragged to earth by the overwhelming desire of private persons to be ready to compete in the marketplace.

Brown's analysis could be extended to consider the way neoliberalism affects any number of other spheres of life; from sport[82] to church,[83] from the food we eat[84] to the news we decide to read.[85] Brown presents neoliberalism as a peculiar form of reason that introduces to society new "economizations" that were not previously there. This totalizing aspiration warrants serious theological critique. It is a theologically live question whether the logic of economization should hold sway even in all matters economic, but it is certainly problematic when it reaches into the parts of our lives which had not been previously considered in terms of profit and efficiency.[86]

---

82. David Goldblatt's sociology of soccer in an English context pays admirable attention to the economic transformation of the game where "the benefits, which are considerable, have been sequestered by the few." Goldblatt, *The Game of Our Lives*, 301.

83. John Drane's examination of how "efficiency," "calculability," "predictability," and "control" drives much modern church practice stands as an early example of how neoliberal logics disciplined ecclesial communities. It is a striking example because of how its final constructive proposals appear even more in thrall to a neoliberal agenda than its critical analysis. In place of a church aspiring to be a rational institution modelled on traditional profit-making corporations, he proposes "we can construct a different sort of authority, based on personal, individual experience." Hence, in "dreaming the church of the future," Drane ends up anticipating the relocated emphasis on self-construction to which neoliberalism ultimately aspires. This underlines again how difficult it is to escape the influence of the spirit of the age. Drane, *The McDonaldization of the Church*, 35–49, 181.

84. Mihalis Mentinis argues that the contemporary cultural preoccupation with food is a neoliberal dynamic at work. The cliché of the Instagram account full of photographs of meals is the surface of how we use food to construct a self defined by consumption, but Mentinis goes deeper to consider the changes in how we eat as rites of passage by which we are inducted into neoliberal capitalism. Our globalized palate is made possible by a vast expansion of the agricultural and logistic industries and made accessible to us through a massive and long-running marketing and media campaign. Mentinis, *The Psyhcopolitics of Food*; see especially the discussion of the celebrity chef Jamie Oliver's repeated attempts to reform the British and American diets in the first chapter.

85. There is little to no regulation of the algorithms deployed by media and internet corporations but the major players—Twitter, Facebook, Google, Baidu, Vkontakte—are all multinational corporations and standard-bearers for globalized capitalism. The influence they can exert is inversely proportional to the oversight applied to them. Frank Pasquale notes that Facebook's intervention into the news feed of American users, prompting them to vote in the 2010 elections, was shown to produce a 0.39 percent increase in voter turnout. This appears to be a dwindlingly small return, but it is, Pasquale argues, "well more than enough to swing the outcome in contests like the 2000 U.S. presidential election." Pasquale, *The Black Box Society*, 74. As this book is prepared for publication, these issues have gained popular traction in the discussion of "fake news."

86. John Hughes's *The End of Work* is a noteworthy text that explores the logic of

Under full-sprinting neoliberalism, people still engage in all sorts of activities that are not reducible to a cost-based self-interest. People still marry those they fall in love with even when the union between the two families offers no apparent strategic or profitable opportunities. People still go walking in the Scottish Highlands without considering how it will provide potential content for their social media stream and with nary a thought for its positive effects on physical and emotional health. People even still leave gainful employment to spend four years researching and writing theological treatises on the dangers of wealth.

Yet the societal structures in which these actions take place are arranged around the economization that Brown identifies. That divorce is no longer even an issue of contention in Western societies indicates the functional ways in which the logic of contract has replaced the promise of covenant. That most of those hillwalkers trek with a mobile phone in their pockets that tracks their every move and aggregates that data into a digital simulacrum of themselves for marketing purposes demonstrates how even our engagement with natural wilderness becomes a site for profit. That the theologian-in-training is likely to be coached by their university to frame their research in terms of skills acquisition to attract the attention of possible recruiters displays how the calculation of personal benefit creeps into to even the most apparently distant of concerns.[87]

As a political project, neoliberalism, to varying degrees depending on time and place, may be associated with austerity economics, or market deregulation, or the transformation of nonmarket institutions along competitive lines, but what holds this motley movement together is the subordination of political discourse to the logic of economic quantification. The economy is what generates our wealth. We can meaningfully describe that wealth-generating circulatory system, as it exists in Ireland and in many other nations besides, as neoliberal. More fundamentally, we can also describe the subjectivity of the citizenry in such places in terms of neoliberalism.

---

capitalism and how it poses problems for very basic ideas of Christianity, namely how work and rest relate to each other. Hughes considers the nineteenth-century English aesthete John Ruskin as an example of a voice that could be marshalled against the logic of economization. Hughes reports that Ruskin worried that we would come to "think of human nature 'merely as a covetous machine' about which laws can be discovered." Hughes, *The End of Work*, 102.

87. It is worth noting that this book started life as a thesis, which was written under the care of a university that made courses on marketing one's "critical thinking and effective communication" skills to potential employers compulsory for doctoral candidates. University of Aberdeen Directorate of Student Life, 'Your Employability', *Aberdeen Graduate Attributes*.

But for theological purposes, it is perhaps wise to grant the objection of my dinner companions and take one step away from the heated disputes about terminology.[88] Whatever about a concerted politico-economic arrangement called neoliberalism, it can be agreed that people living in Western nations increasingly exist as neoliberal subjects. The rationale of economic quantification and monetary valuation predominates not just our political deliberation, but our self-understandings. If we locate the economy within neoliberalism, that matters theologically because it arranges how we view ourselves, our neighbors, and our environment in competitive terms. We are trained to pursue the best versions of ourselves, we must keep up with the Joneses, and in an environment defined by scarcity and risk, we must take care of number one.[89]

We embrace a calculative approach to life so that the metaphors of the accountant become ascendant in our discourse about common goods— "what's the bottom line?"—and the pursuit of wisdom which has traditionally been understood as self-knowledge is transformed into "self-tracking."[90] Thus, the embeddedness of the economy becomes real to us when we think about how we enact neoliberalism in our own lives. Quantification and evaluation are the baselines of this self-understanding. We can identify any number of policy commitments—monetarism or globalization or austerity—that are common features of neoliberal orders, but it is much more significant for the embeddedness of the economy to see how this functions in the life of the individual, in the important decisions we face, in how desire is shaped and formed. To understand neoliberalism on this level, David

88. Brief and accessible arguments have been developed that bypass the critique that talk of neoliberalism represents a slur dressed up in academic clothing. Consider, for instance: Rodrik's argument that academic economics must distance itself from neoliberal political rhetoric, the Institute for New Economic Thinking's symposium on the concept, or Mitchell and Fazi's discussion which, similarly to this chapter, argues that neoliberalism is much more about politics than it is economics. Rodrik, "Rescuing Economics from Neoliberalism"; Mirowski, "This Is Water (or Is It Neoliberalism?)"; Mitchell and Fazi, "Everything You Know About Neoliberalism Is Wrong."

89. "At the risk of bolstering the skeptical economists by adding theologians to their number, the simplest and most accurate way to describe neoliberalism might be in the terms Paul provides us. How are we to understand the New Testament's talk of "powers and principalities"? Consider the diffuse, yet destructive effect of a complex of forces we call neoliberalism.

90. Deborah Lutpon's research into how we engage with technology casts crystal-clear light on how the logic of neoliberalism seeps into every waking (and sleeping) moment of our lives: "Self-tracking may be theorized as a practice of selfhood that conforms to cultural expectations concerning self-awareness, reflection and taking responsibility for managing, governing oneself and improving one's life chances. Self-tracking therefore represents the apotheosis of the neoliberal entrepreneurial citizen ideal." Lupton, *The Quantified Self*, 68.

Beer advises, is "to understand the systems of measurement that act as the mechanisms of competition."[91]

One way of conceiving this creeping, colonizing effect of neoliberalism is to think about forests.[92] We are all familiar with the threat posed to natural rainforests by the incursions of agricultural development. But the existence of forests themselves are radically altered by the intervention of neoliberal capitalist logic, in ways that are generally illuminative. The ideal commercial forest tends towards a monoculture, managed in grids dissected by roads engineered for heavy machinery.[93] The ideal is unattainable however, and the sheer ecological diversity of the forest proliferates.[94] Forest management is a mature discipline dedicated to dealing responsibly with the stubborn insistence of life to spill out beyond the neat grids of cultivated silviculture.[95] When the logic of profit and productivity take over, the natural abundance of the forest becomes an obstacle and a cost to be overcome.[96] The holistic biome is reduced down to a series of neat columns on a spreadsheet representing potential value. To say that something is lost when a wild forest becomes managed is not to engage in idle sentimentality. It is a description of a very deliberate simplifying abstraction, an imaginative leap dedicated to rendering complexity as noise for the sake of efficiency. In neoliberalism, it is not just that we cannot see the forest for the trees, but that the forest is invented by ignoring certain individual trees.

This is a totalizing effect.[97] As the managed forest brackets out all the life-forms that do not yield immediate value, neoliberal subjectivity encour-

91. Beer, *Metric Power*, 29.

92. My thinking here is heavily indebted to Anna Lowenhaupt-Tsing, whose remarkable *The Mushroom at the End of the World* has been hugely provocative as I have wrestled with the diversity and vitality that persists in economic activity even in the face of the apparent neoliberal hegemony. In her extensive discussion of forestry—as a means by which to talk about the mushrooms that fascinate her—she argues that "modern forestry has been based on the reduction of trees—and particularly pines—to self-contained, equivalent, and unchanging objects." Lowenhaupt-Tsing, *The Mushroom at the End of the World*, 168.

93. The early attempts at scientifically informed forestry were desperate social, economic, and environmental failures as they disregarded the complexity of the ecosystem in simple pursuit of efficiency. Scott, *Seeing Like a State*, 11–22.

94. The need for more careful attention to the diversity in forestry is demonstrated in Chazdon et al., "When Is a Forest a Forest?"

95. "Whereas monocultures have excelled at providing large quantities of wood per unit area, this has often come at the expense of biodiversity." Felton et al., "Replacing Monocultures with Mixed-Species Stands," S124.

96. "The reductionist paradigm thus converts a biologically rich system into an impoverished resource." Shiva, *Monocultures of the Mind*, 53.

97. Peter Fleming renders directly what I am trying to argue from analogy: "What

ages us to increasingly apply a solitary logic to the different aspects of our life. That which cannot be measured cannot be managed, so it falls out of our imaginative frame.

Hence, to argue that the best name for the time in which we find ourselves is neoliberalism is to argue that we embrace a way of engaging with the world that is driven, in its deepest logic, by the calculative measurement most commonly associated with market economies.[98] This is the neoliberal revolution—that all of life is increasingly rendered in terms of competitive market conditions. Neoliberalism aims, therefore, towards being a totalized system. It aspires to extend a uniform business culture across the globe.[99] It rests on a certain understanding of the importance of institutions and legality for social stability.[100] It seeks to free markets from interference.[101] It promises to distribute the scarce resources of the world efficiently.[102] Globalization, legality, and an efficiency born of markets are the good things promised by neoliberalism. It presents itself as a universal solvent for economic, social, and political problems. In the words of David Graeber, "the ultimate aim of neoliberal capitalism is to create a world where no one believes any other economic system could really work."[103] Competition is naturalized and efficiencies are valorized. The promise of infinite choice is the rhetoric that drives support for neoliberalism. Plurality, diversity, and

---

makes neoliberalism interesting, if it is at all, is the vast historical continents that it is inherently unable to speak about." Fleming, *The Mythology of Work*, 45.

98. If this were a film, there would be all kinds of zoom and pan shots here for the purpose of foreshadowing. Like Anna Tsing's mushrooms, the discussion of neoliberal subjectivity is going to reappear at the end of this work when our thoughts turn to repentance, which is literally a question of changing our mind, rejecting one way of viewing the world and following the trail of an entirely different approach.

99. "Almost all states, from those newly minted after the collapse of the Soviet Union to old-style social democracies and welfare states such as New Zealand and Sweden, have embraced, sometimes voluntarily and in other instances in response to coercive pressures, some version of neoliberal theory and adjusted at least some policies and practices accordingly. . . . Neoliberalism has, in short, become hegemonic as a mode of discourse." Harvey, *A Brief History of Neoliberalism*, 3.

100. "The world is full of international institutions. Disagreement about definitions, about how old or new the phenomenon, and about its exact impact cannot mask the reality of a growing number and role of international institutions." Smith, "Neoliberal Institutionalism," 217.

101. "The assumption that individual freedoms are guaranteed by freedom of the market and of trade is a cardinal feature of neoliberal thinking." Harvey, *A Brief History of Neoliberalism*, 7.

102. The architects of neoliberalism "believed the model would promote economic efficiency and freedom." Palley, *From Financial Crisis to Stagnation*, 75.

103. Graeber, *Utopia of Rules*, 145.

possibility are the order of the day. The internal contradiction created by the simultaneous promise of never-ending, ever-expanding options that never conflict and the mandate for ongoing, never-stopping competition is held in check by the external threat that the markets must be assuaged. Day-dreaming about lifestyles not based on consumption or ways of working that are not grounded in agonistic struggle are options unavailable to us.[104] The potential negative reactions of multinational corporations and currency exchanges mean that our hypotheticals are limited to tinkering reform of the system we have in place.[105] This is the time we live in. It might be the best of times, it might be the worst of times, but it is certainly an age of endless competition made liveable by the promise of the ever-increasing choice that comes from prosperity.[106] Neoliberal capitalism has brought prosperity to

104. One is reminded here of Brian Brock's comments on the inevitable limitation of choice in such a society. Whatever about having it your way, "You can't go into Burger King and ask for a burger made with sustainably raised beef, pesticide-free wheat, pre-servative-free pickles and lettuce that has not been trucked in a frozen container 1,000 miles. You also can't ask to be served by someone on a working wage, who has been given the opportunity to think for themselves at all during the day, or who has actually learned a skill, like cooking, that they could take to their homes or use to apply for a job at a proper restaurant." Brock, *Captive to Christ, Open to the World*, 64.

105. This is one of the most straightforward explanations of why it is that Irish people did not march, protest, or riot in any significant fashion in the years after the end of the Celtic Tiger. No alternative could be imagined that would draw people to the streets.

106. Dickens famously began *A Tale of Two Cities* with a sentence that situated the plot before the French Revolution. "It was the best of times, it was the worst of times, it was the age of wisdom, it was the age of foolishness, it was the epoch of belief, it was the epoch of incredulity, it was the season of Light, it was the season of Darkness, it was the spring of hope, it was the winter of despair, we had everything before us, we had nothing before us, we were all going direct to Heaven, we were all going direct the other way—in short, the period was so far like the present period, that some of its noisiest authorities insisted on its being received for good or for evil, in the superlative degree of comparison only." Dickens establishes that the age about which he writes is an age of contestation and dispute. Dickens, *A Tale of Two Cities*, 4. That famous piece of writing was adapted during the vintage era of the animated television series *The Simpsons* in an episode that, critically for our purposes, is about labor disputes and the power of worker solidarity. The billionaire owner of the local nuclear power plant, C. Montgomery Burns, is revealed to be employing a thousand monkeys at a thousand typewriters in the hope that they will write "the greatest novel known to man." In the scene in question, Burns takes a sample page from one of the monkeys and reads, "It was the best of times, it was the blurst of times . . ." before discarding it in disgust. The age of neoliberalism is not amenable to Dickensian flights of florid prose. The attempt to expose its hidden meaning through a work of art like a novel is as absurd an aim as hoping that chain-smoking monkeys literally chained to desks might somehow produce an opus for the ages. Even the most impressive efforts will be scrunched up by the owners of capital and tossed aside. The authority to resolve contestation and dispute is relocated from the political realm, to the economic realm.

many of the citizens of the Western world. We embrace the logic of competition because it promises us we can be winners.

The Neoliberal Subject's Theological Problem

If there is no alternative to neoliberal capitalism, it is because no other system can generate such volumes of wealth. The mechanism of market competition refines and streamlines relentlessly, slicing margins, increasing profits, and generating well-being as the rising tide lifts all boats. That is the theory, anyway. Whether or not the smaller boats can survive this swelling tide and what is to be done with those people who own no boats in the first place are questions we can push away for a later day. A sort of magician's trick is pulled when fundamental questions about how to distribute resources gets defined as "redistribution," setting in stone the "prior" rights of the winners to own and possess all that they can stockpile, and framing the conversation about common good as secondary to capital accumulation.

Economic growth is undoubtedly a product of capitalism generally.[107] Neoliberalism, charted in the standard terms of economic evaluation has been successful in generating growth.[108] Beyond the abstracted figures on the page, it is possible to make a specifically theological defense of this political order. Writing about globalized economic markets, Brent Waters praises them, arguing that they promote increased production of goods and services, which are sold at lower prices, generating employment, encouraging capital investment, which all leads to the creation of wealth.[109] The hope of the Christian analysing an economy, according to the economist John Tiemstra, is that she will find a "good story," by which is meant "a plausible account of the causes and effects of certain economic actions, an account that would have meaning to an educated layperson because it would connect to everyday experience."[110] By these lights, neoliberalism has the potential to be rendered as a good story. Critical accounts of neoliberalism decry

---

Kirkland, "Last Exit to Springfield."

107. "Between the year 1 C.E. and the year 1820, living standards in the 'West' (measured with data from Western Europe and the United States) essentially doubled . . . . Over the next 200 years; however, GDP per person rose by more than a factor of twenty, reaching $26,000." Jones, "The Facts of Economic Growth," 7.

108. If we track GDP growth since 1980, when Thatcher and Reagan had both come to power, the average GDP of OECD nations grew from US$8,864 to US$42,173 (2016). OECD, "Gross Domestic Product (GDP) (Indicator)."

109. Waters, *Just Capitalism*, 43–44.

110. Tiemstra, *Stories Economists Tell*, 39.

increased financialization[111] and rising inequality[112] and the growing power of corporate entities,[113] but when faced with the real income changes that make our miraculous smartphones ubiquitous, they can seem like detailed explorations in missing the point.

And here we come to a very tricky point in this argument. On the one hand, especially at the lowest levels of our societies and in the poorest nations, there is absolutely nothing wrong with people desiring to have more. It is not wrong; it is right. Those in Western Europe or North America might have good reason to lament the ways in which economic standards have stagnated or regressed, but in the poorest places of the world, there is a remarkable transition away from absolute levels of poverty in the last generation.[114] If neoliberalism generates wealth, why complain? Get busy making more of it, in a more productive fashion than writing obscure theological texts!

Without denying the very real productivity gains that are hiding behind graphs of rising GDP and without diminishing the ongoing urgency of development work among the poorest peoples in the world, there is a profound theological problem with living as neoliberal subjects. Committing to allowing the logic of market competition to prevail as our primary form of rationality is, on Christian terms, a poor investment. Too much is lost and too much is put at risk. Barth warned that "a morality which has practical success as its reward could finally be one which also makes this

111. Andrew Glyn recounts that since Adam Smith, finance had traditionally occupied a passive role in the economic system, however "financial liberalization and advances in communications encouraged financial innovation and brought finance into much greater prominence." Glyn, *Capitalism Unleashed*, 50.

112. "There was greater inequality wherever one sliced the income distribution; even within the top 1 percent, the top 0.1 percent of income earners was getting a larger share of the money." Stiglitz, *The Price of Inequality*, 2.

113. "If neoliberalism stands for anything," argues Colin Crouch, "it is for a strong separation of state power from commercial markets. If it can be shown that in fact neoliberalism has brought about a dense and opaque entanglement of private corporations with government, the dominant political ideology of our day emerges damaged below its waterline." Crouch, "From Markets versus States to Corporations versus Civil Society?" 220.

114. Branko Milanovic's famous "elephant graph" detailing the relative acceleration of the middle classes in developing economies is an important touch point here. It is also critical to consider the role that China plays in this transformation, as it stands as the largest and most powerful opponent to straightforward neoliberal capitalism. All that is for another book, by another author, but is a powerful reminder that any serious Christian thinking about how to follow Jesus very quickly opens us up to a world of other questions. Milanovic, *Global Inequality*, 19.

reward its goal."[115] The Christian who orders her life in pursuit of growing wealth makes growing wealth the goal of her life. Jesus tells a story about that kind of person and declares them, and their barns, to be foolish.[116] Christianity is opposed to destitution, but it does not follow that Christianity is a supporter of wealth.[117]

When we are convinced that the only way to address questions of material injustice is to respect capitalist conceptions of private property, an easy elision flows from fighting obscene poverty to tolerating obscene wealth. In the social imaginary formed around neoliberal convictions, philanthropy can be expected to play a prominent role. Choice is a driving concern after all, so since Mark Zuckerberg earned his money, it is more desirable that he freely donate hundreds of millions of dollars to schools in New Jersey rather than be compelled to contribute to the education of every young person in America through general taxation.[118]

David Cloutier has interrogated "the neglected vice" of luxury and concluded that "there are strong reasons to be concerned that our society has this disease of excess."[119] The historic testimony of the church is consistent in its vigilance in the face of avarice. Learning to identify what it looks like is made nearly impossible by the incoherence of any sense of when enough becomes too much under the neoliberal logic. It is a fundamental dogmatic claim of Christianity that Creation is surplus, not scarce. There will always be *more* and if we have bought into the idea of self-interest, it is very difficult to justify why that more shouldn't be added to *our* collection. The problem of wealth, as Elizabeth Hinson-Hasty puts it, is "how we think about self in relation to others and the prioritization of an individual's right to make money over against the needs of a larger community."[120] Neoliberal subjectivity, in positing the self as endlessly competitive, puts the accumulation of personal wealth and the increase in aggregate wealth in the place where the Christian might expect to find the common good.

115. Barth, *Ethics*, 170.

116. Luke 12:16–21.

117. I am grateful to Claire Hargaden for her clarifying comments that helped me understand that Christianity is not opposed to poverty in and of itself. After all, Jesus embraced it! Making space for Christianity's historic practice of voluntary begging is a part of, not in contradiction with, our wholesale repudiation of social injustice expressed in material want. Kelly Johnson's work on this issue remains required reading: Johnson, *The Fear of Beggars*.

118. Fascinatingly, at the same time as the phenomenon of the magnate philanthropist re-emerged, a popular opposition to everyday charity among Christians was also flourishing. Lupton, *Toxic Charity*.

119. Cloutier, *The Vice of Luxury*, 203.

120. Hinson-Hasty, *The Problem of Wealth*, 14.

Poverty clearly can be a moral problem. Jesus's gospel was good news to the poor.[121] Yet the Christian response to want is not to license a system of endless wanting. And this is an implicit component of our contemporary economic arrangements. We "now live in societies without an acquisitive ceiling,"[122] where the concept of "enough" is meaningless. As Pope Francis has described it, many of us live in a state whereby we "ignore injustice in a world where some revel, spend with abandon and live only for the latest consumer goods, even as others look on from afar, living their entire lives in abject poverty."[123]

Christians concerned with alleviating that abject poverty must also be concerned with addressing the decadent luxury. The tendrils of neoliberal logic must be tracked and traced and tackled as they deform our deliberation into calculation and tempt us to re-describe all the aspects of our lives in terms of market competition. This is where the totalizing effect of neoliberalism is to be found. When we imagine ourselves as self-interested economic actors, we truncate ourselves and prepare our vision to cut everything out that cannot be represented in terms of quantification. Neoliberal subjectivity's long, winding stretch into how we see the world is the theological problem that must be addressed. In lieu of scarcity, Christianity insists the world is abundant and in place of life as competition, Christianity insists that life is lived in concert.

To say that neoliberalism is a totalizing system is not to say that it is all that there is, but that it aspires to a level of influence where nothing is *entirely* outside its domain. Mark Fisher, in his work, *Capitalist Realism: Is there no Alternative?*, describes neoliberalism as not simply being the only functional option available to us, "but also that it is now impossible even to *imagine* a coherent alternative to it."[124] The totalizing effect of neoliberalism can be considered in how it extends the logic of the market to parts of life that had previously operated on different logic, in how it replaces the contention of political deliberation with the calculation of technical expertise, and, most critically, in how it colonizes how we think about the world, training us to be competitors concerned with self-interest and to aspire to self-destructive levels of comfort. It dominates our imagination. The creeping effect that simultaneously makes it so difficult to analyse and so important to critique is described by Fisher as "a monstrous, infinitely plastic entity, capable of metabolizing and absorbing anything with which it

---

121. Luke 4:18–21.

122. Gregory, *The Unintended Reformation*, 17.

123. Pope Francis, *Gaudete et Exsultate*, §101.

124. Fisher, *Capitalist Realism*, 2.

comes into contact."[125] Christian theology cannot avoid a fight with such a system.[126] If nothing else, the heart of the Christian ontology is laid bare in Eucharist, where the transcendent factor that brings order to the universe is metabolized. If neoliberalism aspires to be a story by which we live, then Christians must take issue with it.[127]

Neoliberalism as Idolatry

In the vocabulary of the Christian church, when we consider how the competitive market logic stretches to become the ordering rationale for all of life, we can see how the neoliberal subjectivity falls into idolatry.[128] The idea that capitalism poses so serious a spiritual threat is not new. Similar arguments have been articulated extensively by figures such as Robert H. Nelson and more recently by Scott W. Gustafson. These scholars extend a functionalist definition of religion and find that under such a lens, market capitalism fits on a spectrum that includes traditionally understood religious systems like Norse Paganism, Christianity, or Buddhism. Functionalists define religion around "how certain ideas and practices function in their lives, that is, the social psychological, and political work that such ideas and practices do to produce the sort of overarching meaning and coherence" offered by traditional religions.[129] For Nelson, "the most vital

125. Fisher, *Capitalist Realism*, 6.

126. That neoliberalism is a complex of factors means that there is no unitary world or space, state or people, market or economy that can be marked out as the nub of the problem. Neoliberalism resists being fixed and stationary. In such a context, an ethics that aspires to laying out some clear principles appears increasingly irrelevant. This is one reason William Cavanaugh suggests, illuminated by reference to the Richard Strauss opera *Ariadne auf Naxos*, that the church cannot withdraw to a "separate enclave" from which it can reflect abstractly on the problems of the world. Cavanaugh, *Migrations of the Holy*, 63–67. He develops these ideas in *Field Hospital*: "The church is called to improvise each performance of space and time, trying to turn the action from a tragedy to a comedy." Cavanaugh, *Field Hospital*, 155.

127. Augustine famously experienced an *apokalypsis* in the midst of "the region of dissimilarity" where he heard the voice of the Lord explain the queer dynamics of the Eucharistic meal: "I am the food of the fully grown; grow and you will feed on me. And you will not change me into you like the food your flesh eats, but you will be changed into me." Such reflections demonstrate both the idolatrous potential in the totalizing impulse of neoliberal capitalism and the inherent centrality that the sacrament has in the church's response. Augustine of Hippo, *Confessions*, 123–24.

128. "Put to death, therefore, whatever in you is earthly: fornication, impurity, passion, evil desire, and *greed (which is idolatry)*" (Colossians 3:5).

129. Cavanaugh, *Field Hospital*, 221; See also Cavanaugh, *The Myth of Religious Violence*, 109–13.

religion of the modern age has been economic progress."[130] He posits economists as a modern priestly class and the advances of science and technology as the symbolic language that has convinced people that the markets must be assuaged and the capitalist order sustained. Gustafson's argument is that capitalism becomes the religious expression of secular societies. Arguing that "secularism is always the by-product of an expanding industrial economy," he goes on to suggest that the concept of indebtedness is at the heart of the religious devotion in the capitalist cult.[131]

Nelson and Gustafson present capitalism as a religious system. By a process of extension, one could argue that neoliberalism functions in a similar fashion. Curiously, neither of these writers engages with Walter Benjamin's brief 1921 essay, "Capitalism as Religion," which presented capitalism as a "purely cultic religion" where dogma and theology play no part.[132] Such a body of reflection would be an unwarranted interruption to the ongoing sacrifice demanded by the market. Capitalism is, Benjamin suggests, a religion where "there is no day that is not a feast day."[133] Yet it is also a religious system without atonement. It is guilt, in the form of debt, all the way down.[134] This is its totalizing claim, which envelops even the concept of a deity. *Etsi Deus non daretur*[135] is the only possible stance capitalism can take to the claim of a God, for "it is a religion which offers not the reform of existence but its complete destruction."[136] Benjamin's capitalism consumes everything until there is nothing left; a parasite inverting the Christian hope that the gospel transforms everything until all is "made new."[137]

In the century that has passed since Benjamin wrote, capitalism has successfully expanded the living standards of billions of people and as a corollary, expanded debt-loads many times. This is not merely a conceptual arrangement. The economic system that Benjamin dubbed "religious" has extracted and processed the mineral and ecological richness of the earth at a pace that would have been impossible in 1921. The age of neoliberalism is totalizing both in terms of preventing imaginable alternatives but also in terms of its vast consumption of created materials. The repercussions of this

130. Nelson, *Economics as Religion*, 329.

131. Gustafson, *At the Altar of Wall Street*, 8.

132. Benjamin, "Capitalism as Religion," 288.

133. Benjamin, "Capitalism as Religion," 288.

134. It is important to remember that the German word *Schuld* means both "debt" and "guilt."

135. "As if God does not exist."

136. Benjamin, "Capitalism as Religion," 289.

137. Revelation 21:5.

age of economic plunder will extend for centuries to come in the form of climate change. The grasp of the neoliberal logic does not simply reach to turn that which had been goods-held-in-common into economized commodities for sale, it reaches into the future by means of the axiomatic assumption that economic growth will be infinite. According to Kerryn Higgs, the neoliberal economic imagination:

> which treats nature as a subset of the economy, underlies numerous unexamined verities of mainstream economics: that the planet is functionally infinite, both as a source of materials and as a sink for wastes, that substitutes for depleted resources will be generated automatically by price increases; and that the limitations of the physical world and the laws of thermodynamics are not relevant to economic processes.[138]

Any force that can bypass the Newtonian limits of the universe is most accurately described as miraculous. Those who put their trust in such a putative force are adherents. In Christian terms, they are waiting on the intervention of a false god bound to fail them. This is the tragedy of idolatry.

In arguing that neoliberalism's totalizing aspiration is idolatrous, we draw on Martin Luther's Larger Catechism. There he expounds on the First Commandment in these terms:

> What does it mean to have a god? Or, what is God? Answer: A God means that from which we are to expect all good and to which we are to take refuge in all distress, so that to have a God is nothing else than to trust and believe Him from the heart; as I have often said that the confidence and faith of the heart alone make both God and an idol. If your faith and trust be right, then is your God also true; and, on the other hand, if your trust be false and wrong, then you have not the true God.[139]

The English theologian Philip Goodchild proposes that money has come to function in a manner similar to Luther's definition of a god. His work offers a philosophically robust account of what it might mean for capitalism to be idolatrous. He argues that money has come to be "the supreme value that all other values are measured by," and in that sense capitalism functions in a Lutheran fashion as the source "from which we are to expect all good and to which we are to take refuge in all distress."[140] Money is a belief system that has won the faith of many, claiming the territory of

---

138. Higgs, *Collision Course*, 16.
139. Luther, "The Large Catechism," 565.
140. Goodchild, *Theology of Money*, 14.

providence that had been previously claimed by the God of the Bible.[141] This is an inherently agonistic dispute. There is no way around Jesus's declaration that you cannot serve two masters (Matthew 6:24, Luke 16:13). Goodchild describes Mammon's attempted usurpation elegantly in an earlier work: "This newly ascendant god, visible nowhere, emergent from the future, executes the murder of God."[142]

Goodchild argues that the market presents itself as a reconciliatory power that brings peace between people based on the cut and thrust of negotiation and compromise entailed by commerce: "The market appears to be a peaceable social institution founded on justice. It recognizes the right of all participants to freedom and property. It mediates potential conflicts between its members by law, contract and exchange."[143] If such a description is taken as true, the neoliberal agenda to extend the competition of this marketplace to areas that had been considered "noneconomic" is almost self-evident. The university strapped for funding because of a failure to flourish under a bureaucratized performance metric has no cause for complaint since the measures being implemented are formally just and equitable. A weakened national health service struggling to compete against for-profit alternatives, which tailor their services to exclude difficult patients and costly treatments, is counterbalanced by the increase in choice and the corresponding expansion of consumer freedoms enjoyed by citizens. Through such rhetorical redistribution, neoliberalism gains support.[144]

Yet Goodchild continues, considering what is first required before the reconciling marketplace can enact its *euangelion*:

> People only maintain their status as participants in the market
> to the extent that they acknowledge the sovereignty of the mar-
> ket system: they become free in the market by renouncing the

141. Quite literally, a note of currency is a promise made by a Central Bank in which we trust when we offer or accept it as a means of payment.

142. Goodchild, *Capitalism and Religion*, 38.

143. Of course, since the arbitration is built on each individual pursuing their own self-interest, it is arguable that this mediation produces the exact opposite of *con*sensus. Capitalism's peace-making capacity cannot rise above the level of calculated cessation of conflict, the provisional transmutation of combat to competition. Goodchild, *Theology of Money*, 131.

144. There is a clear meritocratic logic to all this. Anyone who flounders must, by the pseudo-evolutionary logic of the competitive marketplace, be unfit for purpose. It is appropriate to remember that "meritocracy" was a word coined in a mid-twentieth-century English novel which sought to satirize educational reform. Such etymological insights are all too often lost these days, perhaps because we failed to implement the changes to how we teach people so as to more fully liberate "the innovator who with one stroke can save the labour of 10,000." Young, *The Rise of the Meritocracy*, 15.

freedom to form any social institution that has a superior claim
to that of the rights of property and submission to contracts.[145]

Recalling Luther's warning about what it means to honor a god, real or
imagined, here we see how neoliberal globalized capitalism functions idolatrously. To engage with it, to honor it, to relate to it appropriately means to
approach it as the source of all the good things, the system's "sovereignty."
More than that, it is competitive and jealous about our heart's affections.
It must come first. There can be no other system, force, or person before
it. Wealth becomes our chief treasure. Goodchild exposes, then, the way
in which the liberating promise of neoliberalism—whose globalism will
undo the petty divisions of parochial thinking and whose respect for legal
institutions will undercut corruption and whose markets will cultivate individual flourishing while efficiently distributing resources where they are
most needed—is grounded in a "total and universal war" against competing
forms of authority.[146] To participate in neoliberalism is to embrace the vision of a person who is constituted in competitive trade. To benefit from
the peaceable social institutions of neoliberalism is to grant the view that
the resources are scarce and must be fought for. To enjoy the rights and
freedoms of neoliberalism is to adopt the belief that our deepest desires can
be expressed through commodities. To accept such an account of reality is
to reject the claims of the one Christians call Messiah.

In a recent work entitled *Plundering Egypt*, the American theologian
G. P. Wagenfuhr argues that loyalty to the Christian gospel inherently places
the adherent in conflict with market economies. "To serve God and to serve
money is impossible," he argues, "not so much because serving money is
about consumerism, though that is part of it, but because serving money
is actively engaging in sacrifice to idols fashioned by the myth, symbolism,
and order that money represents."[147] Neoliberalism's myths (for example,
the etiology of primal barter), symbols (not just money, but also the brands
that have become globally ubiquitous[148]), and order (that peculiar form of
economic and political reason that configures all aspects of existence in
economic terms) call for a loyalty from those subject to it that parallels and
competes with the trust called forth by YHWH.

---

145. Goodchild, *Theology of Money*, 131.

146. Goodchild, *Theology of Money*, 132.

147. Wagenfuhr, *Plundering Egypt*, 170.

148. This aspect of neoliberalism is famously the material for Naomi Klein's first
major work. Klein, *No Logo*.

Conclusion: How to Proceed

In this chapter, we have pinpointed the concept of neoliberalism as a dynamic that requires further, sustained theological consideration. Drawing on Karl Polanyi's *The Great Transformation*, we considered how critical it is that discourse around economic matters accounts for the contextual contingencies that sustain particular arrangements of power. Neoliberalism's rise to supremacy was not a default state of humanity. It has historical, political, and geographical explanations. When assessed in this fashion we see that neoliberalism names a nexus of forces that together aspire to offer a total account of our shared life. The attempt to render the life of any given society overwhelmingly in terms of economic markets appears idolatrous. The prioritization of accumulation and profit over goods that cannot be easily described in econometric terms "makes allegiance to capitalism virtually impossible for a Christian."[149]

The question arises as to how to respond. Mark Fisher argues that:

> A moral critique of capitalism, emphasizing the ways in which it leads to suffering, only reinforces capitalist realism. Poverty, famine and war can be presented as an inevitable part of reality, while the hope that these forms of suffering could be eliminated easily painted as naïve utopianism.[150]

Thus, the Live Aid movement of the 1980s, which gained momentum through its depiction of the horrendous suffering of Ethiopians during a famine and civil war, evolved in time to become a brand label, *Product Red*, which sought to be efficiently profitable while maximizing good.[151] Goodchild rules out the possibilities of both secession and confrontation. In the case of the first option, "the strategy of disavowal or forgetting, which recommends that we leave the market behind, merely reproduces the strategy of alienation by which persons are abstracted to become agents in the market," and the second option, "appeals to imperial conquest, a strategy that has been subsumed into the sovereignty of the market institution."[152]

Instead of seeking reform from within, new life outside, or outright revolution, Fisher argues that "capitalist realism can only be threatened if it is shown to be in some way inconsistent or untenable; if, that is to say, capitalism's ostensible 'realism' turns out to be nothing of the sort."[153] A process of subtle demythologization is required; not just attacking this or that aspect

---

149. Ellul, *Money and Power*, 20.

150. Fisher, *Capitalist Realism*, 16.

151. Fisher, *Capitalist Realism*, 15.

152. Goodchild, *Theology of Money*, 133.

153. Fisher, *Capitalist Realism*, 16.

of capitalism and hoping that by heaping up the inconsistencies the system might topple. Besieging capitalism with its own paradoxes has been a profitable micro-industry since Marx, and whenever a siege grows strong, it gets absorbed by the system. Like the evil foe in a superhero film, capitalism gains strength when such weapons are deployed in full-frontal attack.[154]

Rather, the totalized system that idolatrously claims our deepest allegiance must be punctured by an assault from the side. Our faith in the provision of Mammon must be slowly eroded and our doubts encouraged. A direct analogy can be drawn between evangelization and economic awakening. The creed that "There is no alternative" begins to topple when we suspect there's something more than at first appears to be. To show that there is space outside of the system is to destabilize the entire edifice, since its authority stems from appearing total. Fisher cites the example of Peter Weir's film, *The Truman Show*, as an example of a creative work that depicts "a universe of total determinism."[155] Truman Burbank's liberation does not first require the construction of an alternative world, or the destruction of his present world, or the commitment to reform it. Instead, his trust in the world falters sufficiently when he sees it in its reality as an arbitrary human ordering. Only then is he emboldened to faithfully leap into the unknown. That leap is arduous and laden with fear, but when his moment of freedom arrives, it turns out to be as prosaic as opening a door in a wall—because there is a real world outside the totalized system.

It is to ask how such a totalized system might be punctured that we now turn. The austerity politics which has become the norm following the 2008 crash is an intensification of neoliberalism. Protests like the one made at Kilmore Quay are inchoate expressions of a deep dissatisfaction with the demand that we should all become entrepreneurs of our selves.[156] Another way must be possible. The forest must be counted, in all its fullness, not just the profitable trees. In the parables of Jesus, we find a reality depicted that is in direct conflict with the order of neoliberalism. The kingdom of God that Jesus describes in these strange tales is one where accounting practices appear to reflect values antithetical to profit, where investment yields unlikely returns, and where debts are discarded as if they do not matter. When we read the parables of Jesus seriously in the age of neoliberalism, we develop a sneaking suspicion that another world exists. It is to that unseen "outside" that we now direct our attention.

---

154. The neoliberal order "entails subordinating oneself to a reality that is infinitely plastic, capable of reconfiguring itself at any moment." Fisher, *Capitalist Realism*, 54.

155. Fisher, *Capitalist Realism*, 67.

156. Foucault, *The Birth of Biopolitics*, 226.

CHAPTER 2

Karl Barth and the Parables of Jesus

The Time as it is in the Kingdom

INTRODUCTION

The opening chapter undertook an imaginative task that has become second nature to us in this age of digital maps: we zoomed out to attempt a
global view. This was not the mythic "view from nowhere" but an attempt to
peek simultaneously at both an ongoing dialogue within theology about our
capitalist economies and at a wider discourse in Western society about the
health and well-being of those economic systems.[1]

In the next chapter, we consider the recent economic history of Ireland
as its Celtic Tiger era ended and a period of prolonged economic contraction that followed. Three narratives introduce this history: stories that seek
to open perspectives on the lived reality of that transition, which standard
economic accounts might miss. The stories told are local, framed by specific
histories and definite geographies inside a set period of time. This grounds
the theological question of wealth in a concrete location, minimizing the
evasion into abstraction or generality that can beset so wide a question as
how Christians should engage with money.

The themes that were introduced in the first chapter will be considered
afresh in the third. What we will find is that the Irish economy is not unique
in its ability to be rendered narratively. To talk about the economy at all is to
talk in terms of stories. The first chapter examined how we have embraced
a story about the economy that fits more neatly as fairy tale than we are
comfortable admitting. Human societies do not arise out of the truck and
barter of self-interested individuals pursuing their rational interests. Trade
is always embedded in a complex web of relationships and commitments,
most of which cannot be accurately represented by economic quantification.

1. Nagel, *The View from Nowhere.*

Committing to that neoliberal story under the impression that it is social-scientific fact, or political reality, and most fundamentally out of a desire to acquire the riches it promises, poses grave spiritual risks. In telling an overarching tale of a triumphant market, neoliberalism sketches liberal progress through competition, even while reliant on the effective deployment of legal, political, and disciplinary powers to function. We discovered, in consultation with contemporary theological reflection on economics, that this story is not of a default reality, but funds and orients human agents as they shape their world. This means it is actually a story strategically half-told, aiming to suffocate alternative stories. It is easier to imagine the end of the world than to imagine an alternative to capitalism.[2] Neoliberalism weaves a seamless garment from its origin story through to its vision of consummation, enveloping our imagination and memory so as to shape our desire. This is why I suggested that capitalism seeks our allegiance in a way that Christians must call idolatrous.

Christianity is an alternative story about wealth: what it is, how it happens, and why it exists.[3] It is not that Christianity can offer some alternative economic system. There is no "biblical" economic program waiting to be discovered. Neither is it the case that we need to infuse the current system with a little more virtue so that we can achieve some oxymoron like a "Christian capitalism." Rather, as Christians respond to other potential idolatries, they respond to neoliberalism by asserting that allegiance to the one living God is the only viable way to live. The problem Christians have with the idolatry of wealth in a capitalist context is perennial. When we worship things that are not God, we end up worshipping death.[4] Since all creatures and creations have their limits, when those points are reached, idolatry becomes a form of worship bound to spill over into killing.[5] In this light, developing a response to the force that neoliberalism exerts on our thinking and wealth holds over our affections is urgent. Whatever it entails, working out Christian faithfulness in the face of wealth's seductions, which will be explored more fully in chapter 4, will not be achieved through policy discussions or via cultural transformation movements. A multitude of small acts of pointed worship turns out to have much greater possible potency.

The recollection of the story of Jesus, through sacrament and preaching, in prayer and song, and by the reading of Scripture, is at the heart of

2. This is an even smaller ask than imagining the end of capitalism. Jameson, "Future City," 76.

3. Dotan Leshem has written a fascinating account of how early Christian theology shaped our economic thinking. Leshem, *The Origins of Neoliberalism*.

4. Stringfellow, *Dissenter in a Great Society*, 43.

5. Stringfellow, *Dissenter in a Great Society*, 44.

public worship. The stories Jesus told are the material that now concerns us. In these stories we find that the decision to articulate the economic sphere in modes that seem ill-fitting to the modern mind (via parabolic narratives) is not merely an interesting curiosity, or a thought-provoking exercise in method, but the expression of a theological commitment in which the eschatological expectation of God's kingdom is given priority, over and against the normative narratives of the age in which we live. Thus, we do not simply turn to the parables as wise fables, but we turn to them as apocalyptic texts, narratives that intrude confrontationally upon the apparently settled wisdom of this age and of this time. The means by which we will consider these apocalyptic parables is by way of a particular guide: the twentieth-century Swiss theologian Karl Barth.

TIME AND THE KINGDOM OF GOD

As we will see, time is an important register in how Barth reads the parables. The age in which we live is implicitly in question in the stories Jesus tells. Do we live in the era of Caesar or Messiah? As John Swinton has recently argued so powerfully, God's time is bound to conflict with the "Standard Average European Time" of neoliberalism.[6] In God's time, time remains precious, but it is never scarce. Learning how to tell time in the kingdom is one of the things that the parables teach us and that is a training which "properly is a movement away from idolatry and violence towards faithful timefulness."[7]

Neoliberal subjectivity frames the world in terms of competition. Consider where such an imagination leaves us. While we might be inclined to believe that everyone starts from the same line, the reality of capital is that many are actively advantaged and more face obstacles before they even reach the imagined baseline. If we do grant the capitalist fantasy about everyone starting with the same opportunity, the metaphor of competition is brutal. By implication, most will lose out and many of those who win will not triumph through hard work but through a combination of inherited factors. The sharp end of our theological reflection on the neoliberal subjectivity is that the neoliberal age is one where we exist perpetually in debt.[8] Debt is the neoliberal power which operates through time in such a way as to permit Swinton to term it "violence."[9]

6. Swinton, *Becoming Friends of Time*, 23.

7. Swinton, *Becoming Friends of Time*, 65.

8. My work in this section owes a debt, as it were, to the Italian theorist Maurizio Lazzarato. Lazzarato, *The Making of the Indebted Man*; Lazzarato, *Governing by Debt*.

9. Swinton, *Becoming Friends of Time*, 65.

When we posit our lives as that of solitary, self-interested actors who compete against each other for scarce resources, we fire up the furnace in which idols are wrought; we are committing to a lie. Society is not a gathering of individuals seeking to maximize their interest. Instead, relationship is the shape of society and credit is the basis of the *polis*. The direct theological interface here is grace and abundance. Christianity insists that Creation, neither in its origin nor its destination, is a story about scarcity and debt.

Of course, we do not simply imagine ourselves as indebted. Increasingly, we are all bound by debt. We are neoliberal subjects rendered insecure on a very basic moral level by the asymmetry of finance.[10] Burdened by the need to pay back—note how different this language is from the idea of "contributing to society"—our futures are predetermined by the need to live a certain way to honor the debt.

Barth's claim with many of the parables is that the question being posed to us is "In what time do we live?" Neoliberalism is the time of working under perpetual debt, in so many different forms—mortgages that last lifetimes, credit cards that are the simplest way to transform their owners into permanent debtors,[11] and sovereign debt into which we are born, like a fiscal original sin.[12] Debt is a claim on our future because to receive the money implies a commitment to live in such a way as to enable paying it back.[13] Adam Smith's capitalism may have created a *homo oeconomicus* but neoliberalism has forged *homo debitor*.[14]

For Lazzarato, "debt produces a specific 'morality,'"[15] which threads a "promise-default" dynamic into the pre-existing "effort-reward" system that we associate with our economic life. This effort-reward/promise-fault dynamic exerts a constant force on conception of self and our conception of what is possible. As previously noted, Nietzsche reminds us *schuld* (guilt) is

10. Lazzarato, *The Making of the Indebted Man*, 11.

11. Lazzarato, *The Making of the Indebted Man*, 20.

12. Lazzarato, *The Making of the Indebted Man*, 32. Lazzarato explains, "Economists tell us that every French child is born 22,000 euros in debt. We are no longer the inheritors of original sin but rather of the debt of preceding generations. 'Indebted man' is subject to a creditor-debtor power relation accompanying him throughout his life, from birth to death. If in times past we were indebted to the community, to the gods, to our ancestors, we are henceforth indebted to the 'god' Capital."

13. One is reminded here of the "timeless take on time" offered by the Irish stand-up comedian, Dave Allen. "You clock in to the clock. You clock out to the clock. You come home to the clock. You eat to the clock, you drink to the clock, you go to bed to the clock . . . . You do that for forty years of your life, you retire, what do they give? A clock!" Quoted in Garfield, *Timekeepers*, 19.

14. Lazzarato, *The Making of the Indebted Man*, 127.

15. Lazzarato, *The Making of the Indebted Man*, 30.

derived from the concept of debt (and we might add, the Latin root of "debt" is *debita* which also means duty).[16] When social services are financialized, in very concrete senses (both fiscal and social), the recipient of welfare becomes indebted in their acceptance of assistance. Taking on credit and becoming a debtor is how we exercise our freedom, but we are then coerced into living in such a way as to honor the debts we had to take on to become free. As Lazzarato observes, "Even those too poor to have access to credit must pay interest to creditors through the reimbursement of public debt."[17]

There is no more transparent example of how debt constrains and disciplines us than student debt. In the United States, the United Kingdom, and in many other nations, the only way to get ahead is to secure a third-level education, but the only way to access that schooling is to embrace massive debts. The student who graduates with a six-figure student debt that cannot be escaped, even through bankruptcy, is going to govern themselves.[18] They need a job and the best paying job they can get. Squandering their youth on idealistic endeavors is actively *immoral* when society has already extended such privilege to them in the form of a university education. Debt, theologically understood, is not primarily about money, but time, and how we get to spend it. Debt stakes a claim on the future, constraining possibilities in ways that serve the creditor.

The deep theology here is in the claim that debt creates a memory. But this is not the memory that is dedicated to keeping the past alive in the sense of a Seder meal. Rather, the memory of debt is intended to project behavior in to the future.

Christianity deals with memory too. When Christians break bread and share wine in memory of Jesus, we are transparently seeking to re-collect the events of Easter. But we also make a claim that the present is constituted by that specific past event, even though it is not temporally implicated in the superficial causation of the contingent details that make up our lives. The story of our present is determined by the Last Supper and the days that followed in a way that is more determinative than our genetics, or where we went to school, or our emotional state at any given moment. Further, the resurrection is a memory that actively makes our future, in the sense of the future being the domain of possibility. In the era of neoliberalism, the future is shaped by the present. In the kingdom of God, the present is shaped by the future. To help explain this, it will be useful to draw on the work of Stanley Hauerwas.

---

16. Selby, *Grace and Mortgage*, 5.

17. Lazzarato, *The Making of the Indebted Man*, 32.

18. Lazzarato, *Governing by Debt*, 69.

"'Out of all the people of the world I have called you Israel to be my promised people' is the claim that makes time unavoidable for Christians" declares Hauerwas in his essay, "How to Tell Time Theologically."[19] Building on the writing of Oscar Cullmann, Hauerwas argues that Christians, in their claim that they are claimed by the God of Israel, are a storied people. "Few phrases are more significant than 'In the beginning.'"[20] God redeems in time and so redeems time. The cross and the tomb form the fulcrum for all of time. We can think here of Charles Taylor's discussion of "*kairotic* time,"[21] or settle for Hauerwas's description: "On that event all history and nature turns."[22]

Now we begin to see how curious a set of skills are required in telling Christian time. It is not just that Christians rejected the classical Greek conception of a cosmos without beginning. It is not just that they asserted that they had been ingrafted to the narrative line that began with Abraham and Isaac and Jacob. Christians believe that eternity penetrates time. The neat chronology of past, present, and future is called into question by Easter, Ascension, and Return.

God is not timeless. He cannot be because Easter happened. Instead, as Barth puts it, God is

> supremely temporal. For his eternity is authentic temporality, and therefore the source of all time. But in His eternity, in the uncreated self-subsistent time which is one of the perfections of His divine nature, present, past, and future, yesterday, to-day, and to-morrow, are not successive, but simultaneous.[23]

Eternity is not empty. God is the one who has time. He has all the time in the world.

So Hauerwas holds that "since we are human and not God we must learn to live in created time."[24] He has famously said that Modernity names that time when we are told we have no story but the story we make for ourselves.[25] The Christian can never be at home there, in Modernity, because

---

19. Hauerwas, *The Work of Theology*, 90.

20. Hauerwas, *The Work of Theology*, 91.

21. Taylor, *A Secular Age*, 54.

22. Hauerwas, *The Work of Theology*, 91.

23. Barth, *CD III/2*, 437.

24. Hauerwas, *The Work of Theology*, 92.

25. Some variety of this statement—"By modernity, I mean the project to create social orders that would make it possible for each person living in such orders 'to have no story except the story they choose when they have no story.'"—can be found throughout his work. This example comes from Hauerwas, *Wilderness Wanderings*, 26.

"we are embedded in histories we have not chosen but by having our lives storied by God fate can be transformed into destiny."[26] This is not an efficient approach to living our lives and so Christians can never be properly at home in neoliberalism either.

It follows that the Christian life involves telling the time and living in keeping with the time we have been allotted. It is not clear to me whether the time of neoliberalism that Lazzarato describes is properly parasitic on the Christian account or if the formal similarities are coincidental. Regardless, any insistence from the powers that be that they get to shape the future is to be held with almost unmovable suspicion by those who insist they are "never 'boxed in' by history."[27] Time is a gift inhabited in common which cannot be bought or earned. Interest-bearing debt represents the attempt to turn that time into money.[28]

What is clear is that neoliberal power's claim on our future represents yet one more example of the common "proclivity to avoid the reality that we have a beginning and an end."[29] Lazzarato suggests that the society of indebted humanity is "a society without time, without possibility, without foreseeable rupture."[30] Debt as the end of history! Displayed here, we see capitalism's eschatology. But time is ruptured, again and again, as the church gathers to worship. As we enact baptism and Eucharist and preach the Word, through the Spirit, Jesus's fulfilment of the Father's promises becomes real to us. "Worship" is the training that allows us to learn to recognize time and it is also the liberation from the idolatrous claim that capital holds over us. The parables, read aloud and preached upon in worship, stand as paradigmatic examples of how the Scriptures can renew our vision, prying open ways of thinking and being that get sealed shut under the logic of neoliberalism.

We are getting ahead of ourselves however. The task that stands immediately before us is to explain why parables can function as a rich ground in which to begin our ethical investigations, how the apocalyptic register

26. Hauerwas, *The Work of Theology*, 93.

27. Hauerwas, *The Work of Theology*, 100.

28. Hauerwas connects this impulse directly to the invention of the clock. Only after time "could be measured 'exactly'" could we collectively conceive of duration in terms of econometric investment. Once there was no secular, and its creation is inextricably linked to the erection of market bells that ran a different schedule from that of the local church. Hauerwas, *With the Grain of the Universe*, 35–36.

29. Hauerwas, *The Work of Theology*, 102.

30. Lazzarato, *The Making of the Indebted Man*, 47. Lazzarato goes on to say that the Middle Ages saw this clearly; debt was a claim on the future. The usurer was stealing time from God.

allows us to gain traction in concrete situations, and who should guide us as we seek out that parabolic polyvalence which resists simplification.

WHY PARABLES, WHY APOCALYPTIC, AND WHY BARTH?

Parables

It is in the parables that we find some of Jesus's most striking words about money, wealth, and the economy. Fully half of the parables deal with such themes. No substantive theology of wealth can avoid engaging with the parables, not just because of the volume of material related therein to money and economics, but because of the ways in which the questions around these topics are approached.[31] In the first chapter we discerned the ways in which accounts of globalization and contemporary capitalism seek to determine the appropriate words that can be used to describe our reality. Neoliberalism encourages a political and moral stance that treasures responsibility, reasoned after a certain fashion. The parables explode any hope we might maintain of developing such an ethics of principles and propositions. The message is in the medium and by embedding his economic discussion in the form of enigmatic short stories, Jesus teaches us in ways that are complex, open, and resistant to readings that seek only for the bottom line. The parables allow a direct response to the econometric calculation which so often colonizes ethical thought in capitalism.[32]

It is the complex openness of the parables that makes them so enticing as sites of ethical reflection in an age of neoliberal capitalism. In the words of the late Scottish theologian Donald MacKinnon, they go beyond hinting at "unnoticed possibilities of well-doing" and instead reveal the "ways in

---

31. Sadly, it remains possible to write best-selling, popular treatments of the parables that do not engage at all with wealth. In the middle of my doctoral studies, my friend, Alison Chino, very thoughtfully sent me a copy of a best seller she picked up in her local Christian bookstore in Arkansas, a guide to the parables written by members of what was called "The Duck Dynasty." As an Irishman, this was a whole new world to me. It somehow made the parables very simple but left me entirely confused. The book came with a free DVD study guide, but not a word about the prevalence of money in Jesus's teaching. Robertson and Howard, *Faith Commander.*

32. Which is supported by Richard Lischer in his claim that reading the parables with the poor has "uncontested value." The parables do not just occur in settings where wealth and poverty, power and justice are in contention but they were "originally intended to speak to and against systems of oppression." Lischer, *Reading the Parables,* 139.

which things fundamentally are."[33] It is their "peculiar indirection"[34] that makes them so valuable when so much of our ethical thinking is constrained by the bottom line. A parable about a creditor and a debtor is unlikely to be much help to a scholar intending to discover the legal framework by which lending was conducted in first-century Palestine. They are stories intended to transform, and critically, they are stories in which "the transformation is wrought indirectly."[35] One of the ways this works out is that the parable cannot be processed in advance.[36] They are more complex than allegories and they do not function like analogies. We cannot algorithmically anticipate the role that the different characters in any given parable may play via some straightforward symbolic meaning. Thus, MacKinnon warns, the one who manages to convert the "parable into a recipe" is the one who "passes to the side of the goats" in so doing.[37] Whether it is Nathan's parable that cures David's blindness[38] or Jesus's parables that seek to rouse his slow disciples to the task to which he has called them, this is a mode of discourse in the Bible that "shatters the veil of self-induced pretense."[39]

Apocalyptic

Common approaches to reading parables in the last century have either sought out just one point[40] or anticipated many.[41] Reading parables so as to

33. MacKinnon, *The Problem of Metaphysics*, 79.

34. MacKinnon, *The Problem of Metaphysics*, 79.

35. MacKinnon, *The Problem of Metaphysics*, 81.

36. An example of a not entirely convincing effort to determine a precise method for reading the parables exists in William R. Herzog II's ambitious *Parables as Subversive Speech*, which engages in an "experiment" of reading the parables through the tools of modern social science and the philosophy of Paulo Freire. While his assumption that the parables enable "a people so caught up in their context that they hardly see it to step back and gain perspective" is an important insight, the process of codification he borrows from Freire is restrictive in a way that limits interpretations so that they reinforce instead of challenge ideological commitments. Herzog II, *Parables as Subversive Speech*, 259, 266.

37. MacKinnon, *The Problem of Metaphysics*, 86.

38. 2 Samuel 12:1–13.

39. MacKinnon, *The Problem of Metaphysics*, 92.

40. This trajectory was initiated dominated by the work of the German scholar Adolf Jülicher, who rejected allegorical interpretation, insisting instead that the parable is "there only to illuminate . . . one point, a rule, an idea, an experience that is valid on the spiritual as on the secular level." Jülicher, *Die Gleichnisreden Jesu*. Translated and quoted in Hultgren, *The Parables of Jesus*, 13.

41. As Klyne Snodgrass puts it, "Jesus does not need to be saved from allegory.

downplay their eschatological elements must be avoided, but in eagerness to retrieve a range of reading modes, we must also resist downplaying how open the parables are as narratives.[42] The profound challenge that the parables represent can be all too easily missed.[43] A wise assumption as we approach these texts is that they are irreducibly polyvalent. Christian reflection on faithfulness in a wealthy age can begin with the parables because they cannot be knocked into a shape that can give rise to principles or distilled into a moral message. The surplus of the story spills over any instrumental use by which we hope to contain them. The parables are not simple stories engineered to be understood by Palestinian simpletons.[44] The stories are not simple and neither was their audience. They are genuinely perplexing. They often flirt with impiety in how they characterize God, in ways that anticipate an audience capable and willing to reflect deeply and self-critically.[45] They push beyond that. In their complexity, they press even the brightest listeners

---

Parables are allegorical, some more so than others." Snodgrass, *Stories with Intent*, 16. N. T. Wright argues the parables are "functioning at a variety of levels" and are designed "as tools to break open the prevailing worldview and replace it with one that was closely related but significantly adjusted at every point." Wright, *Jesus and the Victory of God*, 175.

42. Don't take me to be suggesting this is an exhaustive model. David Gowler's excellent discussion of twentieth-century "afterlives" of Jesus parables testify to the range of interpretations possible. Gowler, *The Parables after Jesus*, 207–54.

43. The tradition of reading the parables as if they were straightforward has diverse proponents including Abraham Lincoln who is said to have opined that "God tells the truth in parables because they are easier for the common folk to understand and recollect." I'll leave it to historians of America to tell us whether Abe got as far as Matthew 13. Quoted in Hunter, *Interpreting the Parables*, 13.

44. John Dominic Crossan is an example of a contemporary biblical scholar whose work on the parables seeks to highlight both the complexity of the stories themselves and the sophistication with which they were initially received and interpreted. For example: "My own understanding of Jesus' constant paradoxicality in word and deed is, as just noted, to see it as the almost inevitable result of his Jewish tradition turning its aniconic faith onto language itself and thus onto law and prophecy, wisdom and apocalypse. An aphorism such as the last being first and the first last was, for Jesus, a linguistic expression of the Kingdom of God, a paradoxical expression of the relationship between the divine and the human. But such paradoxical aphorisms and narratives could also be heard by those whose understanding was far more political than religious, by someone, for example, who might decide that Jewish peasants were 'the last' and Roman occupiers 'the first' and consider the saying an invitation to holy war. The Jesus tradition, in other words, may well have been remembered by many who heard it literally and read it politically within either spiritual or material, national or international parameters." Crossan, *Cliffs of Fall*, 21.

45. David van Daalen concludes that in the parable of the Talents, "one thing is certain. The master in the parable does not stand for God. It would be blasphemous to suggest that God 'reaps where he did not sow'!" It would also be blasphemous to suggest that God is absent-minded and prone to losing things, but the first parable of Luke 15 is not usually subject to such pre-emptory interpretative regulation. Daalen, *The Kingdom of God Is Like This*, 61.

beyond their competence. Speaking of one of the alarming images for God painted in the parables, Roger White comments, "it is not as though, after profound soul-searching, we will come to find the comparison between God and an absentee landlord easy and acceptable."[46]

The confusion induced by reading the parables is one of the factors that makes them so rich when reflecting on wealth in neoliberal societies. Jesus's divine yarns burst through the iron cage of capitalism. Their irreducibility means they resist co-option. Counter-readings can always be discovered. White argues that they exist to provoke conversion and it is in this mode that we will read them.[47] The apocalyptic register is an obvious response to the totalized ubiquity of neoliberalism. In an age often described as the end of history, the parables remind us that the center of history is found on the cross and that the crucified one can find us whenever we are.[48] In an age when capital appears to reign, the parables often feature a king, because they are intended to reveal the rival kingdom of God. They expose the in-breaking kingdom and thus are ideal dialogue partners as we consider the need to interrupt the dominant discourse of neoliberal capitalism.

To read the parables apocalyptically means to read them as if they reveal something that is concealed. This revealing applies not so much to the stories themselves, as it does to us. We do not find, for example, that the psychological motivations of the characters have roots in childhood trauma, as we might, say, in a contemporary novel. *We* are implicated as the narratives unfurl. This dynamic is described by Lowe as "one of the key ways the gospel contextualizes us."[49] To say that the parables are apocalyptic is not to suggest that they are close relatives to the American pulp fiction *Left Behind* series.[50] The works of Franz Kafka would be a much closer companion, as they invariably involve a protagonist being seized by events that reveal the world is not the way they thought it was and we, the reader, come to have a similar

---

46. White, "MacKinnon and the Parables," 56.

47. White, "MacKinnon and the Parables," 58.

48. Jesus's eschatological vision represented "a vision of history as a whole, a transfiguration of the given world, and not an escape from or a denial of it." Wilder, *Jesus' Parables and the War of Myths*, 140.

49. Lowe, "Why We Need Apocalyptic," 49.

50. Lowe avers that such literature "might better be described not as apocalyptic, but as a form of gnostic dispensationalism." Lowe, "Why We Need Apocalyptic," 50.

disorientating experience as we read.[51] The parables have such conceptual openness because they are stories about Jesus closing in.[52]

In pursuit of these apocalyptic parables, we will approach the material through the prior discussion by a doctor of the church, in this case, Karl Barth. By a close reading of relevant sections of the *Church Dogmatics*, we will seek to hear anew what the apocalyptic good news of the parables has to say about wealth.

Barth

In Barth's *Romans* commentary, he famously declared that "if Christianity be not altogether eschatology, there remains in it no relationship whatever with Christ."[53] While he would come to articulate this in different ways, he never repudiated his elementary commitment to this apocalypse-advent form of God's interaction with the world.[54] If one seeks out the parables to liberate one's imagination from the hegemonic hold of global capitalism as an avenue to explore what it might mean that we live in an age where Jesus is Lord—and Mammon is not—then Barth is an excellent guide. As Douglas Harink has observed, the very structure of the *Dogmatics* rests on the eschatological register: "The entire project begins with 'apocalypse,' that is with the doctrine of revelation which is determined from the beginning to end by the world-dissolving and world-constituting event of God's advent in the cross and resurrection of Jesus Christ."[55]

There is no parable that goes undiscussed in the *Church Dogmatics*, and there is no volume that does not offer some comment on a parable.[56] Yet

51. One can think even of the way in which the Examining Magistrate in the building on Juliusstrasse to which Josef K. must repeatedly present himself in *The Trial* seems eerily to never be the same from one day to the next. K. finds himself in an uncanny world where no fixed points can provide a solid perspective. Consider the contrasts, for example, in the description of the same place in Kafka, chapter 2 and chapter 3, *The Complete Novels*, 30–35 and 43–44.

52. Lowe, "Prospects for a Postmodern Christian Theology," 20.

53. Barth, *The Epistle to the Romans*, 314.

54. Shannon Nicole Smythe's work here on Barth and Pauline apocalypticism is an important companion. "The Spirit's work in liberating Christians for this new life is how their perfect justification in Christ is made subjectively true in present time, even as they await the full realization of new humanity and that of all of creation on Christ's final return." Smythe, *Forensic Apocalyptic Theology*, 227–228.

55. Harink, *Paul Among the Postliberals*, 54.

56. Barth, of course, treats parables elsewhere as well. For example, in the essay, "The Christian's Place in Society" in *The Word of God and the Word of Man*, Barth argues that what marks out the parables from other famous fables, myths, or similar tales

Barth never explicitly offers a systematic treatment of parables.[57] Instead, they are discussed within the momentum of other concerns. His engagement is episodic and incidental. However, there is one clear discussion of the peculiarity of parables that provides lines of enquiry that are taken up elsewhere. It is useful to consider this discussion, centered in §69.

In IV/3, as part of §69, Barth offers the parables as prototypical examples of human words that "even in their whole creatureliness and human frailty either are or may be true words."[58] He goes on to consider the very nature of the parables. The first thing to be said is that they are "little stories which it seems anyone might tell of ordinary human happenings."[59] But not just anyone tells them. Jesus tells them, or as Barth puts it, "Jesus Christ utters, or rather creates, these parables" and in so doing he shares neither simply entertaining narratives, nor profound metaphors, "but a disclosing yet also concealing revelation."[60] They are stories about the kingdom, which stretch the dimensions of everyday life, just as the kingdom comes into the world and makes it new in surprising ways. Drawing on Mark 4:9-12, he highlights the fact that they are examples of insider speech, transparent only to the true followers of Jesus:

> It is also said that the kingdom in its likeness to these events, or these events in their likeness to the kingdom, can and will be heard by those who have ears to hear, i.e., by those to whom it is given to hear (Mk. 4:9f.). That is to say, they will hear and receive the equations or likenesses as such, whereas those who are 'without' will not perceive and understand what is at issue, namely, the 'mystery' of the kingdom.[61]

The stories are not really concerned with ordinary human happenings. They are likened to the kingdom of God and their alien nature is evident throughout. While the subject matter seems humdrum in the large part—women making bread and farmers planting seeds and investors looking for

is "the simple way in which the kingdom of heaven is compared to the world." What resonates in these stories "is the purely miraculous element which inheres in seeing the invisible things of God and understanding them by the things that are made." From the beginning, for Barth, the parables are narratives of apocalypses. Barth, *The Word of God and the Word of Man*, 303, 306.

57. There may be no systematic treatment of parables, but parables of course do play a structural part in the Dogmatics. The entire fourth volume is "framed around an improvisation of the parable of the prodigal son." Cocksworth, *Karl Barth on Prayer*, 180.

58. Barth, *CD IV/3*, 110.

59. Barth, *CD IV/3*, 112.

60. Barth, *CD IV/3*, 112.

61. Barth, *CD IV/3*, 112.

return—certain decisive parables (Lazarus and the Rich Man, The Sheep and the Goats) draw on "the imagery of late Jewish apocalyptic."[62] Even more, the characters behave in odd ways. They are strangely drawn. "To be sure, there are no miracles in the stories. Yet strange things happen."[63]

What kind of stories are these? Are the parables magic realism? The parables are not new stories that remind us of old truths but everyday stories conformed (or distorted?) to give a glimpse of the in-breaking kingdom. The story is told slantwise so that the everyday appears as it has never appeared before, because the everyday is going to appear as we've never seen it before in the kingdom.

Barth is clear that the apocalyptic parables should not be used as raw material for a Christian doctrine of the Last Things because "Jesus narrates, fashions and transforms them" to suit his purposes.[64] As such, these stories should not be utilized as road maps to describe the layout of the final days. Instead, they are of a part with the rest of the more everyday, prosaic scenes found in the other parables. The point is to reveal to us a glimpse of the utterly new thing that is the kingdom.

Barth draws our attention to the fact that even where settings feature mundane scenes, the plot often involves hiddenness (the yeast working through dough, the seed growing under the ground, the opponent who sows tares among the wheat under the cover of darkness). The kingdom of God that is described in these parables is not a project for improving the state of the world. "The new aeon whose dawn is declared by the Word of grace is no mere radiant idea, related to the reality of the old like the mirage to a caravan plodding through a desert which is only too real."[65] It is "no wonderful Utopian dream" and neither is it a particularly "clever and practically illuminating and helpful program for the amelioration of the world or men either generally or in detail."[66] What breaks in is neither a movement of enthusiasm, nor "is there accomplished a new organization of the different forces for good with a view to creating for humanity both individually and collectively a more worthy future."[67]

What happens is "something incomparably more basic and helpful."[68] The parables are stories, and the narratives of stories rely on temporality;

62. Barth, *CD IV/3*, 112.

63. Barth, *CD IV/3*, 112.

64. Barth, *CD IV/3*, 113.

65. Barth, *CD IV/3*, 246.

66. Barth, *CD IV/3*, 246.

67. Barth, *CD IV/3*, 246.

68. Barth, *CD IV/3*, 246.

this action leads to that action, and so on. But the stories of the parables are intended to draw attention to how the action of God is breaking in on the present and sweeping us into a future eschatological reality. As Barth puts it, "This future has begun with the fact that God has fulfilled His covenant with man, that He has loved the world and reconciled it with Himself."[69] Tenses collapse as the election of God before Creation, the last things, and the present come together in stories about missing sheep and hidden pearls. Our future meets our present and absorbs our past as we are brought into this new reality. Barth calls us to note how in the parable of the Marriage Banquet of the King's Son, as the feast is prepared, the oxen and fatlings are already slaughtered. "Not just some things but all things, and not all things in a state of preparation but all things ready" are included in this remaking of all things new.[70]

Thus, Barth's interpretative method for the parables involves reading the tales through a christological lens, attuned to the presence of the kingdom of God. Our expectation should be that the portrait of the kingdom of God that we encounter in the parables will neither be straightforward in depiction, nor in content. It is not enough to say that the tales bend and twist and warp everyday scenarios into unusual perspectives, like narrative Dadaism. We have no reason to assume that what we find depicted can be anticipated ahead of time. There is no necessary overlap between the world we know, populated with the products of human reason and culture and law, and the world that is breaking in. "It is just as though a newly tailored and ornamented garment were ready and we had only to put it on, with no possibility of delay since the old one has already gone to the ragman and is no longer available."[71]

One of the consequences of this is that Barth's interpretation of the parables is unlikely to simply "cash out" with some principles for handling wealth in the contemporary world.[72] Whatever truth lies in the stories of lost coins and seeds sown, it is the truth of this discontinuous kingdom. As Barth reads them, the parables bridge us from this world into the new creation.

69. Barth, *CD IV/3*, 246.

70. Barth, *CD IV/3*, 246.

71. Barth, *CD IV/3*, 246.

72. Such an expectation can be easily found in the literature. David Cowan, for example, concludes his study of the economic parables by declaring that "Jesus' parables rely on the notion that the natural order of things is divinely ordered in some way." Cowan assumes that the parables "rely" on the Jesus for their meaning. The reasoning the led to such a conclusion is obscure and the specifics as to what might be meant by the "some way" is ambiguous, although a few pages later we read that we cannot "say that the market is necessarily of divine provision, though that is definitely a debate worth having." Cowan, *Economic Parables*, 192, 201.

SITUATING BARTH'S PARABLE READINGS:
THE RICH YOUNG RULER

Barth offers us a way into the parables as interruptive narratives that confront us with a logic around wealth, generosity, and faithfulness that is at odds with and an alternative to the logic of neoliberal capitalism. Our engagement with Barth will necessarily range across the *Church Dogmatics*, because that is how he treated the parable material. In §37 of *Church Dogmatics*, Barth offers an extended excursus on the scene from Mark 10:17–31 in which Jesus engages with the Rich Young Ruler.[73] The episode confirms for Barth that God's revelation comes in the form of Jesus.[74] His actions are divine motions, his speech is the command of God. As Barth deploys it in this instance, the divine command is a liberating event, an invitation from the man who is God to live as we truly ought. It cannot be packaged as a system or reduced to principles. Ethics begins when the revelation of God breaks in on us. Thus:

> When we honestly ask: *What* ought we to do?, we approach God as those who are ignorant in and with all that they already know, and stand in dire need of divine instruction and conversion. We are then ready, with a view to our next decision, to bracket and hold in reserve all that we think we know concerning the rightness and goodness of our past and present decisions, all the rules and axioms, however good, all the inner and outer laws and necessities under which we have placed ourselves and perhaps do so again. None of them is identical with the divine command.[75]

The divine command is not an abstract ideal, but a very concrete description of reality, the truth of our existence. Jesus's interaction with the young ruler is enigmatic, in a fashion that is not dissimilar to many of the parables. Jesus's interlocutor goes away "grieving" while the disciples are "perplexed" and "greatly astounded" (vv. 22, 24, and 26). Barth sees here that "the demand of the living divine command made in the person of Jesus aims at the genuine, joyous, and sustained decision of man for this person and therefore at the fulfilment of the one entire will of God."[76] The young

---

73. My reading here is heavily influenced by the prior work of Susannah Ticciati, *Job and the Disruption of Identity*, 35–48.

74. He talks of the "decisive Christological determination of the form of the divine command." Barth, *CD II/2*, 613.

75. Barth, *CD II/2*, 646.

76. Barth, *CD II/2*, 613.

ruler comes to Jesus with questions that anticipate expert opinion ("What must I do to inherit eternal life?") but finds that the one to whom he speaks does not offer advice to be assessed in contrast to other voices. In the course of our lives, we often consult expert opinion for guidance, which appears to be what the rich young man thinks he is doing. But to pose a question to God is to move from ordinary time to eschatological possibility. He came looking for answers, or perhaps even better, consultation. Instead what he found was a questioning that pressed at the heart of his identity, and so presents a demand he must accept or resist and with it Jesus himself.

The "christological determination" of the episode can be seen in how both the obedient disciples and the disobedient young questioner fall under the "judicial authority and power, the *regnum Jesu Christi*."[77] The "ostentatious" fashion in which the young man presents himself in verse 17 is demonstrative of how he has adjusted "himself to the order which is still order even where we are disobedient to it."[78] Once the young ruler places himself before Jesus in this fashion, all is changed. "He cannot and will not reverse or nullify this testimony by his later withdrawal."[79] The kingdom of God is not a voluntary association that you can leave by letting your subscription lie. It is not a mailing list from which we unsubscribe. "It is quite possible to leave or be expelled from a society, but never from the Kingdom of Christ."[80] In a manner of speaking, the young ruler can check out any time he likes, but he can never leave.

The question that the rich young man asks, "Good teacher, what shall I do that I may inherit eternal life?" reveals why he finds the realm of the kingdom attractive. The question is posed, Barth argues, by one who is "sure that in this present fleeting life man has to be and do something definite in order to attain this eternal life."[81] What do you have to do to be an heir? The young man does not pose this question to the cosmos; a sort of soliloquy for the benefit of the universe or the gods or the fates. From his knees, he calls on Jesus for an answer. "For it is in Jesus that there has been concluded between God and man the covenant which forms the beginning of all the ways and works of God, and therefore the objective law under which the existence of all living creatures runs its course."[82] The

---

77. "The reign of Jesus Christ." Barth, *CD II/2*, 613.

78. Barth, *CD II/2*, 613.

79. Barth, *CD II/2*, 613.

80. Barth, *CD II/2*, 613.

81. Barth, *CD II/2*, 613.

82. Barth, *CD II/2*, 613.

drama elicited by the rich young man's question is whether he will submit to the objective law or rebel against it.

The dialogue that follows regarding the fulfilment of the commandments is "at once a preparation and postponement of the communication of the inexorable Word."[83] The verdict is still hidden, so judgement is postponed. In verse 19 Jesus offers the man an indirect answer: "You know the commandments." This is not so much a gentle encouragement as a direct challenge. The tone is rather less of "You already know the answer" and rather more of "You do not yet know the question."

His attempt at observing the law has been an attempt to evade it. In coming to Jesus, "he has really passed him by."[84] The man is revealed to "still be a rebel, determined to go his own way even under this order, allowing the command of God to determine his action but not himself, not subjecting himself to it."[85] Barth's reading of the young man here is reminiscent of the character in Flannery O'Connor's short story *Wise Blood,* of whom it is said, "There was already a deep black wordless conviction in him that the way to avoid Jesus was to avoid sin."[86] Jesus frames obedience in terms of the second half of the commandments because "directing him to his neighbor, they aim to send him to God."[87] "He should *belong* to Jesus—as King of the kingdom in which he lives" but instead he assesses himself "from his own point of view, so that judging himself along these lines he naturally acquits and justifies himself."[88]

Turning to the parallel passage in Matthew 19, Barth highlights that there the rich man asks for specification. In verse 18 he queries: "Which commandments?" In this question attention is drawn to the fact that the Law has an internal and an external component. The commandments that Jesus lays out in Mark 10:19—not murdering, committing adultery, stealing, bearing false witness, defrauding and honoring parents—are the more visible charges in the Decalogue. In Matthew there is the supplement of "love your neighbor as yourself." As Jesus sketches the commandments for the young man, he selects clauses which involve "a concrete doing or not doing."[89] His interaction reverses the internalizing tendency common in later Christian teaching towards rich people, which lingers on the fact that it is the "love

83. Barth, *CD II/2*, 615.

84. Barth, *CD II/2*, 617.

85. Barth, *CD II/2*, 617.

86. O'Connor, *Wise Blood*, 22.

87. Barth, *CD II/2*, 617.

88. Barth, *CD II/2*, 617.

89. Barth, *CD II/2*, 616.

of" Mammon, not Mammon itself, which is the root of all evil. To whatever extent such teaching can be squared with Jesus's words here, love is very much understood as a person's external fidelity to the Law.

Barth is clear that Jesus's selective quoting is not an editing. Barth writes, "In the New Testament sense it is not possible either to love one's neighbor without first loving God, or to love God without then loving one's neighbor."[90] The unity of the internal and external commandments is reflected in the "mystery of the person of Jesus Christ—the unity of the eternal Word with our flesh, of the Son of God with the Son of David and the Son of Mary."[91] Our obedience on one side is revealed in our actions on the other, and vice-versa. Having heard the voice of the Lord, the question is always whether we obey it. This obedience is the answer to the question of how we are to inherit eternal life. This obedience is not some internal spiritual disposition but the "sphere of the most concrete doing or not doing, in dealings with your fellow-man."[92] The rich man paid heed only to the external aspects of the Law, treating them as formal categories to be filled out by his spiritual dedication. His partial agreement is really a full rebellion, evidenced as he turns away from Jesus.

The rich young man is asked to do three things: to sell all, to give the proceeds to the poor, and to follow Jesus. It is this final demand that brings the first two into focus. They serve as the "how to" of the answer to the question about inheriting eternal life, but following Jesus is the content of that answer. "What is required of this man if he is to inherit eternal life? It is required that he should belong to Jesus."[93] He is challenged to not just come to Jesus and fall on his knees before Jesus, but to stay with Jesus. Instead of staying with Jesus, he leaves him. One speculates that he neither sells nor gives. After all, "the freedom for one's neighbor" in the commandments' second table is "freedom for Jesus."[94] Barth summarizes all this in a strikingly clear sentence:

> The two obligations—that this man should sell what he has and therefore become free for God, and that he should give it to the poor and therefore become free for his neighbor—both derive their meaning and force from this final demand, that he should come and follow Jesus.[95]

90. Barth, *CD II/2*, 616.
91. Barth, *CD II/2*, 616.
92. Barth, *CD II/2*, 616.
93. Barth, *CD II/2*, 621.
94. Barth, *CD II/2*, 622.
95. Barth, *CD II/2*, 622.

The refusal to follow Jesus on *his* way and instead to insist on continuing by himself is exactly the point at which the man comes short. He is bound by the responsibilities of wealth, which keep him from grasping his freedom by loving his neighbor. He is deaf to the "command which is also an offer."[96] His riches blind him so that he does not see the Lord who stands before him.

When, due to his "great possessions," he turns from the Lord, it is because he is "captive and bound by regard for other lords and powers beside God."[97] He is possessed by his possessions. Jesus's command, which ties eternal life to poverty, is impossible to grasp without letting our riches go. The disciples marvel at these hard words and wonder, "Who then can be saved?"[98] They are in a moment of crisis, cognizant of all that they have already left to follow Jesus (v. 28) and they begin revising, evaluating, calculating the opportunity cost. The rich young man has found himself in opposition to Jesus's command and now the disciples find they identify with him before being reassured by Jesus's promise in verse 29 that the faithful will receive a hundred times more in the age to come than what they sacrifice in this present age. The confrontation between clock time and kingdom time is disruptive. Their following Jesus after this exchange is as significant as the rich man's sad withdrawal. They have their eyes opened to the true reality and find themselves "regretting their regret" as the veiled implications of what it means to follow Jesus—both the cost and the consolation—is revealed for them as they see in the rich young man a mirror of their own potential selves.[99] The interaction operates like a parable that draws them to a place of repentance and deepened faithfulness.

This extended, close reading of how Barth interprets the Rich Young Ruler interaction serves as a sort of tuning fork for his engagement with the economic parables. Attachment to Mammon is at least the presenting problem of the rich young ruler, who goes away sorrowful when asked to divest his portfolio. Yet as we have seen, the underlying cause of his spiritual crisis is as much incomprehension at Jesus's command as it is comfort with Mammon.[100]

---

96. Barth, *CD II/2*, 622.

97. Barth, *CD II/2*, 619.

98. Willie Jennings's essay on this dilemma is worthy of careful attention. Jennings, "A Rich Disciple?"

99. Barth, *CD II/2*, 630.

100. Barth's interpretation of Jesus's words to the young ruler is evocative of T. S. Eliot, who in his poem "East Coker" writes: "In order to possess what you do not possess You must go by the way of dispossession." Eliot, *Collected Poems 1909–1962*, 187.

Barth maintains that the question of obedience to this objective Lord is the answer to the question about eternal life. Obedience takes concrete form in how we treat our neighbor, hence the dialogue about the second table of the commandments. This discourse cannot be collapsed into a spiritualized reading of finance that says it is all about our inward disposition towards money. But neither can it be read as a legalistic tract laying out principles that must be observed. This is apparent when Barth turns his attention to the second half of the Gospel accounts, where Jesus engages the apostles. With man the inheritance that the young ruler wishes for is out of reach, but with God all things are possible. And those who have discovered Jesus as Lord and sold and given and followed are not thereby whisked away from the world, with some gulf opening between them and those who have not eyes to see. Rather, obedience to Jesus produces new solidarities and destabilizes old certainties. The rich young ruler's sad retreat is a moment in which the apostles see him clearly and in so seeing, see themselves with new clarity. Equanimity with regards to wealth is exposed as a delusion as the rich young ruler walks out of view and untroubled attachments to the comforts the apostles hold dear is similarly voided. They are with Jesus by the grace of God. All they once thought gain, they have counted loss when considered in the light of the new thing they receive as part of following.[101]

Barth's wholeheartedly christological reading of the Rich Young Ruler passage continues in how he engages other parables. The Jesus who we find in dialogue with the young ruler is uncompromisingly certain that he is Lord over the young man, a stance repeated throughout the parables, where Barth finds an "insistent Lord" there depicted.[102] The call to ongoing obedience will find resonance in the sense that the parables are portraits of the in-breaking kingdom and the warnings about the first and the last will prime us to hear keenly Barth's interpretation of the parables as a question of knowing the changing epochs in which we live. To those stories we now turn.

The Parable of the Ten Virgins

The parable of the Ten Virgins is discussed throughout the *Dogmatics*. The main treatment comes in III/2, where time, and its effect on our attitude to our action, is presented as the critical key to the tale. Since the age of new creation is imminent and immediate but unknown, the church must be organized so that it has what it needs to have and does what it needs to

101. Philippians 3:7.
102. Barth, *CD III/1*, 37.

do in the knowledge that this very night all things might change. That is, the church is that community that in this age "exhibits and experiences the lordship of Jesus in the form of the lordship of His Spirit."[103]

The church lives in an expectation—within the parable there is an agonizing wait but the context of the parable established in verse 1 is about the disciples awaiting the kingdom of heaven—focused by the prayer *Maranatha* and "finds its consolation in His promise: 'Behold, I come quickly.'"[104] The parable of the Ten Virgins:

> asks the community whether it is active in relation to the new coming of the Lord, or whether it is merely passive. The ten virgins are supposed to go out and meet the bridegroom. This is the meaning of *upantésis* (v. 1), or *apantésis* (v. 6), and it is implied by the description in v. 10 of their going out to escort the bridegroom and accompany him to the marriage feast with their lamps alight.[105]

The hope of the parable is that when Jesus returns, "the Church of the interim will stand at His side, with its testimony to the whole world."[106] But there is a challenge there as well: we must avoid the tragedy of the five who "having kept their lamps alight for a long time" ultimately have kept them lit "apparently to no purpose" since at the critical moment they "had themselves fallen asleep from weariness" and were left with no oil when the time came.[107] The parable is "controlled by the question whether oil is available to replenish the lamps at the critical moment."[108] The lamps, Barth contends, represent the community's witness[109] and the oil symbolizes Jesus's trustworthy word, that which "makes this witness vital and strong."[110]

Does the community cherish this essential, indispensable oil-burning witness? Even if mediated through our witness, whatever light we offer is "clearly the self-witness of Jesus by the Holy Spirit apprehended in faith and love."[111] This is the critical, solitarily, ultimate characteristic that decides whether the community is tragically absent, rushing to the shops at the mo-

---

103. Barth, *CD III/2*, 505.

104. Barth, *CD III/2*, 505.

105. Barth, *CD III/2*, 505.

106. Barth, *CD III/2*, 505.

107. Barth, *CD III/2*, 505.

108. Barth, *CD III/2*, 505–6.

109. Jerome talks about the illumination brought "in alms and in all the virtues and counsels of the teachers." St. Jerome, *St. Jerome's Commentary on Matthew*, 117:284.

110. Barth, *CD III/2*, 506.

111. Barth, *CD III/2*, 506.

ment the bridegroom arrives, or triumphant (if still bleary-eyed), standing by his side. For Barth, the parable of the virgins is an exposition on how our present life and action (active or passive) is weighed in the balances of Jesus's future and final judgement. Being active witnesses at the *parousia* is the Christian's aim so there is a chronological tension at play in the parable; we must act now—in the *not yet*—as if the Day has come, because the Day may well be about to break in on us. The expectation for or the alertness to that imminent possibility injects our future into our present. The community must "see to it that its relation to the Jesus Christ who was yesterday and is to-day is such that it can only encounter and serve as His community the One who will live and reign for ever."[112]

Barth reads this parable in concert with the parable of the Talents and the parable of the Sheep and Goats. In all three, the characters who receive praise acted with "no ulterior motive."[113] There was "no spiritual strategy."[114] They simply "obeyed without explanations."[115] "They were not occupied with metaphysical considerations. They were simply concerned with men as men, and therefore treated them as brothers."[116] The church that follows the challenging invitation of the Matthew 25 parables will always avoid "an exaggerated estimate of the greatness of the community."[117] It must be content with the consolation of the Holy Spirit, not the consolation of success. If our job is simply to be handmaids "like the virgins at the marriage feast" then that is the job we should do—no more and no less.[118]

Elsewhere, in III/4, Barth again turns to the parable of the Ten Virgins to explicate "the eschatological view of Christianity and the ethics based upon it."[119] Barth proposes the freedom to act in the time available to us as a classic example of freedom in limitation. The time in which we live is the "time ruled by the Lord who has already come but is still to be manifested."[120] It is short, but we can be sure it will be long enough. He draws three main teachings about time that we can gather from the New Testament. Firstly, time is ruled and limited by Jesus. Secondly, time is short. Thirdly, time is

---

112. Barth, *CD III/2*, 506.

113. Barth, *CD III/2*, 508.

114. Barth, *CD III/2*, 508.

115. Barth, *CD III/2*, 508.

116. Barth, *CD III/2*, 508.

117. Barth, *CD III/2*, 510.

118. Barth, *CD III/2*, 510.

119. Barth, *CD III/4*, 580.

120. Barth, *CD III/4*, 581.

"unknown to those who live in it."[121] The parable of the Ten Virgins is one of the passages that presses on this point, intending "not to impress upon us that we are in darkness regarding the future but to make it plain that in this interval we must orientate ourselves by the fact that time is expiring quickly rather than by a known point when it will reach its end."[122] The fact that we do not know the hour is not an invitation to "idly wait with folded hands for the return of Christ" but instead we must in this interim time "hear the call to awaken which is always to be heard when God is at work."[123] It is a call to action, not passivity. To whatever extent it agitates us, to this same extent the call is also a consolation to us.

Barth continuously reads the parable of the Ten Virgins in this vein, as a tale that points us to the urgent need for alertness in the face of the kingdom of God. Christians are those who have awoken. Jairus's daughter was woken from her sleep, while the disciples in Gethsemane could not resist slumber, and Paul calls the Ephesians "dead men" who must wake up. The parable, however, is the clearest signal to this responsibility. "Even the wise as well as the foolish virgins" needed to be awakened.[124] The Christian is not the human who has been woken once but God "wakens him again and again, and always with the same power and severity and goodness as the first time."[125] In this interim age, the church stays alert to its calling and ensures that it is found doing what it should do with its gifts, so that when the Lord returns, we do not tragically miss him while seeking to procure the oil we had neglected.

The Parable of the Talents

The concept of time, specifically urgency, offers a clear path into understanding the kinds of kingdom portraits that Barth finds in the parables. The urgent task is always obedience to the ways of the kingdom. This dynamic is revealed at one point by reference to a quote from Augustine, as part of discussion about the parable of the Talents. The Bishop of Hippo taught, "Your best servant is he who gives attention not (so much) to hearing from you that he might will, but rather to will what he might hear

---

121. Barth, *CD III/4*, 582.
122. Barth, *CD III/4*, 583.
123. Barth, *CD III/4*, 583.
124. Barth, *CD IV/3*, 512.
125. Barth, *CD IV/3*, 512.

from you."[126] The call to be alert in this interim age is echoed again in the parable of the Talents.

In III/2, Barth turns to Jesus's place in relation to time. He claims that Jesus's future is not separated from his past and present. The relevant excursus begins following this paragraph:

> 'I am . . . which is to come.' The consciousness of time inherent in the whole is to be summed up in this phrase of Rev. 18. The future to which we look forward from the present of the man Jesus is, like this present itself, and the past which lies behind it, His time, the time of the man Jesus.[127]

The apostles believe in the coming of the kingdom but they still have to point to it—it has yet to come fully. With direct similarity, the prophets of old gave advance word of the Messiah but they were "unable to make the object of their proclamation visible or perceptible to their hearers."[128] The critical point, supported here by exegesis of 1 Peter 1:16-21, seems to be:

> For Christians living in time the enacted salvation has become past. But in its general revelation it is still future. And in this futurity it is the event which leads Christians forward in time, urging them ahead, drawing them on like a magnet, out of the sufferings of the present time, out of the darkness of the present and into the light.[129]

The kingdom is no longer merely a thing to be anticipated but is present *and* future simultaneously. The parable of the Talents is read in this manner. The Lord has gone into a far country. For Barth, this is the interim period between ascension and return. Before he left, he gave the church his goods to handle, some less than others but all entrusted "in the handling of what is no less genuinely His property and no less valuable."[130] The "profitable use" of mission to which the church is called to direct those resources is not like stewardship at all. The virgins were not vigilant, but slept and the successful investors showed none of the third man's prudence.[131]

As Barth interprets it, the third worker is "positively lazy and wicked."[132] He represents "the community which in the interim period is

---

126. Augustine, cited in Barth, *CD II/1*, 11.

127. Barth, *CD III/2*, 493.

128. Barth, *CD III/2*, 495.

129. Barth, *CD III/2*, 496.

130. Barth, *CD III/2*, 506.

131. Barth, *CD III/2*, 506.

132. Barth, *CD III/2*, 507.

not a missionary community."[133] Such a community will be cast into outer darkness. The tone that Barth strikes here is riven with urgency for the missionary endeavor. The community in this interim period of God's "patience and purpose . . . can never have enough time here and now for the fulfilment of its task."[134]

On the surface at least, this is a traditional and straightforward reading of the text that seems susceptible to the kind of activist agenda commonly found in contemporary churches. But it might be deepened by remembering that the discussion of the parable of the Talents is sandwiched between a discussion of the other two sections in Matthew 25: the parable of the Ten Virgins, and the Sheep and Goats judgement scene. He argues that they all exhibit this dynamic; that the present "interim" action of the church is shaped by the future (but already achieved) consummation. Hence, the community's integrity will be revealed in the future, at the judgement scene, upon the arrival of the bridegroom. It is the community's present action that will reveal their integrity: "it is because they knew Jesus as their Brother and God as their Father that they fed the needy, gave them drink, clothed and visited them."[135] The specific scene of Matthew 25:31–46 is "the *Magna Carta* of Christian humanitarianism and Christian politics" because it diagrams what it means to be a group of people who follow Jesus "who has come, and will come again."[136] The present experience looks back to the past when Jesus came and forward to the future when he will return and so acts in generosity knowing that he is with us still. The dilemma involving investment in this parable rests on the drama created by the overlapping aeons that Christians inhabit. The stewards trusted with the talents and the disciples included among the sheep are scenes of such significance due to this dynamic of chronological simultaneity. Barth's interpretation of the parable of the Talents, taken in line with the parables that precede and follow it, and its challenge to consider in what aeon are we investing, is sharpened to such an extent that it cannot be reduced to an agenda of simple proclamation evangelism.

Barth's interpretation of the parable of the Talents makes little reference to the narrative ambiguity at work in both the accounts of Luke and Matthew. The third investor insists that the master is a "harsh man" (Luke 19:24, Matthew 25:21), but there is no evidence external to his subjective testimony that supports this assertion. In fact, when the master sees the return

133. Barth, *CD III/2*, 507.
134. Barth, *CD III/2*, 507.
135. Barth, *CD III/2*, 508.
136. Barth, *CD III/2*, 508.

made by the first two investors, he does not merely pay them their wages, but goes further, inviting them to "enter into the joy of your master" (Luke 19:21, 23). In other words, he does not simply promote them as employees but embraces them as friends. Their reward is not just a bigger pay packet or a higher place in an organizational chart, but the warm ushering into a sharing of the spoils as partners. What kind of harsh man is as generous with relationship? When the third investor presents his defensive strategy and explains it based on the character of his master, the master responds by respecting his words. He says, "I will judge you by your own words" (Matthew 25:22). The standard by which he responds is not his own standard, but the servant's. Remembering Martin Luther's definition of a god as the one from whom "we are to expect all good," the servant stands towards this master in a stance far from worship.[137] The master is not admitting that he is a harsh master, but instead is acknowledging that he is seen as a hard master. He goes on, before issuing his verdict: "You knew, did you, that I was a harsh man, taking what I did not deposit and reaping what I did not sow?" (Matthew 25:22). When read in the light of the ambiguity of the third servant's testimony, traditional readings of the parable as a straightforward invitation to stewardship are subverted. His failing is not a poor dividend. Instead, the parable becomes a tale about how our preconceived notions about God can blind us to the call of God, the invitation of God, and the friendship of God. If we insist that he is a tyrant, then we will see a tyrant. If we determine in advance, from reason or tradition or whatever other source, that God is a certain way, then our ability to be alert to the God who will surprise us in this interim age washes away.

The judgement that comes at the end of this parable is not the action of a divine despot. In an excursus in II/1, Barth explores the idea that God's righteousness is one "which judges and therefore both exculpates and condemns, rewards and also punishes."[138] In a brief survey through the biblical literature, he finds that judgment is a constituent part of God's righteousness. It is the other side of the coin we know as mercy. This is true in the Old Testament and in the New.

He connects the man from Matthew 22:13 who had no wedding garment with the "unprofitable servant who has buried the talent entrusted to him instead of exploiting it."[139] Both are "cast out into the outer darkness where there is weeping and gnashing of teeth."[140] (The foolish virgins from

137. Luther, "The Large Catechism," 565.
138. Barth, CD II/1, 391.
139. Barth, CD II/1, 392.
140. Barth, CD II/1, 392.

earlier in Matthew 25, the inhospitable "goats" from later in Matthew 25, and the fig tree in Matthew 21 are all classified in similar ways.)

The parable of the Talents is directly slotted in to this wider exegesis of a major theme that Barth locates throughout the Scriptures: "the mercy of God is the judgement which we certainly will not escape without faith."[141] Contrary to the third investor, the righteousness of God does not call us to dwell on damnation averted, but salvation secured. "We are already invited by this summons to give ourselves to God who lives for us and saves us by His life for us."[142] While Barth does not explicitly interrogate the reliability of the third servant's testimony within the narrative of the parable, these comments do arrive at the same conclusion. When God's faithfulness confronts us, "our own characteristic reaction to it is always unfaithfulness. We are revealed as foolish virgins, as unprofitable servants, as the murmuring stiff-necked idolatrous people of Israel."[143] The one who is unfaithful has vision that is untrustworthy and discernment that is not plumb, and we can miss or misinterpret the goodness of God and see it as something else.

As the kingdom of God breaks in on the world, it changes our sense of time. It alerts us to the untrustworthy nature of time as we construe it. The groom is returning. The master is returning. We must live now with the ethics of the not-yet. That we can conceive of risking that life is what faith is. Barth explains:

> It is necessary that faith should remember the abyss from which it has been saved and over which it is poised in order that as effective faith it may praise God as the One who has found man in his utterly lost condition, snatching him from the grip of death and translating him into life; in order that it may give honor to free mercy in the freedom in which it has accomplished the unexpected and incomprehensible; in order that it may be bound in total obedience to the God who owed it nothing and to whom it owes everything.[144]

Perhaps the third (lazy) servant is the inverse of what we ought to be, even if he is an accurate portrait of who we presently are. He is blind to the untrustworthiness of his present grasp of time. This prompts him to trust in the "abyss" of his own understanding. He cannot see the Good News that God is asking him to participate in his kingdom. Just like the rich young ruler, we are called to see that the invitation is secure. What risks there are,

141. Barth, *CD II/1*, 392.
142. Barth, *CD II/1*, 393.
143. Barth, *CD II/1*, 393.
144. Barth, *CD II/1*, 393.

are not real threats for us. It is not the case that one step might bring us into faith and another into damnation. Rather, faith and reward are built on top of the damnation that *was* our destiny. To see faith and reward right, we must know the story. But the past is not effective in our present and therefore damnation is not ahead of us in the future. We live now as people entrusted to invest ourselves for the sake of the kingdom, and that is a task we should encounter with joy.

The Parable of the Sheep and the Goats

The alertness, the wakefulness, and the sense of urgency required in this interim age can only be found through an encounter with Jesus. The rich young ruler got half the way there in approaching Jesus and asking him for help, while kneeling. But the realization of where we are and who we are always comes as a result of God's intervention. It is when the Father embraces the younger son that the depth of his crimes is revealed. Even when we think of Paul, "it is not a new revelation of the Torah, let alone a revelation of conscience or the like, but a revelation of the living Jesus Christ" that brought him to his knees on the road to Damascus.[145] Saul becomes Paul when he realizes he is persecuting Jesus, not just the community of The Way. And the separation of the goats from the sheep is based on "what they have or have not done to Him in the person of the least of His brethren."[146] It is only in relation to Jesus and his mercy that the depth of our unrighteousness can even begin to be discerned.

Who we are, ultimately, is only known in the ultimate encounter with the ultimate One. In this sense, the parable of the Sheep and the Goats is perhaps the clearest example of the three parables found in Matthew 25 of the dynamic whereby our actions now are determined by our trust in future, a trust in a verdict that is accomplished already, even if it is not yet manifest.

The above discussion, from IV/1, has a counterpart in III/2. Barth considers the Matthew 25 parables to demonstrate that the church is the community that realizes it lives in the age between the resurrection and the *parousia*. The resurrection and the *parousia* represent our present in the sense that they are the realities in which we live. The parable of the Sheep and the Goats is one more angle on this dynamic. The sheep represent those communities that had hope "for this Judge, and rightly so."[147] Jesus is hidden in the present, but the sheep community is the group that

145. Barth, *CD IV/1*, 392.
146. Barth, *CD IV/1*, 392.
147. Barth, *CD III/2*, 507.

looks with eager anticipation for the day he is revealed and acts in the present in the light of this anticipation. The help that they offer the least of his brethren is help extended to Jesus himself because "they represent the world for which He died and rose again, with which He has made Himself supremely one, and declared Himself in solidarity."[148] The test that determines whether you are a sheep or a goat (as there was a clear dividing line between being a wise or foolish virgin, or a wise or wicked investor) is the extent to which one "has succored its Lord by giving unqualified succor to them in this needy world."[149]

The rich young ruler was directed by Jesus to look again at the commandments, to realize how his responsibility to God was wrapped up in his responsibility to his neighbor, and vice-versa. This parable underlines this point. In IV/1, Barth argues that the love of God and the love of others are distinct but inseparable commands for the Christian. "The following of the divine loving in Christian love would be incomplete, indeed it would fail altogether—and we must remember the very sharp warnings on this point in the First Epistle of John—if it did not take this twofold form."[150] Love of God has first place, love of others second, but either on their own is incoherent. This is revealed in the parable of the Sheep and Goats. The "criterion at His judgement will be the question what we have done or not done to Him in the person of the least of His brethren."[151] Yet it is important to remember that the least of his brethren:

> are not identical with Him, but they are witnesses which we must not overlook or ignore, witnesses of the poverty which He accepted to establish that fellowship between God and man which is given to the world and gives light to the Christian community, witnesses of the wealth which in Him is given secretly to the world and openly to the Christian community in that fellowship.[152]

Love of the other, on the horizontal plane, is not equitable with the love of God on the vertical plane, but it is the hallmark of that love for God. Love for God is also the source of the love for neighbor.

The parable depicts the nations gathering around the king's throne. Jesus Christ *is* the kingdom. "The *basileia* [Kingdom] cannot be separated

148. Barth, *CD III/2*, 508.

149. Barth, *CD III/2*, 508.

150. Barth, *CD IV/1*, 106. 1 John 4:8: "Whoever does not love does not know God, because God is love."

151. Barth, *CD IV/1*, 106.

152. Barth, *CD IV/1*, 106.

from Him any more than it can from God. This is true in the absolute sense."[153] Yet it is also true relatively speaking as well. Where two or three are gathered in his name, there he is too, and therefore, where his community of followers are, the kingdom will be (in some sense) present.[154] "This is why it can be said in Lk. 10:16: 'He that heareth you heareth me.'"[155] It is in light of that relative, representational presence of Jesus in the community of his followers that we can better understand the logic driving the Sheep and the Goats parable:

> That is also why the nations assembled for the Last Judgement in Mt. 25:31–46 are asked by the Son of Man concerning their attitude to His brethren and judged accordingly. What they have done, or not done, to the least of His brethren, they have done, or not done, to Him. It is not merely that there is a solidarity between Himself and His brethren. But He Himself is hungry and thirsty and a stranger and naked and sick and in prison as they are.[156]

The kingdom of God is a central concern for the Synoptics. The language falls away after the Gospels. This is not because it is no longer relevant, but because *ekklesia* is the place where we most likely encounter *basileia*.[157] "The community lives, not only because, but as Jesus lives, the Kingdom of God in person."[158]

It is this king who "was hungry and thirsty and a stranger and naked and sick and in prison as His brethren were."[159] When Jesus promises to be with his followers to the very end of the age, this "does not indicate merely a third or further added to the two or three, and therefore a numerical

---

153. Barth, *CD IV/2*, 658.

154. It is important to note that for Barth, the kingdom is associated fully with Jesus. The kingdom is entirely present in the presence of Jesus and this shapes all Christian understanding of the times in which they live. John Webster explains this well, citing Barth from IV/3: "The church does not view history as a permanent, principled, dialectic between *providentia Dei* and *hominum confusio*. Rather, it views history in the light of the 'new thing', God's grace in and as Jesus Christ; this enables it to see history as delimited and shaped by the already achieved overcoming of confusion. 'In Him there is not the clash of two kingdoms, but the one kingdom of God in reality.'" Webster, *Barth's Moral Theology*, 144–45.

155. Barth, *CD IV/2*, 658.

156. Barth, *CD IV/2*, 658.

157. *Ekklesia* is Greek for church, literally the "called-out people" and *basileia* is Greek for kingdom, or realm.

158. Barth, *CD IV/2*, 659.

159. Barth, *CD IV/3*, 758.

increase."[160] Jesus's presence with the community is obviously not another seat filled. Rather, his presence is the root of the gathering itself. Its sheer existence relies on the presence and activity of Jesus and his Spirit. Since the parables are portraits of the kingdom, the King is the main character. The parable of the Sheep and the Goats illuminates this. All the nations are summoned by the King and they gather around him. They are not asked if they were generous in general, or followed Christian principles of steward-ship, or maximized their profit.[161] They are asked if they fed the hungry, watered the thirsty, welcomed the stranger, clothed the naked, tended the sick, and visited the prisoner. "What did the peoples either do or not do to them? They did it, or did not do it, to Him, their King."[162] This is a logic that is decidedly not consequentialist, but actions still matter. Good intentions and efficient systems have no intrinsic moral value in themselves. It is not the volume of water being drunk, but the giving of the water that counts.[163] This line of inquiry re-occurs throughout Volume IV and always appears along with Luke 10:16 and the conversion of Saul in Acts 9:4. Barth reads this parable as the basis of "Christian humanitarianism" because it is the basis of Christian ecclesiology.

If there is a distinctive Christian wealth ethic it must consist of prac-tices determined by an allegiance that lies primarily with the kingdom of God, as against more seemingly apparent realities. The powers of this age are futile in the face of the time of God's kingdom. The parables, as Barth reads them, do not give rise to starry-eyed plans for economic utopia, nor even spiritual counsel to soften the long journey trod by hard-working pragmatists. The parables tell of a kingdom that reorients the people who populate it (not individual citizens, which is axiomatic to both the an-thropology and politics of late capitalism) so that the accepted norms are called into question. The great economic virtue of prudence is built on the wisdom of planning for tomorrow based on what has happened yesterday and today. That virtue is relativized, if not annihilated, by a Lord who scat-ters seed even on rocks, who welcomes back wayward sons, who pays all the laborers the same wage, and who strikingly and unequivocally divides the world into "sheep" and "goats."

---

160. Barth, *CD IV/3*, 758.

161. Such an approach is a dead end because of how it transforms "supreme folly first into desirable duty, and then into legislated duty." Illich and Cayley, *The Rivers North of the Future*, 58.

162. Barth, *CD IV/3*, 758.

163. One is reminded on Barth's claim that "love to the neighbour is weighed, not measured." Barth, *CD I/2*, 447.

For Barth, all three parables in Matthew 25 concern how the church tells the time. The parable of the Ten Virgins exposes alertness to time as a critical aspect of the active mission of the church. We must be roused and have oil to burn when the bridegroom returns. In the parable of the Talents, the ambiguity of the interim time is emphasized. If we allow what appears to be to determine our actions, we will end up trapped by our preconceived notions, as the third servant was. In this light, Barth's reading of the Sheep and the Goats parable is a manifesto for how the church lives in this interim time. Against the common preconceived notions of any generation, Christians commit to living in true time, under the reign of this insistent Lord. If Christian humanitarianism is grounded on Christian ecclesiology, it all first relies on Jesus making himself present to us.

UNRUFFLED AUTHORITY, CHALLENGE, AND REVOLUTION

In his parables, Jesus displays a complicated attitude towards wealth. Money, capital, and profit are common themes running through the stories about assets, investment, and harvest. Taken as a whole, the parables do not yield an ethic that coheres straightforwardly with the lives of Christians in the contemporary West, immersed as they are in neoliberalism. When Jesus addresses the prudent, barn-building farmer of Luke 12:16–21, confirming that his toil amounts to nothing more than that he is a "fool," Christians in the West hear a warning about their own lives. Barth's most extensive and focused discussion of the complexity of Jesus's attitudes towards wealth that engages with the parables comes in §64. As part of his discussion of "The Royal Man," Barth unpacks his concept of Jesus's "*gelassenen Konservativismus*,"[164] which is woven into the revolutionary prospect that is the kingdom. I propose the term "unruffled authority" in an attempt to capture this idea in English.

Just as the parables are "little stories which it seems anyone might tell of ordinary human happenings,"[165] the Royal Man is "the One who is ignored and forgotten and despised and discounted by men."[166] If this strange man is Royal, then his reign must be over a curious kingdom. Indeed, it is "an in-

164. The phrase is translated into English as "passive conservatism" by Bromiley. This is accurate on a word-for-word basis, but leaves the reader imagining Jesus as a character that Marilynne Robinson cut from a novel at the drafting stage. I have sought to get at the meaning by translating "*gelassenen*" as "unruffled" and replacing "*Konservativismus*" with "authority," to get at the sense in which Barth deploys the phrase in relation to societal power structures. Barth, *Die Kirchliche Dogmatik IV/2*, 194.

165. Barth, *CD IV/3*, 112.

166. Barth, *CD IV/2*, 169.

considerable and from the human point of view an insignificant kingdom" which is "hidden like leaven in three measures of meal (Mt. 13:33), like the treasure in the field (Mt. 13:44), like the grain of mustard seed which is smaller than all other seeds (Mt. 13:32)."[167] This kingdom is not discovered through observation, "nor can it be proclaimed directly, or, as we should say, 'historically.'"[168] Only those with eyes to see will find it. The unexpectedness of this lowly and despised Royal Man and his inconsiderable kingdom is reflected in the people whose eyes and ears God has opened. The people who are drawn to the proclamation of God's coming kingdom by God's despised and lowly anointed King are the lowly and despised of the land:

> Throughout the New Testament, the kingdom of God, the Gospel and the man Jesus have a remarkable affinity, which is no mere egalitarianism, to all those who are in the shadows as far as concerns what men estimate to be fortune and possessions and success and even fellowship with God.[169]

Granting that James is widely regarded to be the New Testament text most explicitly concerned with this aspect of Jesus's ministry, Barth locates the same dynamic throughout the New Testament, citing the Pauline corpus, the Sermons on the Mount and the Plain, and the parable of the Rich Man and Lazarus. Upon reflection on the wide spread of the New Testament teaching on this topic, Barth warns, "there should be no softening of the starkness with which wealth and poverty are there contrasted and estimated (as also in Jas. 5:1f.) even in the economic sense."[170] "Softening" however, is an idea that needs to be rock hard. To hear Barth's warning and then respond by simply seeing the teaching of Jesus in, for example, the Beatitudes, as an economic teaching would be a softening of another kind. Jesus who is meek and humble of heart does not set himself simply against all those who are content to be vastly wealthy and surrounded by the poor. Jesus's challenge extends "to everything that counts as human greatness and littleness, strength and weakness"[171] and that challenge is at its sharpest when it encounters "the possession of moral and religious righteousness."[172] Thus, to avoid the "softening" that Barth warns against is to remember that "in every sense, irrespective of the concrete form taken

---

167. Barth, *CD IV/2*, 167.
168. Barth, *CD IV/2*, 167.
169. Barth, *CD IV/2*, 169.
170. Barth, *CD IV/2*, 169.
171. Barth, *CD IV/2*, 169.
172. Barth, *CD IV/2*, 170.

by riches and poverty, that the hungry and thirsty and strangers and naked and sick and captives are the brothers of Jesus in whom He Himself is either recognized or not recognized."[173]

Thus, it is a softening to obscure the economic aspect of the New Testament teaching, and it is a softening to emphasize it at the expense of the other ways that human beings can gather to themselves a false sense of righteousness.[174] But to grasp properly the challenge that Jesus poses to all the accumulated wealth that human culture generates—from economic to social status to moral authority—requires grasping "the pronouncedly revolutionary character of His relationship to the orders of life and value current in the world around Him."[175] To grasp this requires a close reading of the dialectical excursus that runs from page 173 to 179 of §64 in IV/2. What we find there is that from a certain angle Jesus can be seen as a character who tolerates the orders of his society without ever celebrating them. From a different angle, he can be portrayed as someone who challenges the orders of his day without ever seeking to annihilate them. Yet neither of these perspectives, alone or together, can truly grasp the peculiar revolutionary movement that the kingdom of God represents.

The revolutionary stance that he takes cannot be compressed into a theory or a system.[176] Jesus is too radical to even be safely classified as something the world identifies as "radical."[177] Whether he was a foe of existing ideologies was obviously a live question around the time of his arrest, but no one confused him with an ally. "He did not range Himself and His disciples with any of the existing parties."[178] In every realm of human life—politically, economically, morally, religiously—Jesus was profoundly unsettling to the different groupings because he possessed "a remarkable

173. Barth, *CD IV/2*, 170.

174. George Hunsinger's comments on Barth as a corrective to liberation theology would be an example of how this theology can fruitfully play out in practice. Hunsinger, *Disruptive Grace*, 53.

175. Barth, *CD IV/2*, 171.

176. Keen readers will note how my years in Aberdeen left me deeply indebted to Phil Ziegler's way of seeing these things: "Jesus resists assimilation of his lordship to the patterns of this age, saying, 'If it is by the Spirit of God that I cast out demons, then the kingdom of God has come to you' (Matt. 12:28). Accordingly, the Christian's political service to Christ's reign can and must be politics by other means, a politics of the third pneumatological article of the church's ancient creeds, we might say." Ziegler, *Militant Grace*, 66.

177. The argument here comes close to Marion Grau's idea of a "third," countereconomic space discovered or created through the figure of the Trickster. See especially Grau, *Of Divine Economy*, 174–81.

178. Barth, *CD IV/2*, 171.

and employees dependent on their good will, of masters and servants and capital and interest, as though all these things were part of the legitimate status quo."[192] The steward of Luke 16 is not declared a "deceiver" but instead receives an "unqualified prize."[193] In the same parable "we are told to make friends with mammon (even the unrighteous mammon)."[194] While we should be clear that this "was certainly not an invitation to maintain and augment our financial possessions as cleverly as possible" in the fashion that later came to be associated with Calvinism and the Protestant work ethic, nonetheless, "it is obviously not a summons to socialism."[195] When he is sought for arbitration in the question of the brothers' shared inheritance in Luke 12:13–21, Jesus parses covetousness from a hunger for justice. In Mark 14 Jesus "takes it as almost axiomatic that there must always be poor people" which is, Barth suggests, "a thought which has given an illusory comfort to many in subsequent periods."[196]

In all these spheres, Jesus grants space for the orders to exist. This acknowledgement should not be stretched, however. He does not deny the connection to parents, nor the reality of a legal system, nor the commerce of the marketplace, but "there is also no trace of any consistent recognition in principle."[197] Any respect extended is merely provisional. It is toleration in the true sense of the word—Jesus allows these things which are not part of his agenda to persist. His position toward these orders can be summarized by saying that he "acknowledged them and reckoned with them and subjected Himself to them and advised His disciples to do the same; but He was always superior to them."[198]

When we consider this superiority, it prompts us to reconsider the spheres of order just previously discussed. While Jesus tolerates the existence of the family and the temple, of the state and the market, his supremacy over these powers comes through in his actions and words. He pays the temple tax, but he does it to avoid offense and not "on the basis of an unqualified recognition."[199] Jesus was making "an unmistakable assault on the order of the family" when in Mark 3 he asks who his mother is and who are his siblings. In questions of religious propriety, he claims in Mark 2 that he is Lord

---

192. Barth, *CD IV/2*, 174.
193. Barth, *CD IV/2*, 174.
194. Barth, *CD IV/2*, 174.
195. Barth, *CD IV/2*, 174.
196. Barth, *CD IV/2*, 174.
197. Barth, *CD IV/2*, 175.
198. Barth, *CD IV/2*, 175.
199. Barth, *CD IV/2*, 175.

over the Sabbath and more generally in Mark 7 explains that chasing mere external purity is a foolish pursuit since, as Barth puts it, "it is not what is without but what is within that really defiles a man."[200] This same dynamic is found in the political sphere. Among other examples cited, Barth makes the astute observation that "although Pilate, like the high-priests, made a case against Him," Jesus offered no defense.[201] Their jurisdiction was not sufficient to demand a corresponding response from him. He did not have to answer their accusations. He was not disengaged—he made enemies exactly because of his engagement. But there was an unruffled authority in all the interactions with the figures and institutions that claim our deference.

In the specific domain of economy, Barth locates "some striking breaches of the contemporary (and not only the contemporary) industrial and commercial and economic order."[202] Certain parables display that unreal quality that has already been discussed. For example, why did the farmer sow seed without care, "scattering his seed irrespectively over the path and stony ground and among thorns as well as on good ground"? Why should the servants of Luke 17 declare themselves "unprofitable when they have done all that they are required to do"? What possesses the king in Matthew 18 to forgive the steward who has defrauded him so preposterously? What trade union negotiations must be in the background when the vineyard owner decides in Matthew 20 to pay a daily rate across the board, even to people who had only worked an hour? In Luke 12 we find the sensible farmer who invests in a new barn infrastructure and then is "described by God as a fool—simply because he has the unavoidable misfortune to die before his enterprise can be completed." Barth, laden with sarcasm, raises as his final example the clearing of the money changers from the temple. Jesus does not "seem to have a proper understanding of trade and commerce" in this story and his verdict that it represents a den of thieves "is rather a harsh description for the honest, small-scale financial and commercial activities which had established themselves there."[203]

These examples are signals of "the real threat and revolution which the kingdom of God and the man Jesus"[204] represent for economics, for religion and state and family, and all the other orders of the world that present themselves as natural and fixed and universal. Something more than toleration on the one hand and challenge on the other is at work here.

200. Barth, *CD IV/2*, 175.
201. Barth, *CD IV/2*, 176.
202. Barth, *CD IV/2*, 176.
203. All of these examples are from Barth, *CD IV/2*, 176.
204. Barth, *CD IV/2*, 176.

The real revolution in question cannot be discerned by simply observing instances that fit this description or counter-instances that correspond to another description. To perceive this "deeper consideration" Barth proposes it is best to read Jesus's words and actions through Mark 2:21–22:

> No-one sews a patch of unshrunk cloth on an old garment. If they do, the new piece will pull away from the old, making a tear worse. And people do not pour new wine into old wineskins. If they do, the wine will burst the skins, and both the wine and the wineskins will be ruined. No, they pour new wine into new wineskins.

What can be discerned by the way that Jesus tolerates orders in the world, while maintaining his supremacy over them is that "all human orders are this old garment or old bottles, which are in the last resort quite incompatible with the new cloth and the new wine of the kingdom of God."[205] With Jesus, a new time has come into being. Barth presents parables in general in similar terms; the kingdom breaks in in such a fashion as to undermine any expectation that it will be continuous with what we have known before. In the parables, with the kingdom, it is as if "a newly tailored and ornamented garment were ready and we had only to put it on, with no possibility of delay since the old one has already gone to the ragman and is no longer available."[206] This dynamic of a new thing that bursts the boundaries of the old thing is at work in the way Jesus's sovereign lordship over the orders of the world (including the economy) is displayed. Approaches that seek to soften the negatives of our economic system or to overturn it in pursuit of some fresh start are both rendered irrelevant in the face of the new reality revealed in Jesus's lordship.

Both conservative and progressive thought agree (or perhaps more precisely, hope) that "there is a certain compatibility between the new and the old, and that they can stand in a certain neutrality the one to the other."[207] The "invading Kingdom of God" is an "alienating antithesis to the world and all its orders" and there is no space for the neutrality beloved of progressives and conservatives.[208] Jesus's unruffled authority is exposed at the points of penetration where the insistent Lord puts the human orders to the test.[209] He remains undisturbed in his challenge, but his challenge

---

205. Barth, *CD IV/2*, 178.

206. Barth, *CD IV/3*, 246.

207. Barth, *CD IV/2*, 177.

208. Barth, *CD IV/2*, 177.

209. He stands "absolutely free from all ideology and partisan politics (since Christ the king transcends all this-worldly conflicts with a royal freedom)." Congdon,

profoundly disturbs us. Jesus lives among these competing human spheres, but his proclamation creates the "radical and irremediable unsettlement introduced by the kingdom of God into all human kingdoms."[210]

Turning again to the domains of temple and family, state and economy, Barth now sees a much more cataclysmic interaction between Jesus and the orders of his day. In this final reading, we have gone beyond the on-the-one-hand-and-then-the-other approach but now can clearly see the "radical antithesis of the new thing which was actualized and appeared in Jesus."[211] The conversation about the destruction of the temple and its rebuilding in three days resolves with the clear understanding that while Jesus "honored the temple as the house of God and was even jealous for its sanctity, He could not ascribe to it any permanent place or significance in the light of what He Himself brought and was."[212] Not even the temple can stand in the face of the new age. In all these spheres of worldly power, what Jesus does is a form of "ignoring" and "transcending."[213] In the realm of family ties, Jesus himself stood as a counter-example to the normative pattern by remaining unmarried and prophesying that there would "be others who would remain unmarried for the sake of the kingdom of heaven."[214] What louder verdict can be placed against the temporary nature of the family than Jesus's teaching that there will be no marriage in the resurrection? And where politics is concerned, Barth probes the mystery of the profound revolution that Jesus accomplished. The followers of Jesus are not to resist evil, they are to turn their cheek when hit, give their cloak when their coat is taken, and walk an extra mile when a soldier impels them to carry his load. They are to avoid judging, love their enemies, always pray for their persecutors, and remember at all times that God causes the rain to fall on the just and the unjust together. Barth ponders: "what political thinking can do justice or satisfaction to this injunction and to the One who gives it?"[215]

But the tension between the new wine and the old wineskin is most evident in the economic order, which "was simply but radically called in question by the fact that neither He Himself nor His disciples accepted its basic presupposition by taking any part in the acquisition or holding of

---

"Following the Deacon Jesus in the Prophetic Diaconate," 146.

210. Barth, *CD IV/2*, 177.
211. Barth, *CD IV/2*, 177.
212. Barth, *CD IV/2*, 177.
213. Barth, *CD IV/2*, 177.
214. Barth, *CD IV/2*, 177.
215. Barth, *CD IV/2*, 179.

any possessions."[216] The ground for the normal economic activity that Jesus observes around him and acknowledges in his parables is swept from under his apostles. Fishermen and tax collectors—people familiar with the bustle of the marketplace—are called into a different way. They abandon their assets to take up with Jesus. And yet in Luke 22 we are told that they lacked for nothing. They wanted for nothing, even as they wanted nothing. This was "not due to acquisition or possession" but through the provision of God.[217] The confidence that this provision is real is testified to "by the most primitive post-Pentecostal community" which we learn in Acts 2 took up the challenge.[218]

When this radical economic teaching is taken seriously, with its recommendation to make no plans for tomorrow because tomorrow will take care of itself, a suspicion arises that Jesus might not have been taking economics seriously. "Surely there could be no sound or solid economy, either private or public, without this laying up and taking thought?"[219] Barth rejects that line of thinking. Jesus did teach these things, so we must take them seriously. We can admit that they do not translate into policy for nation-states and at the same time recognize that his words about money are "strangely illuminating and pregnant and penetrating."[220]

The subtlety of Jesus's economic teaching, which is so resolutely stubborn in the face of our creative efforts to reread it as clear-cut or as practically useful highlights how "the concept of mammon," no matter how central to our reading of the New Testament, cannot become the "basic schema for all the blessedness or otherwise of man!"[221] The problems of greed, the indignity of poverty, and the social toxicity of wealth inequality were well known before Karl Marx, Rage Against the Machine, and Thomas Piketty. Jesus was certainly familiar with such issues. Recognizing the cruelty of a world where a few people have much and many have little, we might expect Jesus to offer some resolution. If not directly, we could hope that his spiritual teaching might yield some insight that could be transformed into an unassailable lever for redistributing justice. The radicalism

---

216. Barth, *CD IV/2*, 177.

217. Barth, *CD IV/2*, 178.

218. Barth, *CD IV/2*, 178; Along these lines, Joseph Lear has published a superb argument that the famous sharing-all-in-common passages from Acts 2 and 4 have a significance in the broader writings of Luke that is often underestimated. Lear makes a convincing case that eschatology and ethics are bound together in Luke-Acts. Lear, *What Shall We Do?*

219. Barth, *CD IV/2*, 178.

220. Barth, *CD IV/2*, 178.

221. Barth, *CD IV/2*, 178.

of the revolutionary Jesus transcends even this trajectory. Whatever justice comes with the kingdom, it does not follow the logic of the justice of the world. The kingdom will do more than merely reverse the momentum of wrongful economies. It is the sheer scale of the challenge that Jesus poses to the assumptions about how our economic world "naturally" works that prompts us to dismiss it as utopian, unrealistic, or irrelevant. The fundamental provocation that Jesus brings is so great that the pragmatist can seem reasonable or even honorable in her rejection of this divine economics. But Barth is clear. "The royal man Jesus" penetrates "to the very foundations of economic life in defiance of every reasonable and to that extent honorable objection."[222] With such a dramatic and untamable message, it is no surprise that the church, has "again and again stifled and denied and even forgotten" the hardness of Jesus's words.[223] When the church cannot even remember it, never mind live it out, it is to be expected that the world disregards it also. But the church has never fully escaped this "unsettlement which it has within itself" and the world cannot completely hide either.[224] The mere "presence of this man has meant always that the world must wrestle with this incommensurable factor."[225]

It is not enough to say that Jesus relates to the orders of his day in an unpredictable fashion. He fully revolts against any order of predictability. We can say that Jesus's initial engagement with these powers is quietly positive, at least to the degree that it is not openly antagonistic. But this positivity is always limited. The fact that he is Lord over the temple and the family, the synagogue and the market, and certainly Lord over the rulers, means that there are counter-balancing words. For every instance where Jesus appears to be affirming the way things are, there are staunch, uncompromising words that devastate the status quo.

The truth of Jesus's position cannot be calculated, however, by counting up the positive comments and contrasting them with the negative. Paying close attention to each atomic instance of toleration or devastation from Jesus in relation to wider society does not add up to the full picture. The crisis that he brings is "more radical and comprehensive than may be gathered from all these individual indications."[226] That Jesus has words of both toleration and critique for the structures of the world should not lead us to believe that the kingdom comes by gradual improvement. Ameliora-

222. Barth, *CD IV/2*, 178.
223. Barth, *CD IV/2*, 179.
224. Barth, *CD IV/2*, 179.
225. Barth, *CD IV/2*, 179.
226. Barth, *CD IV/2*, 176.

tion of injustice and hardship is no bad thing, and is certainly not to be opposed. But even our best efforts will fail to keep the wine permanently. The reign of God is not a tinkering or an adaption of what is already here. No such approach can be squared with the imagery of new wine and old wineskins. The positive toleration that prompts Barth to speak of a passive conservatism, or unruffled authority, does not allow us to make peace with the world. Rather, the single lines that can be measured as "for" or "against" the orders of the age (whichever age that may be) point us towards the fact that Jesus places all human orders in the dock. The reason Jesus cannot be pinned down in a conservative or liberal camp, a capitalist or socialist camp, a Hellenist or Semitic camp, a Blur or Oasis camp, is that Jesus is superior to them all. Barth's "passive conservatism" is his way of describing the theme within the Gospels that shows Jesus posing "the unanswerable question, the irremediable unsettlement introduced by the Kingdom of God into all human kingdoms."[227]

What Then Can Be Said?

If Jesus indeed stood in judgement over the economy of first-century Palestine, then we must suspect the same fate also awaits twenty-first–century neoliberal capitalism. The insights gathered from considering Jesus's transcendent revolutionary stance towards the orders of family and cult, state and economy, now cut even deeper. In his reading of the parables Barth's analysis offers us a way to interpret Jesus's critique of worldly economics without falling into two wide traps and underlines one cornerstone of ethical thinking about wealth.

This insight saves us, first, from building a critique that insists the economic injustices we encounter are so great that we must start again, brushing everything aside to create a fresh slate. No Christian ethic can offer a consistent defense of massive wealth inequality, yet Jesus did not respond to the drastically unfair distribution of assets in his day by calling for a peasants' uprising.[228] In fact, vineyard owners and investors play starring roles in his parables. That Jesus acknowledges his economic reality in all its ambiguity is not a license for unjust economics. In the same way, regardless of how harsh a critique we levy against twenty-first–century neoliberalism,

---

227. Barth, *CD IV/2*, 177.

228. As Richard Horsley describes the social context of Jesus's ministry, "the immediate Palestinian context of Jesus' mission was highly politicized, filled with periodic popular unrest and protests, movements and outright revolts against the imperial order that had been imposed by the Romans." Horsley, *Jesus and Empire*, 13 See also 35–54.

we are never licensed to disregard the positives and successes achieved under its reign. From MRI scanners to smart phones to jet fighters, capitalism has facilitated an ambiguous and complex social arrangement.[229] This reading provides a way to begin the articulation of ethics on a positive word. The dynamic of unruffled authority both grants that the world of everyday finance, wealth, investment, fraud, and harvest that we encounter in the parables is not to be dismissed with blanket opprobrium, nor can it be embraced with uncritical welcome.

Deeper again, Jesus's stance towards these orders is, second, predicated on the boundary that he represents to them. These institutional orders may have potency, but this is sourced in the delegation of power from God, and it is limited by God. Their pretense is toward permanence but their true nature is that they are always fundamentally contingent. Remembering such contingency saves us from imagining that we can find some ironclad principles that can guide us, such that we can arrive at socialism with a human face, or compassionate capitalism, or any other attempt to cast the complexity of social orders as an idyll. The radical contingency of the orders suggests the quest for principles will tend towards instability, easily overtaken by change.[230]

The cornerstone that we encounter from a close reading of this material is the scrutiny with which we must examine our perceived notions about the overlap between the in-breaking kingdom and the world that we take as a given. Barth presents Jesus as a radical who is so radical that we cannot even put him in the "radical" category. The "insistent Lord" insists he is Lord over all our systems, which prevents our ethics from being subsumed into another political project. We are reminded that whatever ethic we articulate, it is wont to be destabilized by this royal man. No ethic we generate can ever stand on its own. It is always required to acknowledge the possibility of divine rejuvenation or rebuke. After all, the logic of the kingdom is not on a spectrum with the logic of the world. It is like a new wineskin, to be used in a grand banquet.

Or to make the same point more explicitly, Barth's reading of the parables shows us that they are valid and valuable sources for ethical thinking

---

229. It is essential to remember that the neoliberal narrative of innovation often obscures the role of state involvement in these technological advances. See: Mazzucato, *The Entrepreneurial State.*

230. Christopher Holmes echoes this point when he argues that Barth's "hesitancy to apply principles derived from the divine economy and to posit them in relation to our economy does not necessarily lead to abstraction or formalism. Rather, such a hesitancy is itself a bulwark against abstraction and formalism." Holmes, "Karl Barth on the Economy," 204.

about wealth. This is exactly because they do not prescribe some meta-economic approach that will install justice (for example: outright revolution); nor do they prescribe an intra-market approach that will make peace with injustice. They go beyond the standard left/right dichotomous responses to present us with this scandalous proposition: we are not left on our own to make up an answer to the question Jesus provokes in us about wealth. In the parables, we find stories of the kingdom where the logic of the gospel breaks in on the lives of characters just like us. The parables cannot be co-opted by one side or the other of any given economic debate because God will continue to break in on those who listen to them, destabilizing their dangerous contentment by revealing the contingencies of the systems they think secure and permanent. Barth introduces us to apocalyptic parables, and apocalyptic parables are the stories that Christians in the neoliberal West need to be telling and retelling.

It is commonly held that the parables take the world of the ordinary and every day and make it strange. Yet reading after Barth, we begin to see the ways in which the parables actually serve to, using Donald MacKinnon's words, "make the strange into the merely (but emphatically not quite) trivial."[231] Jesus's stories do this so as to allow us to "approach the unutterable profundities of the familiar, in order to learn to see that familiar anew."[232] In rare moments we can see the economic system in which we live as absurd—we glimpse the futility of our dozens of different kinds of breakfast cereals or we hear tell of the horrors of east Asian sweatshops—but in the parables a deeper revelation occurs. There is not just condemnation here but grace. For MacKinnon, the unutterable profundity is exposed alongside its "means of its transformation."[233] They are the pronouncements of a king whose kingdom is coming and is already here, and in pursuit of that treasure, it is wise to go and sell all that we have so that we can secure a place in it.

In this chapter we argued that in the face of the monopolistic hold that neoliberal logic can exert on our ethical imagination, the parables, especially when read in an apocalyptic register, can offer fresh ways to engage with questions of wealth. We have proposed Karl Barth as our guide in that journey, because of his attentiveness to such themes. In that dialogue on the Rich Young Ruler we saw the Christocentrism of Barth's readings of Scripture, which is continued when he turns to consider the parables. But we also considered the theme of time as the point where

---

231. MacKinnon, *The Problem of Metaphysics*, 121.

232. MacKinnon, *The Problem of Metaphysics*, 121.

233. MacKinnon, *The Problem of Metaphysics*, 121.

Barth's reading of these divine yarns and the Christian's position within the prevailing economic system overlap.

In the three parables considered from Matthew 25, this arrangement of concerns—Jesus's apocalyptic exposing of time—can be seen from three perspectives. In the parable of the Ten Virgins, the attentiveness to the imminent end of the age is expressed in terms of communities equipping themselves with the resources required to be witnesses. Do we have the oil to keep our vigil (even as we sleep)? In the parable of the Talents, we saw how the anticipation we experience in this in-between time is determined by how we view our Lord. Is he a profiteering, savage capitalist to be feared, or is his business, to which we are called, of a different order? In the parable of the Sheep and the Goats, the end has arrived and remains a mystery to those who are called to account based on how they conducted themselves. The overlap of the ages is as obscure as the acts of eschatological charity that the sheep did not know they were performing. Only when the Lord reveals the truth of things can the truth of things be known. It is that *apokalypsis* upon which we wait.

Thus, if the problem of wealth is often reconstituted in the parables as a question about the age in which we live (and the putative Lord under whom we serve), it remains for us to turn back to the economic realm and consider how we might redescribe the world in which we find ourselves in the light of the narrative parables and their apocalyptic impact. With this in mind, in the next chapter we will turn our attention to the small nation state of the Republic of Ireland and seek to retell its recent economic history not in terms of the numeric, quantitative logic of public square economics, but as stories about particular people in particular places. Statistical accounts of the economy shape our discourse and inform policy but too easily slip away from the concrete reality of lives lived. The period known as the Celtic Tiger (1994 to 2008) and its aftermath (2008 to the present) is the apparent age in which the Irish people live. How might their history be retold in the light of the unruffled authority of the "insistent Lord"?

CHAPTER 3

Telling Stories About Irish Money

Narrating the Past

INTRODUCTION

In Claire Kilroy's acclaimed novel set around the Irish financial crisis, *The Devil I Know*, the lead character Tristam observes that "money kills the imagination."[1] This thought comes to him as he walks through a car park full of executive cars: all alike, all black. But the thought also illuminates Irish public discourse since 2008. An economic crash wrought from the commitment to a zealous adherence to neoliberal capitalism has been followed by a doubling down on the very same principles that created the disaster. As this book goes to press in 2018, Ireland was again posting positive economic growth figures which were reliant on a largely unaddressed property bubble.[2]

The "insistent Lord" who weaves the parables offers us a way of thinking about wealth in an entirely different register. The logic of the kingdom of God, unveiled in the parables, is disjunctive with the logic of the neoliberal market. It offers us a renewed imagination for considering wealth and justice. Jesus, as Barth shows him to us, stands over every system and hence, after considering his parables, we can be bold in reconsidering and redescribing sites within the neoliberal economic system.

Theological engagement with economic thinking faces an immediate problem. In this chapter, we seek to get below the surface appearance of wealth, economic activity, and capitalism. How do we do this? There is a disconnect between theological thought and economic analysis. Economic

---

1. A sort of fantastic moral fable, this is one of the most perceptive novels written about Irish society at the end of the boom. It is especially sharp in its depiction of Celtic Tiger avarice as a form of addiction. Kilroy, *The Devil I Know*, 211, 236.

2. Burns et al., "Rebuilding Ireland."

analysis relies on a confidence in our ability to quantify. The initial assumption of economics is that allocation and exchange of resources is a critical problem because resources are scarce.[3] Any adjudication is already a quantification.

Theology, as a basic guiding assumption, denies that the world is marked by scarcity. It utilizes entirely different language by declaring that creation is superabundant. Genesis speaks of surplus, but even more determinative, the resurrection testifies to an excess so vast that it could transform even the most dismal of sciences.[4] In this chapter we press such theological insights onto a particular economic narrative—the story of Ireland after the 2008 crash—and describe it accurately, but through a language alternate to the standard econometric vernacular, a refusal to "see like a market" that is also being attempted in other quarters.[5]

During the Celtic Tiger's peak, in April 2005, the Irish Minister for Health, Mary Harney, delivered a speech to the Irish Medical Association where she confidently declared that Ireland now out-spent Britain with their NHS and even Germany, with their world-leading healthcare system. Ireland, she announced, spent 70 percent more per capita on healthcare than Italy. These claims, which seemed too good to be true, were entirely false. In a press release issued later, it was explained that Harney was working from memory based on an article she had written almost three years before. That particular article had dealt with Ireland's projected spending, not actual spending. Equipped with the apparent accuracy of percentage growth and economic specificity, Irish political leaders were utterly disconnected from reality.[6] Ironically, the political vernacular for economic discourse promises scientific precision but often presents misleading vagueness.

The parables are surely meant to be read as ethical teaching, but they are as far removed from a corporate "Best Practice" document as can be imagined. Theology as talk of God is talk of that which cannot be bound. Economics as a science of measurement can only talk about that which it can bind, and hence much of life is left out of its evaluation. Here we

---

3. One thinks of the influential definition of Lionel Robbins that "the forms assumed by human behavior in disposing of scarce means" make up the domain we call the economy. Robbins, *An Essay on the Nature and Significance of Economic Science*, 15.

4. Bell, *The Economy of Desire*, 149.

5. An example of an investigation that fleshes out what is meant by econometric vernacular is Fourcade and Healy's recent paper on the rise of what they call "Ubercapital," the calculable accumulation of a person's digital footprint that increasingly shapes real-world possibilities available to individuals. Fourcade and Healy, "Seeing like a Market," 10.

6. Kerrigan, *The Big Lie*, 75.

encounter the sharp point of Karl Polanyi's work: "instead of economy being embedded in social relations, social relations are embedded in the economic system."[7]

This is another way of approaching the insight gleaned from following Barth's readings of the parables.[8] There is a logic at work in Jesus's narratives that does not mesh with the modern rationale. It has a trajectory that does not parallel the arcs of the stories we tell. This is not a theological problem to be interpreted away, but the basis of a theological perspective that demands investigation. In the language of computing science, the incongruence of the parables is a feature, not a bug. The parables are the sharpest expression of how Jesus's teaching clashes uncomfortably with the wisdom of our age. These odd stories puncture the hegemonic hold that neoliberal capitalism aspires to exert over our imagination. As they echo in our thinking, we are bound to approach economic description from a different direction, with a different vocabulary, looking to find different things. Pearls of great worth are hidden out of sight if we use only the econometric vernacular of our day.

So instead of giving a pragmatic priority to economic language or seeking a hypothetical third language where economics and theology can meet, the approach advocated for here will be the fostering of dialogue between the disciplines that prioritizes narrative. Jesus's divine yarns can illuminate the ethical difficulties of wealth, but to have eyes to see requires finding new words to speak.[9] By electing to describe the recent history of the Irish economy without extensive reference to economic indicators like GNP and GDP, or through other economic frameworks, the goal is not to discount the validity or coherence of economic ideas but to foreground the embeddedness of economic activity. Theological ethics goes awry with abstraction. No slight against economics is intended by locating the perspective of this study on a plane where the human stories can be described.[10] Rather, the determination to find the story positions this approach as a practical unroll-

---

7. Polanyi, *The Great Transformation*, 60.

8. Reconsidering the story of the end of the Celtic Tiger in this way, after reading Barth on the parables, puts into question Kathryn Tanner's claim that Barth's "criticism of capitalism remains almost entirely formal." Specifically, she is addressing the arguments made in *Church Dogmatics* IV/4 where Mammon is described as a lordless power. What we find here is that even if Tanner's reading of that narrow slice of the *Dogmatics* stands, that wider project is always exegetical at base. The substance of the argument is always found in Barth's careful engagement with the Scriptures and the tradition. Tanner, "Barth and the Economy of Grace," 182.

9. Or as Stanley Hauerwas is fond of saying, "you can act only in the world that you can see, and you must be taught to see by learning to say." Hauerwas, *The Hauerwas Reader*, 699.

10. Nor is it a guarantee that the alternative narrative will stay on track!

ing of a theological conviction about the plenitude and gratuitous generosity of God's creation.[11] The abstracting step that simplifies complexity and allows the economic sciences to proceed is an impoverishing step if taken alone. A theological engagement demands a different sort of attention. To draw the economy in its richness into view is to draw the economy into the path of the parable-telling Jesus, and this requires an intention to depict the economy as a story as well as a datum.

To make this move is not to advance into uncharted waters. Social scientists, historians, and theologians have made these points and points like them before. A critical examination of economics reveals the extent to which its numericalized imagination sits atop stories, narratives, and myths. To respect the value in econometric thinking demands that we flesh it out with a keener attention to rich contexts than data models can offer.

Famously, Adam Smith posited that in every age men displayed a "propensity to barter, truck and exchange one thing for another."[12] Widely debunked as history, this idea persists as myth. Polanyi famously judged that "no misreading of the past ever proved more prophetic of the future"[13] than the one offered by the Scottish philosopher.[14] Smith and other mod-

---

11. Even though, as Gerry O'Hanlon puts it in one of the few theological treatments of the Irish crash, "there is no simple connection between the Mystery of the Blessed Trinity and fiscal stimulus packages," theology continues to have a fundamental interest in our shared economic life. O'Hanlon, *The Recession and God*, 52.

12. Smith, *An Inquiry into the Nature and Causes of the Wealth of Nations*, 25.

13. Polanyi, *The Great Transformation*, 45.

14. In *The Great Transformation*, Karl Polanyi declares that "in spite of the chorus of academic incantations so persistent in the nineteenth century," until that age there had never been a society that even aspired to operate under the control of markets. As previously noted, Polanyi's book charts how it came to be that the market took pride of place in popular conceptions of society. Karl Polanyi, *The Great Transformation*, 45. David Graeber launches a similar revision project in his work, *Debt*. After citing many examples of economic textbooks postulating a hypothetical pre-currency barter society, he directly engages Smith's etiology in which a "tendency to slip from imaginary savages to small-town shopkeepers" is clearly visible. We start with a story set, so to speak, a long time ago in a galaxy far away and we end up with the corner store where we buy our milk. What is at work here is not merely a teaching aid to understand the tri-fold purpose of money, but the presentation of the economy as a field set apart, "which operated by its own rules, separate from moral or political life." Graeber contends that this narrative faces a critical challenge—"there's no evidence that it ever happened, and an enormous amount of evidence suggesting that it did not." An explanation can only persist in the face of so fundamental an obstacle if it serves some critical purpose. Graeber and Polanyi, by different routes, both suggest that the discipline of economics relies upon assuming that "'the market' naturally exists." We awake into a world of globalized finance and through the means of the origin story of barter, as far back as our imaginations stretch, we see that it is as it ever was. Granted our markets are more complex and varied, but they are markets nonetheless, scaled up from the bartering primitives. Like a

ern economists who follow him in postulating a distant, unreachable past where bartering gave rise to currency are advocating a "primal myth."[15] Like all myths, it is intended to "shape agents' moral stances by directing attention, framing conceptual priorities" and in the case of the tale Smith tells, it situates "the stated and unstated analytical presuppositions that orient contemporary economic discourses."[16] Thus, this story tells us from where we began and in so doing, it legitimates the state we are now in. Smith's deistic "invisible hand" may be the best-known aspect of his protology, but much more decisive is Smith's insistence that the market is original and the source from which wider society springs. By making the pursuit of exchange value the cornerstone of the communal life, the marshalling of the market becomes a process of subduing natural forces. The pursuit of the common good is reimagined as the pursuit of profit. If the market is prior to politics, it is a fool's game to seek to wrestle it into some shape that we decide is best, as foolish as trying to keep the tide out until it is more convenient for us.

The origin story of economics begins with bartering, and positions the market as the foundation upon which politics and society rests. This local variety of the story—the Irish boom to bust tale—begins with ingenious economic policy positions that lure foreign investment into the country and ends with economic policy that is tragically outstripped by that same flow of global capital, leaving Ireland at a severe loss when the reckoning begins in autumn 2008. The order that Smith established is present here. The market is the pre-existing natural force that must be seduced. Politics is the tool by which we collect the run off of this natural resource—a canal by which we channel it or a but by which we accumulate it—but always in response to the forces that existed before us and will linger after us. Thus, the origin story of the Celtic Tiger as a thing that happened, irreducibly inexplicable, and the crash as an unfortunate and unforeseen side effect of something that was happening somewhere else, legitimates and concretizes the political and economic arrangement. Our recent past holds a determinative power over our immediate present and our distant future.

Origin stories matter. Protologies determine eschatologies. The endings are contained in the beginnings. This is true for modern myths of superheroes and the more ancient myths of the major religions. It is also true in the case of the myth told by the discipline of economics. By positing the

---

sort of financial Newtonian law of motion, the debtor pays the creditor and the investor takes a slice of the profits. Graeber, *Debt*, 26, 27, 28, 44.

15. The work of Brian Brock is influential in this argument, and Brock is clear that no pejorative connotations are intended by either "primal" or "myth." Brock, "Globalisation, Eden and the Myth of the Original Markets," 403.

16. Brock, "Globalisation, Eden and the Myth of the Original Markets," 402.

nonexistent bartering village, economics can detach the market from the seams of shared life. Isolated, the market is now amenable to study by the Enlightenment methods that evolved into economics. The myth legitimates the entire discipline.

Theological engagement begins by reattaching the seams of shared life to the abstracted market. The myth can be contested. The market is not a natural phenomenon, but something we construct out of our shared lives. It is "embedded" in the political disputes and religious commitments and the many other social relations that make up human community. Polanyi maintained that "distribution of material goods is ensured by noneconomic motives."[17] Noneconomic motives drive economy. There is a difference—no matter what the formal description says—between a loan made to a cousin and a loan made to a stranger.[18] And noneconomic criteria are also means by which economies should be analyzed. The embedded nature of market interactions is not quantifiable by economic measurement. Yet those market interactions are real. The Celtic Tiger is not to be judged based on whether graphs that can be drawn around it go in the right direction, nor are the negative consequences of the subsequent crash to be limited to that which can be aggregated in diagrams. Origin stories matter. To consider the *giving us daily bread* aspect of Christian conviction, the origin story that prevails in capitalism and globalization at large and in the Irish economy specifically must be interrogated.

In recent works on the theology of economics, this effort to overcome the temptation to grant the markets the first word has been widely recognized and approached in numerous ways.[19] In this chapter, we will seek to follow the lead from these and other theologians and approach a discussion of the Irish economy that foregoes any ambition to comprehensive accounts. Instead, drawing on a range of sources and prioritizing narrow, specific events or apparently marginal phenomena, an attempt will be made to sketch the recent economic history in its very embeddedness.[20] Our at-

17. Polanyi, *The Great Transformation*, 279.

18. Graeber, *Debt*, 22.

19. Goodchild, *Theology of Money*, 29, 75–76, 201; Long, *Divine Economy*, 4–5; Bell, *The Economy of Desire*, 31–33. And although not explicitly dealing with wealth, economy or capitalism, Craig Keen's *After Crucifixion* repeatedly touches on such issues, and its internal rhythm is established by five prose interludes. Keen, *After Crucifixion*, 34–36, 66–73, 110–20, 159–62, 196–207.

20. What is being approached here is not dissimilar to Katrine Marçal's re-examination of capitalist assumptions by means of investigating the labor that does not get noticed. "Adam Smith never married. The father of economics lived with his mother most of his life. She tended to the house and a cousin handled Adam Smith's finances. When Adam Smith was appointed as a commissioner of customs in Edinburgh, his

tention will be drawn in unusual directions and to peculiar perspectives once we begin considering the stories after Barth's reading of the parables and the realization that the logic of the kingdom clashes with the philosophy of neoliberalism. If it is true that beneath the econometric surface of modern market thinking lies an origin story comparable to other "primal myths," then an approach that seeks to place aspects of the larger story of recent Irish economic history in the foreground will be theologically fertile.

A Word on Sources

One of the exasperating aspects of history is how it never ends. If a project's remit involves "recent economic history," it will invariably require a comment on sources. While the broad brushstrokes of recent Irish economic history have been well documented, much remains unexplored. Dealing with such recent events demands, then, that a wider range of sources are drawn from than traditional academic works.

In this chapter, four main categories of source material are utilized. Firstly, below the text lies an extensive engagement with Irish economic history.[21] Social scientific accounts of the Celtic Tiger and its demise are also commonly consulted.[22] If 2008 saw the beginning of a recession across Ireland, it also gave rise to a mini-boom in publishing popular books about why the Celtic Tiger came to an end.[23] For the large part however, the value of these sources lies in their combined representation of how the crisis was understood and interpreted. The popular books were the books being read by commuters on buses and discussed on radio

---

mother moved with him. Her entire life, she took care of her son, and she is the part of the answer to the question of we get our dinner that Adam Smith omits." Marçal, *Who Cooked Adam Smith's Dinner?*, 16. It should be clearly noted that the present author relied almost entirely on his wife to work menial administrative jobs in sometimes awful conditions to put food on the dinner table while he sat and read and mused about neoliberalism's corrosive effects on contemporary life during his PhD at Aberdeen.

21. Representative works include: Bielenberg and Ryan, *An Economic History of Ireland Since Independence*; Daly, *Industrial Development and Irish National Identity 1922–1939*; Garvin, *Preventing the Future*; Whelan, "Ireland's Economic Crisis"; Ó'Gráda, *A Rocky Road*.

22. Kirby, *Celtic Tiger in Collapse*; Kitchin et al., "Placing Neoliberalism"; Mercille, *The Political Economy and Media Coverage of the European Economic Crisis*; McCabe, *Sins of the Father*; O'Hearn, *Inside the Celtic Tiger*.

23. McWilliams, *Follow The Money*; MacSharry and White, *The Making of the Celtic Tiger*; Clinch, Convery, and Walsh, *After the Celtic Tiger*; Murphy and Devlin, *Banksters*; McDonald and Sheridan, *The Builders*; O'Toole, *Ship of Fools*; Cooper, *How Ireland Really Went Bust*.

programs. They acted as interpretative keys for wider society as people sought to make sense of the sudden downturn and they are therefore essential as we seek to describe the recent economic history as it was experienced. Newspapers (which increasingly live online) often write history's first draft and day-to-day reportage plays a critical role in informing this chapter. The final category of sources gathers together those cultural artifacts that engaged with the economy, ranging from newspaper reports to comedian's sketches, to plays and novels. For example, familiarity with the character of Michael Fitzgerald in John Michael McDonagh's 2014 film *Calvary* would aid anyone's understanding of the Irish economic boom and crash.[24] Such appeals to nontraditional sources are of a piece with the broader intention of reconnecting analysis of economic life with the aspects and angles that are often lost in abstraction.

Inspired by Barth's reading of the parables from chapter 2, and informed by this source material, the rest of this chapter will seek to localize the problem of wealth within the context of the Irish economy since the start of the Celtic Tiger, but most specifically since the 2008 crash. The story of the Irish crash has been told and retold working from the assumptions of neoliberal logic. Yet following after the christological-apocalyptic reading of the parables in chapter 2, we are emboldened to approach this story from a new angle. What shape does the story take after being reminded by the insistent Lord that the people and their motivations, not the abstractions and their percentages, are the focus of our ethical thinking?

Three specific events will draw our careful attention, each drawing out themes that will resonate through subsequent chapters, and which give rise to theological assessment. Each of the three analyses will focus on "parables"; accounts of particularly illuminating events in a prose form which prioritizes the narrative over econometric graphing.

Parable 1: It Began Off-Shore

> There once was a nation that went to war, but after many years of conflict sat down with their counsellors and realized that even with their ten thousand men, they still could not oppose the army coming against them with twenty thousand. The war ended and the many men went home to their cities and took jobs and found love and sought to start families. There were not enough homes for all the newlywed couples and so the leaders of the nation gathered together a well of money. Stewards were

24. McDonagh, *Calvary*.

appointed to share out the money to builders and to buyers. Soon, there were enough homes for all the families.

Years passed, and another war came and went, but the well of money did not run dry. The newlywed couples became old and their children grew up and married and needed places to live. Eventually, people forgot why the well of money was gathered in the first place. The stewards had been entrusted with it for so long that the people agreed to let them act as if they owned it. People began to value the well of money more than the homes it helped create. One day, the stewards in charge of the well heard of a small land where their well could go deeper and hold more money and so with the help of the people in that land, they moved it all the way over into the new country.

From that new place, the stewards could share the money out all over the world. They no longer just built homes for newlyweds in their home city but magnificent roads and fine palaces and elaborate mazes of yet more money. The well was larger than it had ever been, much larger than the first people who dug it could have imagined. But still there was not enough money in it to do all the things the stewards were hoping to do. They grabbed money from here and from there to keep the well full but as soon as they had it, they shared it out again, certain that in time it would come back to them larger than before. The people in the well's new home were very impressed with the skill of the stewards and marveled at the magnificent new well they had in their midst. People from the original city also noticed and it came to pass that some very senior stewards arrived one day and announced that they would do whatever it took to join this well to their well. Things had never been better.

A day came however when the well was looking empty, but there was nowhere to go to find money to fill the well. Worse, on that day, no money came back to them from the people they had shared it with. The next day, the same thing happened, and the day after that. It seemed clear that the well was now truly empty and that there was no way to fill it back up.

But, there remained many people whom the stewards had borrowed money from to keep the well filled up when the days were good. These people soon came knocking, noticing that their share had not come back to them. The people in the well's new home were now very distressed, because it would surely not be long before those angry people looking for their share would stop knocking at the stewards's door and start knocking at theirs. When things looked very desperate, the people of the new city were saved. A judge had heard about the case and she

had ruled that although the well was dug into the new city, because its chief stewards lived in the old land, the old land would
have to pay the price of everyone who deserved their share. A
sigh of relief went up around the city, loud enough to startle the
birds in the air and the fish in the sea.

Depfa Bank and the Continuing Relevance of Borders

In the long boom at the turn of the new millennium, innovative finance
products were making fortunes for shareholders all over the globe. Among
the algorithmically calibrated credit default swaps and the complicated
hedging positions that would garner so much of our attention in the aftermath of the bursting of the bubble, some of the major players in the brewing
storm came from unusual places. One such unlikely place was the rather
anonymous modern office building on the north shore of Dublin's river
Liffey that was home to Depfa Bank. Deutsche Pfandbriefanstalt (Depfa) was
established in 1922 to provide credit for residential construction in Prussia
in the aftermath of World War I. In 1991 it was privatized, as a part of a
German Federal government initiative that sought to liquidize public hold-
ings that did not serve public functions.[25] In an account of the privatization,
written in 1999, it was a success. The early years of this newly constituted
Depfa bank had "been characterized by dynamic growth"[26] and it was an
example that showed, from that time's perspective at least, that "privatization is advantageous for all parties."[27]

In 2002, the Irish government passed law that allowed a restructured
Depfa to base itself in Dublin's International Financial Services Centre
(IFSC).[28] The IFSC was a late 1980s initiative between the then *Taoiseach*,
Charles Haughey, and the broker Dermot Desmond to attract finance firms
to Dublin to compete as a regional European hub for the industry alongside London, Frankfurt, and Paris.[29] In Ray MacSharry and Padraic White's
insider's tale of the economic boom, *The Making of the Celtic Tiger*, we find

25. Another book could be written on how the provision of mortgages to young
families came to be construed as something other than a public good. Gruber and von
Stein, "Privatisation in the German Banking Sector," 271.

26. Gruber and von Stein, "Privatisation in the German Banking Sector," 275.

27. Gruber and von Stein, "Privatisation in the German Banking Sector," 278.

28. McCreevy, Central Bank Act 1971 (Approval of Scheme of Depfa Bank-Europe
Plc and Depfa Bank Plc) Order 2002.

29. The *Taoiseach* (Irish word for chief) is the head of the Irish government, an
equivalent to a prime minister. For those who want to ever say this word out loud, it is
pronounced "Tee-shock."

that the IFSC was modelled on "the success of Bermuda in creating jobs in financial services."[30] It would be an off-shore style finance center, on-shore in the center of a European capital.

In its new home, Depfa continued its stellar growth. It quickly became Ireland's largest bank, lending to public bodies around the world,[31] including a deal to create a pension fund for teachers in Wisconsin that went awry with the crash.[32] Business was so lucrative for the 396 staff that the average salary in 2005 was almost €230,000,[33] a figure so large that the average industrial worker would need eight years of earnings to achieve it.[34] Two years later it was targeted for a takeover by the German bank Hypo Real Estate, for €5.7 billion. Depfa remained based in Ireland and continued its business model of lending for long-term public-sector capital projects which were funded by surfing shorter-term money markets. The "credit crunch" popularly spoken of with the collapse of Lehmann Brothers immediately affected that short-term flow. Depfa, which "in theory" was "an ultra-safe institution" quickly approached insolvency.[35]

At the end of September 2008, as each of the six Irish banks faced the same liquidity crisis, news broke of a series of bank collapses across Europe. On September 29 it was announced that the German government, in alliance with the banking industry, would issue an initial bailout of Hypo Real Estate for €35 billion. The bank "blamed its problems on its subsidiary Depfa."[36] By early October, when the bailout was finally enacted, the figure had risen to €52 billion and would eventually settle at around €100 billion. Fintan O'Toole unpacks the implications: "It was pure luck (for the Irish) that Depfa had been taken over in September 2007 . . . . If Hypo had not taken over Depfa twelve months before the collapse, the problem would have belonged exclusively to little old Ireland."[37]

Depfa started as a local bank that would help young Berliners to buy a home, and it ended as a global concern, resident in Ireland, owned in Germany, doing business everywhere, and being effectively regulated nowhere. By considering the story of Depfa—why it came to Ireland, why it collapsed,

30. MacSharry and White, *The Making of the Celtic Tiger*, 324.

31. Ewing, "Which Banks Hold Europe's Troubled Loans?"

32. Duhigg and Dougherty, "From Midwest to M.T.A., Pain From Global Gamble."

33. Beesley, "Directors of Depfa Bank Get €34m Pay Package."

34. Central Statistics Office, The Average Industrial Wage and the Irish Economy 1938–2015.

35. O'Toole, *Ship of Fools*, 149.

36. Murphy and Devlin, *Banksters*, 187.

37. O'Toole, *Ship of Fools*, 149.

and why it did not bankrupt the country—the global nature of the very local Irish economy can be exposed.

The case of Depfa's collapse is instructive in a number of senses. Firstly, it brings us very close to conceiving of how the crash endured by the Irish economy could have been different. The counterfactual thinking that flows from imagining that Hypo Real Estate did not take over Depfa allows us to assess the responses that were made to the collapses that did happen under the authority of the Irish government. As it stands, the banking guarantee crippled the economy.[38] On one hand, if the shortfall had been twice as big, one wonders how the state could have continued to function. Yet on the other hand, such potential losses may have rendered a guarantee futile and the remaining options (which would likely include banks folding) might have been less painful over the long term. Such hypotheticals are beyond the purview of this book. Yet Depfa does illuminate two factors that are pertinent to it.

As we consider the Irish economy as a tool to grapple with what it means to be wealthy Christians, we are inextricably bound up in a conversation about globalized neoliberal capitalism. Ireland's story is peninsular to the major movement of politics and economics across the globe. Among those who tend to see globalization positively, the story of Depfa is *almost* a happy one. A regional bank with a limited agenda slowly and responsibly grew until it ended up funding infrastructure in California,[39] local government initiatives in Paris,[40] and many other beneficial construction projects around the globe. It moved to Ireland to benefit from a small island nation intent on competing in a global market. By examining the significance of that move, the case of Depfa reveals the continued relevance of both geography and borders to the global market.

It is a common trope in popular treatments of globalization that due to technological developments, location is less and less important. Thus, Thomas Friedman holds in his bestselling book *The World is Flat* that "homesourcing to Salt Lake City and outsourcing to Bangalore were just flip sides of the same coin-sourcing. And the new, new thing I was also learning, is the degree to which it is now possible for companies and individuals to source work anywhere."[41] As this argument goes, wherever

38. The decision to guarantee the deposits in Irish banks in full was intended to bolster the system to get through a temporary blip. What it resulted in, instead, was that the "Irish state took on the problems of the Irish financial system" in its entirety. Ó'Riain, *The Rise and Fall of Ireland's Celtic Tiger*, 247.

39. Duhigg and Dougherty, "From Midwest to M.T.A., Pain From Global Gamble."

40. Lazzarato, *The Making of the Indebted Man*, 17–18.

41. Friedman, *The World Is Flat*, 45.

you can secure broadband internet access, a smartphone, and a computer, you can set up and do business. Some version of this thinking might be at work when a bank such as Depfa, with historic roots in Prussia, relocates to the quays of the river Liffey. The 1,315-kilometer distance between Berlin and Dublin shrinks under the instantaneity of email. Both bases are firmly within the Eurozone. Distance and sovereignty are apparently transcended by capitalism.

Yet the location of Depfa was absolutely central to the business that it undertook. The shift from funding housing developments in Berlin to building motor ways in San Diego was a shift in what was valued which required a shift to a new jurisdiction. In Germany, under the *landesbank* regulatory culture, Depfa could not have pursued and secured the new business it found once it had moved to Dublin. The German system did not value such speculation. The IFSC was described as the "wild west of European finance"[42] and its "facilitative business climate" entailed "light-touch, if not entirely absent financial regulation."[43] In the IFSC, the question of what value an institution offered was determined by shareholder return. Depfa was not simply based in Ireland, but in the IFSC zone where it could gain particular tax advantages.[44]

The case of Depfa offers this critical nuance on the easy stories that we tell about globalization. Even if hyper-text transfer-protocol is interpreted the same way around the world, the web does not make the world "flat." It mattered that Depfa's offices were in a very specific, small region, east of Connolly train station and south of the East Wall Road in a specific, small city in Western Europe. Laws applied to that space that did not apply elsewhere in Ireland.

It follows that since location still counts, borders do as well. In the work of thinkers like Philip Bobbitt, the coming end of the nation-state is often assumed. The collapse of Depfa, a relatively small bank, cannot falsify such a broad claim, but it can chasten it. Bobbitt argues that "states are losing control of their sovereignty, especially if this is conceived in territorial terms."[45] Yet Depfa's collapse did not result in a deepening of the Irish sovereign debt crisis. Rather, responsibility for resolving the collapse fell to Germany. The traditional nation-state, during a crisis in the rapidly evolving experiment that is the Eurozone, retained its sovereignty,

42. Downey, "The Financialisation of Irish Homeownership and the Impact of the Global Financial Crisis," 128.

43. Downey, "The Financialisation of Irish Homeownership and the Impact of the Global Financial Crisis," 128.

44. Cudden, "Dublin," 165.

45. Bobbitt, *The Shield of Achilles*, 806.

even in the face of territorial complication. Germany, as nation-state, saw it as a matter of self-interest to take on the shortfall in Hypo Real Estate and by extension the debts of Depfa. If Depfa had to be geographically within the domain of the IFSC to get into the mess, it had to be within the sovereignty of Germany to get out of it.

Bobbitt's claim is that "the globalization of markets, owing to advances in computation, invites the rapid transience of capital, [and] reduces the autonomy of the nation state to manage its own currency and economy."[46] Due to this and other tensions such as terrorism and climate change, Bobbitt foresees an era of constitutional adaptation. The Depfa case stands as an example of a useful counterfact for thinking about the Irish economy, while also serving as a reminder of the importance of political sovereignty in a globalized economy. In 2008, the sovereignty of nation-states such as Germany was such that territorial location and distance would be overridden in times of crisis. Paradoxes proliferate as the nation-state struggles to keep up with the flow of capital. The borderless flow of currency was the very reason that German regulators could not trace the flaws in Depfa's business plan and it was due to the rapid transience of that capital as it fled that the collapse occurred. Depfa is one of the many points in the recent history of the Irish economy where the connectivity between the local and the global becomes evident. By considering the narrow frame of the economy of this small island state, there are plentiful access points into broader, bigger conversations.

The Politics of Commitment to Foreign Investment

Since the government of Seán Lemass in the 1960s, Irish economic policy has had a sustained commitment to open trade. A critical aspect of this policy has been attracting foreign direct investment into the country. Government agencies such as the Industrial Development Authority (IDA) had developed sophisticated sales techniques, which were allied to a young English-speaking population, the firm commitment to be part of the emerging European open market, and a favorable tax climate. Taken together, it made for an attractive proposition and in time, the technique began to bear significant fruit. American dollars flooded into Ireland, so that by 2002, 93 percent of the funds invested in the EU arrived in Ireland.[47] Undoubtedly, the long-term strategy of attracting foreign investment had begun to pay off.

46. Bobbitt, *Terror and Consent*, 87.

47. Ruane and Ugur, "Trade and Foreign Direct Investment in Manufacturing and Services," 175.

Yet the benign narrative that can be plotted by means of such statistical snapshots is troubled when we look for their real-world effects. In 2008 multinationals accounted for 88 percent of Irish export sales yet they employed only 7 percent of the workforce.[48] In other words, the unglamorous stalwarts of farming and food production employ as many Irish people as Intel, Pfizer, Google, and the other much-vaunted multinationals based there. The corporation tax policy central to attracting such investment means that the exchequer received only €2.8 billion in tax on €109.64 billion of exports.[49] Apart from significantly boosting GDP figures, this foreign direct investment makes a surprisingly minor contribution to the Irish economy. More troublingly, the vast majority of the productivity arising from these multinationals in Ireland is funneled out of Ireland.

The IFSC, where Depfa was based, was a central component in this broader policy. Passing specific law to attract a firm was perfectly consistent with the wider commitment in Ireland to winning foreign investment. Whatever problems exist when such a strategy is applied to computer component manufacturers or pharmaceutical firms is amplified when applied to the abstracted industry of global finance courted by the IFSC. It now hosts "over half the world's top 50 financial institutions" and "eight thousand funds with $1.5 trillion in assets."[50] Bear Stearns, one of the pillar institutions to collapse in 2008, based three subsidiaries running two investment funds and six debt securities in the IFSC, "for which every dollar of equity financed $119 of gross assets."[51] In their own reports, Bear Stearns declared that they were regulated by the Irish Financial Services Regulatory Authority but the regulator's understanding was that its remit was to cover just the six Irish banks. As Shaxson summarizes, these huge funds were "effectively regulated nowhere."[52] There are tangible economic benefits, both direct and indirect, to attracting foreign investment. Yet the political strategy of Ireland has, for generations, seen no difference between a euro invested in shadow banking activities of the kind that prospers in the IFSC, and a euro invested in more significant and concrete economic activity. Bear Stearns and firms like them flocked to the IFSC to do business by the quays of the river Liffey in a way that they would never have been allowed to operate in their home nations. Whatever profits they made in Dublin were transported away, after paying only nominal tax. They employed few people, contributed

48. McCabe, *Sins of the Father*, 98.

49. McCabe, *Sins of the Father*, 98.

50. Shaxson, *Treasure Islands*, 186.

51. Shaxson, *Treasure Islands*, 186.

52. Shaxson, *Treasure Islands*, 186.

little to infrastructure, and engaged in high-risk practices that they falsely positioned as being backstopped by Irish governmental regulation. The question of value, outside of spreadsheets, in terms like the common good, was never raised. Economic activity in and of itself was prized.

Framed in this fashion, the remarkable success of the Irish strategies of attraction appear to be considerably more shortsighted than visionary. The profit is exported, the risk is imported. Ireland, as a society, tolerates this under the impression that it is the most favorable outcome it can hope to achieve. Whether that is an accurate impression or not, the ability of these firms to dictate terms (as they have done in the IFSC) and then move if the terms no longer suit (as famously occurred with both Dell and Fruit of the Loom), creates an insecurity inherent within the economic system that demands account.[53] The political hope of a foreign direct investment model based off a low-tax base is that a trickle-down effect will be initiated by the stable, well-paid employment created by the incoming firms. Whether those jobs are plentiful, stable, or trickling down is all up for debate. Even if they are, underlying this economic policy is a formulation of the state that is literally the servant of capital, meeting its legislative, regulatory (or lack thereof), and material needs to win its favor and deliberately nihilistic in its disciplined refusal to ask what all this busy business is for.

Foreign Investment Shaping Tax Policy

This subjugation of the state to the needs of capital is perhaps most clearly seen in reductionist tax policy. At the founding of the state, Irish economic policy was driven towards self-sufficiency and an austere distance from the perceived excesses of other western nations. Kevin O'Higgins, Minister for Justice in the first government famously declared, "I think that we were probably the most conservative-minded revolutionaries that ever put through a successful revolution."[54] Tax policy was central to the reversal of these commitments in the 1960s, and the emergence of contemporary Ireland's open policies. In 1956, a tax relief on exports was introduced which gave a 50 percent tax remission on export sales.[55] In 1958 this relief was doubled to 100 percent. The measure held full effect for fifteen years and offered reduced relief for a subsequent five years. Padraic White, later the

---

53. Consider: Nesbitt and Guider, "Dell Confirms Plans to Shed 1,900 Jobs in Limerick," and Aughney, "Final Spin for Fruit of the Loom in Donegal."

54. Costello, "The Role of Propaganda in the Anglo-Irish War 1919–1921," 20.

55. Barry, "Foreign investment and the politics of export profits tax relief 1956," 60.

managing director of the IDA, argued that this favorable tax policy became the "most distinctive investment incentive" Ireland offered.[56]

The use of tax policy as a means of economic development spread to other sectors. In 1981, tax policy was extended to encourage property development. Contemporaneous reports held that the allowance offered a "tax efficient outlet for investors and a valuable shelter for people with existing rental income."[57] In effect, investors could secure tax-free rental income on any property they bought, for a decade, in practically any urban area of Ireland, whether commercial, industrial, or residential. Furthermore, any excess relief could then be extended to other property either previously owned or later purchased. The developer Simon Kelly explained it with the hypothetical purchasing of a retail unit in Tallaght, a growing suburb of Dublin:

> A group of investors would get together to buy a shop or office for, say, £100,000. The [annual] rent on that kind of development would have been between £8,000 and £10,000. The investor would receive a tax break of £80,000 against their tax bill, which translated to a tax saving of £40,000. The tax saving would form the deposit on the shop, and a bank would lend the balance of £60,000. The result of this was that you got the shop for free, and the tenant would pay back the bank debt.[58]

It is hard to imagine how money could be lost on such deals. It is also hard to account for how a tax regime that so resolutely served the interests of those with capital could be politically viable.

One such scheme assured all commercial, domestic, and rental property development in the western counties of Longford and Leitrim, along with large portions of Cavan, Roscommon, and Sligo, of immediate tax relief on half of every euro spent in building, and then thirteen further years of more humble discounts.[59] This certainly encouraged building but it is questionable whether that construction met real market demand. The 2006 census (two years before the crisis broke) reported that almost 22 percent of all housing in Leitrim and Longford was vacant.[60] These demographic discrepancies repeat all over the country. Ennis is the principal town of the rural county, Clare. Regional politicians, surely informed by the property

56. MacSharry and White, *The Making of the Celtic Tiger*, 187.
57. McCabe, *Sins of the Father*, 43.
58. Kelly, *Breakfast with Anglo*, 22.
59. McCabe, *Sins of the Father*, 53–54.
60. McCabe, *Sins of the Father*, 55.

mania, gave zonal planning permission for houses to cater for a population of 100,000. The town itself only has 27,000 residents.[61]

Over this period, Irish governments "halved capital gains tax, reduced capital acquisitions tax, brought corporate taxes lower and introduced a series of income tax cuts."[62] In 1998 and 1999 the "taxes on profits from residential development and on development land were halved to 20 per cent."[63] Alongside these broad and in some cases, universal measures, Ross lists some of the niche allowances created by the Celtic Tiger-era governments:

> Capital allowances were on offer for hotels, holiday camps and holiday cottages, sports injury clinics, third-level education buildings, student accommodation, multi-storey car parks, park and ride facilities, crèches, private hospitals and nursing homes.[64]

The effect of these fiscal instruments was to tilt the entire national economy towards property development and acquisition, fueled by ready supplies of debt. By 2006, the construction industry represented almost a quarter of all activity in the economy.[65]

While these forms of tax incentives did not garner widespread attention, one branch of Irish tax policy became infamous in the aftermath of the crash. The so-called "Double Irish" was a means by which corporations could characterize profits as stemming from intellectual property and thus shift those profits to Ireland before transferring them elsewhere.[66] Regardless of where the profits were actually made, they would be booked through Ireland on the way to an even lower tax regime. "Structures such as those used by Google and Apple also often involve further shifting of IP [intellectual property] income from low-tax countries like Ireland to even lower or zero-tax countries."[67] The existence of these loopholes attracted firms to Ireland and it certainly hindered other states in their economic development, since the profits, when they do eventually get repatriated, are no longer eligible to be taxed, having already been thoroughly processed (at rates as low as 2 percent) in Ireland. Under pressure from the

61. McWilliams, *Follow The Money*, 42.

62. Ross, *The Bankers*, 123.

63. Ross, *The Bankers*, 123.

64. Ross, *The Bankers*, 124.

65. Ross, *The Bankers*, 124.

66. Loomis, "The Double Irish Sandwich," 836–42.

67. Graetz and Doud, "Technological Innovation, International Competition, and the Challenges of International Income Taxation," 401.

European Commission, Ireland began a six-year process of phasing out the "Double Irish" in October 2014[68] but maintained its contentiously low corporate tax rate of 12.5 percent.[69]

The operating assumption behind tax stimulus policies of the kind that Ireland has relied upon is that the market should not be hindered.[70] The state embraces the corporate perception of tax—choosing to see it as a negative phenomenon, an obstacle to growth, a barrier to business. Alternative conceptions could be imagined whereby tax payment is seen as a positive—contributing to the common good, establishing long-term stability, developing critical infrastructure. How a society construes tax reveals much about what it values. An economic policy reliant on canny tax law is an economic policy that in many respects is cannibalistic. Encouraging futile housing estates and empty multistory car parks and allowing tax evasion on a global scale may, in the long course of econometric calculation, have benefits. But the underlying capitulation to the logic of the market undermines the very notion of the state as the guarantor of the social good.[71]

The Colonial Resonances of Neoliberal Capitalism

Ireland is a postcolonial nation. What this legacy means is still debated. For our purposes however, there is an unavoidable analogy to be drawn between the historic subjugation of Irish society to the priorities of its larger neighbor across the Irish Sea and its present position in relation to the much larger and more diffuse priorities of global capitalism. The cycle of boom followed by bust that has marked Ireland's economic history since independence is continued and even exaggerated in the recent era with the adoption of neoliberal economic orthodoxy. There are more disjunctions than similarities

68. Boland, "Dublin Ditches Double Irish to Save Low Tax Regime."

69. Irish popular discourse often engages the challenge of maintaining low corporate tax rates. A search through the newspaper of record finds ten discussions in the first three weeks of May, 2014. A representative example would be: Paul, "UK Takes on Ireland with Lower Corporation Tax Regime."

70. Nicholas Shaxson's summary statement may be too bold, but it nonetheless points at an important connection between light-touch attitudes to regulation and low-tax economic policies. "In truth, the term tax haven is a bit of a misnomer because these places offer an escape not just from taxes but from many other rules and regulations too." Shaxson, *Treasure Islands*, 6.

71. Article 6 of the Irish Constitution: "All powers of government, legislative, executive and judicial, derive, under God, from the people, whose right it is to designate the rulers of the State and, in final appeal, to decide all questions of national policy, according to the requirements of the common good." Republic of Ireland, *Bunreacht na hÉireann*.

when we compare imperialism with global capitalism.[72] There is, however, the same attempted total grasp of the social domain; the turning of society towards the servicing of narrow, external aims. Ireland in the colonial era (and afterwards) was "Britain's larder"[73] and in the globalized era is a "treasure island" for tax piracy.[74] No strong correlation is required for the humble claim being made here—that neoliberal capitalism frames the social imaginary of contemporary Ireland and in this way it echoes the effects of colonialism.[75] They are both dominating forces that achieve their aims by framing the political possibilities open to a people. It was on this level— a contestation of the imagination—that the Gaelic cultural revival played such a central role in the independence movement.[76] W. B. Yeats did not lay out an economic policy and Dubhglas de Híde did not get embroiled in conversations about British import levies. The deep question which informs the nuts and bolts of legislation and treaties is the prior question of possibility. By thinking about Ireland's location in relation to global capital as an analogical recapitulation of colonization, space may be created in which alternatives can be conceived. We can discuss what it is we value.

The Irish economic crash of 2008 was a direct consequence of the crash that began in the New York stock markets. Neoliberal capitalism left the entire Western world vulnerable to dramatic economic fluctuations but Ireland's commitment to a particular kind of regulatory culture and fostering of a particular form of finance industry meant it was especially prone to collapse.

72. One thing they certainly do have in common is that the breadth of usages of both terms and their cognates defies simple definition! Samir Amin draws explicit reference to the utility of such vagueness in his discussion of how globalized capitalism aspires to a totalization comparable to imperial projects: "This absence of precision lets us understand that we are confronted with an inevitable condition, independent from the nature of social systems: globalization will impose itself equally on all countries, no matter what their fundamental choice—capitalism or socialism—and it will thus act like a natural law produced by the shrinking of the global space." Amin, "Capitalism, Imperialism, Globalization," 157.

73. A description used by British government officials as late as 1947. McCabe, *Sins of the Father*, 90.

74. Mercille and Murphy, *Deepening Neoliberalism, Austerity, and Crisis.*

75. Following Taylor, a social imaginary here is "the ways people imagine their social existence, how they fit together with others, how things go on between them and their fellows, the expectations that are normally met, and the deeper normative notions and images that underlie these expectations." Taylor, *Modern Social Imaginaries*, 23.

76. "Many no doubt joined the revival for social reasons, attracted by dances, concerts, sports and outings rather than by any love of the Irish language or history. But through its theatre, literature, Irish festivals, 'pilgrimages' to sacred spots, summer schools in the West, it acted as a major socializing influence on the young, orienting them away from British metropolitan culture to a visionary Ireland based on the Gaeltacht." Hutchinson, *Dynamics of Cultural Nationalism*, 291–92.

The example of Depfa illuminates how geography, policy, and sovereignty have continuing relevance, even within the most globalized of capitalisms. It was how those questions related to each other that meant Depfa's collapse did not fall to the Irish state, which had very real consequences both for people living on the Atlantic coast in Donegal and people living in apartment blocks in Dortmund. Recalling this, and focusing on this, represents a shift in attention from the heady days before the crash when profitability was the (sole) evaluating criterion for Depfa. Regardless of how abstract the products become or how obtuse the financial modelling may be, Depfa and institutions like it are still in the business of facilitating living, breathing people engaged in embedded economic activity. The elision of attention involved in considering Depfa's bottom line without reference to its methods or its consequences represents a narrowing of vision similar to that which commonly occurred during the Irish colonial experience. The economic activity of society was not subject to assessment or evaluation on any level lower than what the dominating force demanded. Under the rule of Britain, the markets needed beef and beef was produced. Under the rule of globalization, the markets needed capital and capital was produced. To book no value beyond what is considered necessary is another way of insisting there is no alternative. Possibility and the potential of different futures evaporate under the relentless pressure to meet present demand. Economic policy committed to attracting foreign direct investment resonates with imperialism in how commitment to the larger, external force comes at the price of being able to ask pressing questions about concepts like the common good. Economic policy extracted from geography and sovereignty is utopian, certain to topple. The consequences of this for Ireland soon became clear.

PARABLE 2: ROBBING YOUR OWN BANK

There once was a man who was famous across all the land for his wise and brilliant business sense. He was often invited to sit in the seat of honor and crowds came to him so he could teach them. Rulers paid him homage and judges sought his counsel. And whenever he would speak, he would remind people that he was a man born of humble beginnings and that the world was there for everyone's taking, if only they had the courage, like he did.

Behind closed doors, this man did many deals. Some of those deals were wise and some were foolish. In all of them however, his belief in himself never wavered. Although he lived in the new city, in the place where that first well of money had been relocated, he thought to himself proudly that he had mastered the techniques of those stewards long before they ever thought of them. All of his business was conducted at speed, moving gold from here to there and silver from this pot to that, making sure that every time he shared some money out, he got much more back.

Soon after the first well of money had recently run dry, this businessman's well was found to be empty too. The people grew angry with him, because the judges had ruled very clearly that if the businessman could not pay back to those from whom he had borrowed, the city would have to pay his bills. The bills were so large that many people would go without food and heat for a very long time before they were cleared.

But when the time came for the man to make an account of himself, he was able to prove that he had had no malice in what he had done. He had not hidden away vast troves of gold while the wells ran dry. In fact, he confessed, shamefacedly, he had so deeply believed in the strength of the wells and the speed of his skills that he had invested all his treasure in making the wells strong. His belief, he admitted, was so firm that he had some-times stolen from the well to buy himself a bigger slice of the well. He had had his friends who were also businessmen conceal his thieving, because all he ever trusted in was the strength of his own wells.

The people of the city went hungry. They were cold in the winter. They had no festivity for years, no feasts, and no lavish parties. The wells were broken. There was no money to put in them and if there was, they could no longer contain it. He had stolen from his neighbors. He had damaged the city wells. He so loved being thought of as a master that he could not imagine he could go wrong. He loved his wells too much and now they were forever broken. The man spent his elderly years watching his neighbors suffer and he awaited a day when a judge would pass her verdict.

The Greatest Small Bank in the World

Anglo Irish Bank was founded in 1964, targeting an emerging market offering banking services to small businesses. It remained a niche figure in the Irish banking industry before entering a period of sustained growth in the 1980s, under the leadership of Sean FitzPatrick. It "played up the fact that it was a small but plucky bank willing to take business from bigger players."[77] With a model similar to that of Depfa, funding long-term loans with short-term credit, Anglo Irish grew consistently in the years leading up to the Celtic Tiger and quite explosively afterwards. In 2007 they had posted profits of over a billion euro, the twenty-second consecutive year of profitability.[78] To place that figure in context, in 1987, the first year that Anglo Irish was a publicly listed company, the annual profits were IR£1.45 million.[79] Those 2007 profits before tax were a 46 percent increase on 2006.[80] Anglo began to receive international acclaim. The stock price rose from less than €1 to peak at €17.60 in May 2007.[81] It was named the best performing bank in the world as late as 2007.[82] The centrality of the ambitious chief executive, Sean FitzPatrick, to Anglo's successes meant that Anglo was informally known as "Seanie's Bank." The awards and plaudits came to him as well. In 2002 he was named the Irish Businessman of the Year.[83]

Anglo's growth was based on lending to property developers and speculators. Their approach was aggressive. They said yes to loans that others turned down. They built loyalty by factoring equity built up in previously successful loan deals as security for new loan initiatives. Thus, property speculators were able to cumulatively roll over large sums of credit which satisfied risk criteria because it was backed up by personal guarantee. When some deals involving the property developer Paddy Kelly started to go awry in late 2005, the bank's internal risk report concluded, "Paddy Kelly's net worth gives comfort."[84] That Kelly's net worth was largely built on lines of credit drawn from Anglo seemed to escape the bank's notice. In fact, convincing developers like Kelly to continue drawing down more debt was the essence of Anglo's remarkable annual reports on profitability. Kelly's son Simon, in his memoir of bankruptcy, records how Anglo strongly opposed debtors paying back their loans in full: "Lose money or make a mistake on a deal, and a banker might get a little irked. Pay them off—even at a time when they were trying to cool things down—and they would go bonkers."[85]

---

77. Carswell, *Anglo Republic*, 12.

78. Lynch, *When the Luck of the Irish Ran Out*, 3.

79. Carswell, *Anglo Republic*, 16.

80. Anglo Irish Bank, "Annual Report and Accounts 2007," 2.

81. Saigol and Smyth, "The Men behind the Anglo Irish Scandal."

82. Wyman, "10th Annual State of the Financial Services Industry 2007," 22.

83. Lynch, *When the Luck of the Irish Ran Out*, 135.

84. Carswell, *Anglo Republic*, 82.

85. Kelly, *Breakfast with Anglo*, 156.

When the credit crisis reached Irish shores at the end of September 2008, no full reckoning of the scale of the crisis seemed possible. There was a need to act, as deposits fled from all of the banks. The Irish government consulted with expert advice and were advised that under a stress test, the accumulated bad loans on the books of Irish Nationwide, Irish Life & Permanent, and Anglo Irish Bank could together total as much as €5 billion.[86] Merrill Lynch had produced a report on Anglo Irish Bank that suggested that at most 3 percent of their loan book was impaired.[87] The extent to which these reports underestimated the risk can barely be overstated. Informed by such wayward expertise, however, at 3:30 AM on September 29, 2008, the Irish government announced "an unprecedented two-year blanket guarantee of the debts and deposits of the top six banks."[88] The Minister for Finance, Brian Lenihan, boasted that this would turn out to be "the cheapest bailout in the world."[89] When it was formally withdrawn on March 29, 2014, Anglo Irish Bank no longer existed and the total direct cost of the bailout rested at €64.1 billion.

Anglo Irish Bank's collapse can be grouped with many of the financial institutions that failed when liquidity sources dried up in September 2008. The English bank Northern Rock had collapsed a year before the wider global crash after its ability to shore up long-term loans with short-term credit failed in September 2007. Anglo's end came about in a similar fashion. As already discussed, the Dublin-based Depfa bank fell in the same way. Anglo is notable due to its influence in the creation of the Irish credit bubble and for the scale of its losses, but it is illustrative of the deeper dysfunction that was found in the Irish economy at the tail end of the Celtic Tiger. Even after the bank guarantee, Sean FitzPatrick remained in control of Anglo Irish Bank. It was only with the discovery that he had dubiously borrowed €129 million from the bank and deliberately concealed the loans from auditors that he was forced to resign.[90] Even such corruption is not out of place in the recent history of Irish banking. What is notable about the disguised loans is the purpose to which they were put. He largely invested the money in Anglo Irish bonds. Michael Lewis notes that this bizarre investment strategy continued as late as April 2008.[91] He unpacks the significance of this detail:

86. Carswell, *Anglo Republic*, 279.

87. Carswell, *Anglo Republic*, 216.

88. Lynch, *When the Luck of the Irish Ran Out*, 191.

89. O'Toole, *Enough Is Enough*, 7.

90. Lyons and Carey, *The FitzPatrick Tapes*, 220.

91. Lewis, *Boomerang*, 102.

"The Irish *nouveau riche* may have created a Ponzi scheme, but it was a Ponzi scheme in which they themselves believed."[92]

There are many anecdotes that reveal insights about FitzPatrick as a character and there are an increasingly large numbers of stories that captures Anglo Irish Bank as a culture, but no single story better broadens out and captures the psychology of the Celtic Tiger like FitzPatrick's hidden loans used to purchase stakes in the very company he had dubiously taken them from. Ireland's was a fêted capitalism with the shakiest of foundations; a growing economy that was stealing from itself, a crash waiting to happen.

There is, then, a fundamental irrationality on display in the latter years of the Celtic Tiger. The impairment of discernment demonstrated both in FitzPatrick's loans and in the institutional inability to even create regulatory checks to limit such abuses of power is so stark as to warrant comparison with blindness. Anglo Irish Bank's sustained scale of growth was so dramatic that external investors were discouraged from interrogating the core business methods. Anglo's competitors were so preoccupied with the threat posed to them that they were reckless in their pursuit of market share. Anglo's own staff were so richly rewarded, both financially and in terms of status, that they could not apply the brakes. It was in the interest of no one to covertly withdraw money from a bank to then invest it back into that very same bank but no one thought it was in their interest to protest. It was in very few people's interest to issue a complete guarantee of bank deposits, even for a bank like Anglo Irish that had no domestic business. Yet this was done, without protest. The final days of Anglo Irish Bank are important to consider because their insanity must be accounted for.

Corruption and Community in Ireland

When read in sequence, the mini-publishing boom in books that explained (in hindsight) how the Celtic Tiger faltered share a notable commonality. In each of these many books, the same names continue to appear. The impression is created that four overlapping spheres were brokers of power in the Irish economy in the run up to the crash. There was a tight circle of journalists, a tight circle of property developers, a tight circle of bankers, and a tight circle of politicians that interacted with each other, symbiotically aligning and competing to achieve their individual ends.

Frank McDonald and Kathy Sheridan's *The Builders* was subtitled "How a small group of property developers fueled the building boom and

92. Lewis, *Boomerang*, 103.

transformed Ireland."[93] The only book written by a property developer is Simon Kelly's *Breakfast with Anglo*,[94] which features anecdotes of partnership, rivalry, and close relations with all the major figures that grace the cover of McDonald and Sheridan's work. Kelly describes how he was treated as a friend by his representative bankers at Anglo Irish.[95] Those bankers, in turn, maintained close relationships with political leaders. As it became clear that he would become *Taoiseach*, Anglo bankers positioned themselves as trusted guides to Brian Cowen as he grappled with imminent new responsibilities. "On 24 April 2008 Anglo hosted a special private dinner . . . so that Cowen could meet Anglo's board members and executives."[96] They joked about horse racing and discussed the economy and the next day Cowen became leader of the Irish government.[97] It was not just bankers who were close to the political leaders. Shane Ross recounts the jarring detail that "Ireland's most controversial property developer, Sean Dunne" was a guest of honor of the then-serving *Taoiseach* Bertie Ahern at a British government event organized to honor Ahern's centrality in the Northern Irish peace process.[98] Such orchestrated diplomacy is an unusual place to find a well-to-do builder. Julien Mercille's work demonstrates how closely aligned the leaders of the Irish media were to the "political and economic establishment."[99] He quotes a reporter who stated that journalists "were leaned on by their organizations not to talk down the banks [and the] property market because those organizations have a heavy reliance on property advertising."[100] No vignette better illustrates the proximity of politicians to the journalistic class than the claim that the economic commentator David McWilliams makes in his book *Follow the Money*. On the evening of Wednesday September 17 2008, less than a fortnight before the bank guarantee, the Minister for Finance, Brian Lenihan, showed up at the suburban home of McWilliams. He sat at the family's kitchen table, peeling garlic bulbs and chewing on them, explaining that they "gave him strength and kept him healthy and alert."[101] He said he felt isolated from his offi-

93. McDonald and Sheridan, *The Builders*.

94. Kelly, *Breakfast with Anglo*.

95. "The offers came thick and fast." Kelly, *Breakfast with Anglo*, 87.

96. Carswell, *Anglo Republic*, 159.

97. Carswell, *Anglo Republic*, 160.

98. Ross, *The Bankers*, 113.

99. Mercille, *The Political Economy and Media Coverage of the European Economic Crisis*, 20.

100. Mercille, *The Political Economy and Media Coverage of the European Economic Crisis*, 23.

101. McWilliams, *Follow The Money*, 15.

cials, suggested he was struggling to get up to speed with a job he was not trained for (he was a barrister with no economic experience before taking the post), and that the emerging financial crisis had disorientated him. "He leaned over and, in a hoarse voice, almost whispering, he said, 'What would you do?'"[102] Newspaper columnists, in the ordinary course of democratic politics, do tend to influence public policy through their published words. It does not normally happen over their kitchen tables. Even the fiercest defender of the place of journalism in the public square would deny that the influence should be this direct and unmediated.

It follows, then, that the unsettling decisions, scandals, and outright corruption revealed in the aftermath of the crash bore signs of this interwoven, overlapping elite. An arrangement (discussed in the next section) whereby Anglo's shareholding was manipulated to reduce the influence of one business magnate, Seán Quinn, involved off-loading those shares to a "golden circle" of ten property developers, who all knew each other, did business with each other, and against each other.[103] The Byzantine arrangement by which Seán FitzPatrick warehoused his loans from Anglo on the books of Irish Nationwide on days when results were published was coordinated with Michael Fingleton, his opposite number in Irish Nationwide.[104] Alan Dukes, who was the Minister for Finance who had overseen a bailout for Allied Irish Bank in 1985 was appointed by the government to become a director of Anglo Irish Bank after nationalization.[105] The business leader Denis O'Brien, who was implicated in a corruption scandal involving the politician Michael Lowry, became the owner of a range of major Irish media outlets in the turbulent markets after 2008.[106] Bertie Ahern, *Taoiseach* during the majority of the Celtic Tiger, resigned in the midst of a corruption scandal. Subject to various accusations of malfeasance throughout his career, Ahern had been nicknamed the "Teflon Taoiseach" since no accusation ever stuck to him. This changed in 2008 when rumors that had circulated for years were confirmed and it was revealed that while serving as Minister for Finance in the late 1980s, he had accepted large financial gifts from a range of influential businessmen. At the time, Ahern was struggling with personal financial difficulties after the breakdown of his marriage. As he recounted those events from the perspective of 2008, he characterized the

102. McWilliams, *Follow The Money*, 16.

103. Lyons and Carey, *The FitzPatrick Tapes*, 145–57.

104. Cooper, *Who Really Runs Ireland*, 216–19.

105. Carswell, *Something Rotten*, 80–87.

106. Moriarty, "Report of the Tribunal of Inquiry into Payments to Politicians and Related Matters, Volume II."

gifts as a "dig out" from friends.[107] Public support deserted him and in May 2008 he resigned as leader of the political party *Fianna Fáil* and as *Taoiseach*. He remained a parliamentarian until the 2010 general election, when he retired from politics.

Whether the protagonists were politicians, journalists, bankers, or business people, this small sampling of the contentious dealings that have come to light in the aftermath of the crash demonstrate how the same limited group of people are at the center of the story of both Ireland's economic expansion and its contraction. In Ahern's description of the events that ultimately led to his downfall, an empathic reader can almost see the sense in which this corruption is a form of community. His sincere testimony is both that he behaved in a way unbecoming for the Minister of Finance *and* that he was merely accepting the support of his dear friends at a trying time in his life. The "golden circle" who purchased Seán Quinn's stake in Anglo were known to Quinn, and were friends with each other. The heads of the six banks, including Fingleton and FitzPatrick, saw each other socially. The journalists who reported on the tribunals that investigated Denis O'Brien's business dealings became employees of O'Brien as he purchased the largest newspapers and radio stations in the country. Elites form in all societies, especially relatively small societies such as Ireland. What is curious about the corruption of the Irish elite is how convivial it appeared to be. Illegality is represented as loyalty to friends, corruption is not self-interest but communal concern. The common good cannot be protected when corruption is misconstrued as community.

The communal concern that business leaders are called to is the wellbeing of their stockholders and stakeholders and this cannot be served by orchestrating complicated fraud. The communal concern that politicians are called to is the wellbeing of their citizenry and electorate and this cannot be served by becoming quite secretly indebted to a powerful circle of patrons. This convivial elite was an aggressive repudiation of responsibility. And from a theological perspective, the communal corruption that characterizes Ahern and his pals, Fingleton and FitzPatrick, Quinn and his Golden Circle, is subject to an even more trenchant critique. To care only for those who care for you is insufficient.[108] Jesus's teaching leaves us no space for comfort when we meet the demands of those who are like us. The politician satisfied to merely answer the demands of her electorate has still drawn a line connecting her responsibility to people who are like her and people who can benefit her. As corrupt power goes, there is something thankfully

---

107. Clifford and Coleman, *Bertie Ahern and the Drumcondra Mafia*, 317.

108. Matthew 5:46–47.

benign about the inept financial misdeeds of Irish leaders. Yet there is no space for the other in the culture of leadership revealed in this elite. The corruption denudes the very coherence of democracy but Christian ethical reflection drives us deeper than practices that meet the standards of democracy.[109] The gulf that opens up in these tales of scandal is the large territory where the interests of the wider community, the many, especially the poor and the downtrodden and the marginalized other, are displaced.

How to Think About Justice

To date, six people have been jailed as a result of the banking crisis in Ireland. At the same time as these few trials are brought before juries, the Irish justice system has fought an ongoing battle against other forms of financially based crime. In the years 2008 to 2016, 65,235 custodial sentences were handed down for the failure to pay fines.[110] In 2016, twenty-two debtors were committed to prison.[111]

This wild discrepancy should not be taken as a signal that the courts have not been engaged in the clear-up after the crash. The Commercial Court has presided over vast numbers of cases dealing with company liquidations, mergers, and fraud. These judges are "writing the first draft of the demise of the Celtic Tiger" as they see case after case that illuminates the inside history of how business was conducted.[112] More sharply, some might argue that the deepest injustice in the number of imprisonments over private indebtedness is a judiciary that misuses custodial sentences so recklessly, jailing people who pose no real public threat. In such a reading, it would be a travesty twice over if high profile imprisonments were sought for the sake of appearances.

The discrepancy still stands however, and it calls into question the hope that even if parliamentary politics is awry and if corporate governance is sloppy, the justice system should be one impartial place where right is seen to be done. When we consider how those guilty of petty theft or drug dealing are treated in comparison to those responsible for the economic

---

109. "Ultimately, the exercise of corruption is intrinsically undemocratic because it seeks to bestow unfair and unjust advantage to the few." Byrne, *Political Corruption in Ireland 1922–2010*, 238.

110. O'Keefe, "9,000 Jailed for Not Paying a Fine"; and Irish Prison Service, "Irish Prison Service Annual Report 2016," 34.

111. Irish Prison Service, "Irish Prison Service Annual Report 2016," 34.

112. McDonald, *Bust*, 5.

collapse,[113] we are reminded of the pirate's famous answer under questioning from Alexander the Great: "Because I do it with a little ship I am called a robber, and because you do it with a great fleet, you are an emperor."[114] The corruption and collusion that is a matter of public record between leading Irish banks was responsible (in part) for a long depression with rocketing unemployment, a consequent devastating alteration to public finances, and years of austerity and political instability.[115] It wounded the nation. Corruption was not new to Irish shores. A series of government tribunals ran through the 1990s investigating corruption scandals across a range of industries that implicated senior political figures. The slow-motion criminal prosecutions involving Celtic Tiger industry leaders moves on a different register of time than the rapid market responses that leave people redundant and see social services cut.[116] For all the work being done in commercial courts, the power distribution in Irish society is clearly seen in the different ways that the justice system treats someone who cannot pay a television license bill and someone who orchestrates cataclysmic banking fraud.

While Jesus's parable in Luke 18 about the unjust judge and the persistent widow may be a superficial source of consolation for those who stubbornly refuse to give up on the idea of justice, one's thoughts after corruption in Ireland turn more naturally to the Old Testament prophets and their railing against perverted judges.[117] The most direct route into the hardship caused by the crash—the route that our econometric imaginations have primed us for—may be tables of statistics about impoverishment rates or jobs lost. Yet the bias and priorities of the criminal justice system is an alternative way in. FitzPatrick is the symbolic representation of a corporate culture that was lauded for a business model that consisted of cannibalization.[118] FitzPatrick's shady deals are not problematic simply because they might have harmed Anglo Irish shareholders, or because they reveal a potentially crooked financial sector. It was representative of a political economy that privileged a very few at the expense of the very many. It exposes what justice looks like in Ireland. Those spending short sentences in prisons around Ireland for parking fines unpaid and dog licenses lapsed are

113. McDonald, *Bust*, 231.

114. Augustine of Hippo, *City of God*, 148.

115. Cooper, *How Ireland Really Went Bust*, 165.

116. Byrne, *Political Corruption in Ireland 1922–2010*, 179.

117. Luke 18:1–8. In the Old Testament one thinks of Micah 3:9–12 or Amos 5:7–13.

118. FitzPatrick avoided conviction when his trial was finally completed in May 2017. Brennan, "Sean FitzPatrick Acquitted on All Counts after Direction of Trial Judge."

testimony to that in a visceral and tragic fashion. The question of how the wider community of the very many experienced and reacted to the crash is explored with the next parable.

Parable 3: Public Protests for a Bankrupt Billionaire

There was once a small village that had very little going for it. Some people were shopkeepers and a few people worked as teachers, but most were farmers with modest harvests. But then a man in their town began to dig a hole in his garden and he found that people would bring him money if he let them take away the stones he dug out. With the money that he gathered, he started a small factory making this and then another making that. He gave jobs to all the people in the town. They still had their farms, but now they also had work in his factories. The shopkeepers were happy because people had more money to spend in their shops and the teachers were happy because their students were able to do much better now that they could afford their books.

As the man's factories grew, so did his pots of money. He bought a hotel and some horses and then a helicopter and a jet. He paid all his workers on time every week so people were happy for him to be doing so well. They were proud that the man came from their town. They were proud to work for him.

In time, the man met stewards from the city, who had learned how to use wells of money to make more and more money. He gave them his money so they could grow it for him. Now every season, his factories produced plentifully and he received pots of treasure back from the stewards in the cities. He said to his soul, "Soul, look at how well I run my factories. If I ran those stewards' wells I could make more money than they ever could." So, he began to give the stewards more and more of his gold, hoping that in time, all the wells would be full of nothing but his money and then no one could stop him from taking the wells for himself.

But before he achieved this the stewards realized his plan and stopped it. They emptied out all his gold and this left all his affairs in disarray. With the pots and the wells mixed up, he could no longer support his factories and before long he was left without any money at all. The factories were taken away. The horses were sold. A prince from a distant desert bought his airplane.

But all was not lost, because his neighbors remembered when their little village was very poor. And they were still grateful for the jobs he had made for them in his factories. And so, they gathered together in the streets of their village and put the man on a stage and chanted slogans in his honor and sang songs about the good old times. They had priests and athletes and singers stand to give speeches about how good at business the man had been. He sat on the stage with the crowds of people down below him and he could not help but shed a tear. Things were bad and they could get worse, but he would always have his friends.

Quinn as the Totemic Job Creator

As with every other shared narrative, the Celtic Tiger story was plotted around characters. Heroes arose, like Sean FitzPatrick, the head of Anglo Irish Bank. Antiheroes also appeared, like Michael O'Leary, the combative boss of the discount airline Ryanair. One of the businessmen who rose to celebrity through this era was Seán Quinn. He portrayed himself as a common man made good. Matt Cooper contends that "the romantic rise of Seán Quinn was a story that many people loved during the era of the Celtic Tiger."[119] Quinn's business empire began with a back-garden quarry in 1973 and expanded into building materials, pubs, hotels, glass, radiators, wind power, office space, and many other interests.[120] His public presentation was as someone who pulled himself up from nothing:

> We came from a very simple background and we tried to make business always simple. We don't believe in too much fuss, I don't use a mobile phone, I play cards in a house at night where you have to go out into the front street to go to the toilet.[121]

Wealth cannot be understood separate from the politics in which that wealth is generated. The politics from which Seán Quinn became wealthy were politics that gave rise to mass protests on the streets in support of him, populated by the very people who risked losing their livelihoods because of his speculation. These protests represent a strange flurry of popular enthusiasm for a larger-than-life local personality. Yet they also express something of the kind of capitalism that is at play in Ireland. Quinn is not just a peculiarly exaggerated case of a neighbor who has fallen on hard times but a

---

119. Cooper, *How Ireland Really Went Bust*, 170.

120. Lyons and Carey, *The FitzPatrick Tapes*, 99–105.

121. Lyons and Carey, *The FitzPatrick Tapes*, 112.

totemic representation of a "job creator."[122] To the protestors who faced the grey clouds of an Irish October, Quinn himself is the source of economic vitality in the region. The laborers mistake the employer as the one who labors. The Quinn protests reveal the way in which contemporary Irish imagination is thoroughly captivated by the myths of neoliberalism, and its Irish expression which is so concerned with property.

Quinn's approach to business seemed to pay great dividends. He was widely considered to be the wealthiest man in Ireland. In 2007, *The Sunday Times* Rich List featured him as the twelfth wealthiest person in the UK or Ireland.[123] By that point he had a net worth somewhere around €4.5 billion.

He had also built up a significant interest in Anglo Irish Bank by purchasing CFDs, "contracts for difference" on the firm. A contract for difference is an asset that offers a "geared play on a stock."[124] An investor can take out a small option on a stock, either short or long, the yield of which ratchets up if the investment accurately anticipates the market. Thus, "a CFD can be described as a leveraged financial instrument whose value is based on the future price change ('the difference') of an asset."[125] The alternative also holds, of course. The losses can be catastrophic. CFDs are complicated and high-risk investment devices.

The attraction of CFDs for Quinn seems to have extended beyond potential profitability. CFDs are constructed as options on shares and it meant that he did not have to list himself publicly as a shareholder of Anglo. Quinn was already heavily invested in commercial property across a number of countries. He also owned an insurance company and a health insurance company. There would be rational reasons for him to consider a takeover of Anglo Irish and CFDs were a vehicle that allowed him to anonymously build up a position over time.

In early 2007 there was speculation that Quinn had a 5 percent stake in Anglo Irish. That spring, the share price reached €17.53.[126] Such a position would have been very valuable. The actual position he had built up

---

122. The widespread belief that captains of industry, and not laborers, are the ones who generate wealth and create jobs is not restricted to the secular realm. During the 1990s, the prominent Bishop of Oxford, Richard Harries, published a book about the problem of wealth for Christians which specifically addressed "those engaged in the creation of wealth," meaning those who owned and managed concerns of free enterprise. Harries, *Is There a Gospel for the Rich?*, 74–87.

123. Carswell, *Anglo Republic*, 106.

124. Coogan, *Guide to Hedge Funds*, 124.

125. Corbet and Twomey, "How Have Contracts for Difference Affected Irish Equity Market Volatility?," 559.

126. Carswell, *Anglo Republic*, 108.

however was much more dramatic. In reality he had "gambled somewhere between €2 billion and €3 billion on Anglo Irish" and now controlled up to a quarter of the stock.[127] Yet with the gathering pessimism over the future viability of the financial markets, the Anglo Irish share price began to fall during 2007. This saddled Quinn with enormous losses but it also massively increased the risk of a further free-fall in the share price.[128] If Quinn cut his losses and sold out his stake, the very existence of Anglo Irish would be in question.

The management at Anglo Irish Bank were absorbed in resolving this dilemma. Having been approached repeatedly by the bank, Quinn agreed to off-load 10 percent of his holding and to convert the remaining CFDs into stock which were to be held by his family members. The shares that Quinn released were purchased by ten prominent Anglo clients, using loans of €451 million made by Anglo.[129] The intricacies of this arrangement are now the topic of many chapters in books on the Irish financial collapse. This corruption and widespread moral failure seems to capture the strange days at the end of the Celtic Tiger. To pay for the stock conversion Quinn blatantly "dipped into the reserves of Quinn Insurance."[130] The banking regulator was privy to this deal.[131]

The Quinn Group outlasted Anglo Irish Bank, which was nationalized in January 2009 and absorbed into what became known as the Irish Bank Resolution Corporation. The trading position on Anglo was disastrous however. Shares that had been trading at €17.85 a few years previously were valued at €0.21 at the end. Quinn seemed unperturbed, confident that the Quinn Group's high level of profitability would see it through. In an interview around this time he suggested that such setbacks were not serious obstacles because of his perspective on life: "I finished school at fifteen, I've never seen myself as some high-flier. I just live a very simple life with my wife and five kids and that is what is important to me."[132] Yet in March 2010 the Quinn Group was placed in administration. The decline in domestic construction and losses in their international property portfolio were the immediate causes.

The response to this decision was remarkable. As is standard practice, administration entailed the removal of Seán Quinn and his children from

127. O'Toole, *Ship of Fools*, 203.

128. Lynch, *When the Luck of the Irish Ran Out*, 188.

129. Murphy and Devlin, *Banksters*, 114.

130. O'Toole, *Ship of Fools*, 204; Lynch, *When the Luck of the Irish Ran Out*, 188.

131. McWilliams, *Follow The Money*, 122.

132. Murphy and Devlin, *Banksters*, 120.

any role in the management of the Quinn Group. Staff protests followed, not at the prospect of losing their jobs as a consequence of irrational decisions made by a billionaire, but at the prospect of keeping their jobs without the charismatic leadership of that billionaire. The humble self-image that Quinn presented was held even more passionately by the thousands of people who worked for his companies, who firmly saw him as the creator of an economic revolution in the border regions of Cavan and Fermanagh. Quinn declared bankruptcy in January 2012. Amid ongoing accusations of hiding assets, he was convicted of contempt of court in November of that year and sentenced to nine weeks in prison. His son was also convicted on the same charge and served a twelve-week custodial sentence.

In the months leading up to these sentences, public rallies were held in Cavan, where much of the Quinn Group was based. These protests were not like the ones we have grown familiar with around the world in recent years. There were no hooded youths in Anonymous masks, no tear gas, and no carnival atmosphere with steel drums. They were largely free of heavy policing. They did not take place in the capital city but in a provincial town. Their rallying cause was not austerity cuts, or economic sovereignty, but justice for a put-upon billionaire.

The protests were an authentic grassroots expression of local discontent with what was thought to be the unjust treatment of a community leader who also happened to own his own private jet. Almost 10,000 people crowded down the narrow streets of Ballyconnell (population: 747) and chanted in support of Quinn. Quinn sat tearfully on a makeshift stage, flanked by prominent priests and sporting figures (not politicians or financiers) as speech after speech lambasted corrupt leaders and greedy businessmen. Estimates hold that between 5,000 and 10,000 people attended these marches in support of the Quinn patriarch and his family.[133] Up to that point these were the largest public protests made anywhere in Ireland in response to the crisis.

There are fascinating factors at play that bear on local politics and the Northern Irish Troubles that help to explain this totemic value that Quinn came to represent for the people in that region. On one level, these protests can be read in the gracious light of Bob Crachit and his hungry family praying for Ebenezer Scrooge.[134] They testify to an intricately woven community spirit that rallied around their friends in a time of need. Yet most fundamentally, it reveals a delusion that seems to be common in capitalist accounts of creation, where harvest is hard-won and profit is

---

133. Reilly, "At Least 5,000 Attend Rally Supporting Quinn Family in Co Cavan."
134. Dickens, *The Christmas Books*, 48.

the result of straining battle. Quinn is a prototypical self-made man. An early school leaver, he is self-formed. He credits his success to discipline he learnt while competing in Gaelic football. He became a master of the game, the captain of the Fermanagh county team. His brother became the head of the national association. He became a sort of personification of the Gaelic games. In every aspect of Quinn's self-presentation, the apparent humility serves to communicate the message that he is just like you or me, he worked hard just as you and I do, but things really paid off for him. The crowds rallied because without him, it was thought, nothing would pay off in the region again.

This self-made man elides into the myth of the job creator. The productivity of the factories that turned out roof tiles and bottles, radiators and cavity blocks became attributed to his visionary ability. Thus, to remove Quinn is to remove the productivity and prosperity that came from Quinn. It is this aspect of the story that demands our sustained reflection. When the protests resonate in this key, they curiously remove the protesters from the story. After all, it was not Quinn that made the factories productive, but the laborers. In marching and chanting in honor of the entrepreneur, they enacted their neoliberal version of the plea, "When did we do this, Lord?"

Quinn and his family fought one battle for the legacy of the Quinn Group and the IBRC fought another, but neither fought for the sake of the workers. The humble celebrity that is Seán Quinn obscures the reality of Quinn as a man given to irrational and irregular business practices, who accumulated vast wealth for himself and his closest companions, while endangering the livelihoods of thousands of his near neighbors. The besieged visionary that is Seán Quinn obscures the reality that it was Quinn's employees who generated the profitability that was attributed to the Quinn empire. The critical question that the collapse of the Quinn Group raises is how do we account for economic growth (and retraction) while accounting for all the agents involved; employees as well as entrepreneurs, laborers as well as leaders?

Property Economics as a Machine for Debt

The crash of 2008 brought an end to a period of sustained economic growth that represented a "Golden Age of modern Irish economic history."[135] This era was marked by GDP growth, GNP growth, increasing employment, reducing public debt ratios, and a raft of other signifiers of economic health.[136]

135. Clinch, Convery, and Walsh, *After the Celtic Tiger*, 180.
136. Kirby, *Celtic Tiger in Collapse*, 32–35.

A speculative property boom was at the heart of the expansion, and at the heart of that property boom was a concerted tax policy.

Without the global financial crisis, over the matter of property alone, Ireland's boom was almost certain to bust. Between 1985 and 2006, property prices in Finland and Italy rose by 50 percent, in France by 75 percent, in the UK by 140 percent and in Ireland by almost 250 percent.[137] In the five years from 2004, new house completions in the Republic of Ireland averaged over 75,000 homes a year.[138] To put this figure in perspective, that is just under half the completion rate over the same period in England,[139] a country with over thirteen times the population, and undergoing a property boom of its own.

When the crash came, beginning in late 2007, but accelerating apocalyptically in September 2008, the Irish economy was devastated. Independent of the global financial collapse, the Irish property market had crashed. As Michael Lewis summarizes it: "since 2000, Irish exports had stalled and the economy had become consumed with building houses and offices and hotels."[140] As already discussed, convinced that this was a temporary blip caused by global factors and not an internal structural problem precipitated by the global tremors, the government's initial response was to issue a guarantee on all bank deposits *and* bank bonds.[141] In the days and weeks that followed, regardless of government positioning, it became clear that this was not a temporary blip.

The jump in unemployment arising from the construction slowdown simultaneously prompted a decline in income tax revenue and an increase in social welfare payments. The fiscal devices that had encouraged construction through the boom now served to perversely exacerbate the state's precarious financial situation. The tax base had evolved to rely heavily on revenue associated with construction industry activity.[142] The global credit crunch was not primarily causal in this breakdown, but a catalyst that ac-

137. O'Toole, *Ship of Fools*, 101.

138. "Annual Housing Statistics Bulletin 2008," 43.

139. During this period, on average England saw 159,714 new builds annually. Therefore, in the late period of the Irish property bubble, Ireland was building 47.7 percent of the houses that England was producing, even though Irish population is just over 7 percent of England's. Department for Communities and Local Government, "Live Tables on House Building—Statistical Data Sets—GOV.UK."

140. Lewis, *Boomerang*, 91.

141. Lewis is very clear how curious a decision it was to guarantee bonds as well as deposits. Lewis, *Boomerang*, 114–16.

142. "Furthermore, Ireland's tax base had been altered during the later periods of the boom to collect more and more tax revenue from construction activity." Whelan, "Ireland's Economic Crisis," 10.

celerated the effects of the underlying problems. All this meant that real GDP declined by ten percent and the deficit expanded to unmanageable levels.[143] An IMF and EU bailout package was initiated in 2010 which entailed deeper and more severe austerity budgets. At the time of this writing in 2018, the Irish economy is still severely hampered by high levels of private indebtedness and the public debt burden taken on in the aftermath of the bubble bursting.

That bubble inflated because of people's trust in the viability of an economy based around profit derived from rent. In the ordinary course of things, real estate speculation works by leveraging equity to secure a mortgage that allows asset accumulation in the form of property that can be rented out for profit. When this market is functioning, it can be an efficient way to distribute resources. Long before the crash, it had stopped functioning efficiently in Ireland.

In Ireland, the commitment to property development became uncritical. The property bubble meant that debt overwhelmed the system. That bubble was made possible because the market for property became the focus of the hopes of the society, an idolatrous commitment to self-defeating actions. Ireland's recent economic history is an example of credit-based speculation on a fundamental of human life (shelter) which created a devastating cycle of debt. That cycle was made possible by unchecked, uncritical, and unfounded faith in invisible hands administering material gain.

Thus, the recent story of the Irish economy is that of an economy mired in debt, in pursuit of profit from rent. Adam Smith himself famously declared that "landlords, like all other men, love to reap where they never sowed, and demand a rent even for the natural produce of the earth."[144] He cited the leasing of rocks that were home to wild, naturally occurring kelp as a particular egregious example of local landlord theft in the Scotland of his day.[145] These rocks yielded a harvest without human intervention and were often even below the high tide mark. Yet the political power of the landowner created a context where a rent could be extracted. Smith was analyzing a stable property market, not one in crisis like Ireland in 2008. This indicates that even in a normally functioning property market, real estate trading involves ethical complications.

When Quinn took out his options on Anglo Irish stock, he was taking a position on a company whose remarkable profitability rested on the servicing of this property speculation bubble. When the Quinn Group went

143. Whelan, "Ireland's Economic Crisis," 10.

144. Smith, *An Inquiry into the Nature and Causes of the Wealth of Nations*, 65.

145. Smith, *An Inquiry into the Nature and Causes of the Wealth of Nations*, 161.

into liquidation, the thing that swallowed up the majority of most worker's paychecks were the mortgages they had taken out in "a rush to get on the property ladder."[146] Quinn's exploratory attempts at finance profiteering were made on the back of debt that was already crippling his employees.

Real estate investment markets can serve to widen inequality. An integral assumption of the property speculation market is that long-term investment in land and property will hedge against inflation. Buying a house removes the cost of rent and promises the possibility of equity.[147] Yet this possibility is not open to everyone, especially in a time of market exuberance. Those who do have such resources to hand can accumulate more property and add rental income to balance sheet growth. Over the medium term and especially over generations, without intervention, this dynamic leads to the emergence of a capital-controlling class.

That the ability to invest in property is limited based on access to capital, and that this ability can be a chief opportunity to accumulate further capital, leads to the second complication. The material resources at the disposal of landlords make them an influential group within the political sphere.[148] In the Irish instance, the close collaboration between property developers and politicians did not even take place behind closed doors, but was conducted out in the open, most notably in party political tents erected at the Galway races where speculators paid up to €4,000 for a chance to dine with elected representatives, especially with those from the ruling party.[149] Government policy prioritized strengthening the profit potential of the residential property market over the provision of social housing.[150]

The political influence that comes with the accumulation of capital creates a double negative effect on those who are excluded from wealth.

---

146. In her post-boom novel *The Forgotten Waltz,* the Irish novelist Anne Enright captures the way in which the achievement of a mortgage became a critical life goal for young couples. "The day we moved in, Conor was inside in among the boxes, sitting at his laptop like a demented organist, cursing the internet connection. I didn't complain. We needed the money. The next few months were all about work and there was something frantic and lonely about our love in that little house (don't get sentimental, I tell myself, the sockets moved in the wall every time you stuck in a plug). We clung to each other. Six months, nine—I don't know how long that phase lasted. Mortgage love. Shagging at 5.3 per cent." Enright, *The Forgotten Waltz,* 27.

147. Piketty is especially clear on how this dynamic exacerbates inequality. Piketty, *Capital,* 454–55.

148. The spheres also commonly overlap. 20 percent of parliamentarians are landlords. O'Sullivan, "Nearly One in Five TDs Are Landlords, Registry Shows."

149. McDonald and Sheridan, *The Builders,* 18–19.

150. Byrne and Norris, "Procyclical Social Housing and the Crisis of Irish Housing Policy."

The worker cannot easily accumulate the reserves needed to engage politically. "The capitalist can live longer without the worker than can the worker without the capitalist" and this is so in a large part because the "landowner and the capitalist can make use of industrial advantages to augment their revenues" where the worker "has neither rent nor interest on capital to supplement his income."[151] The worker who needs to earn wages to provide housing is discouraged from industrial agitation by the imminent arrival of rent day and is discouraged from political agitation by the inability to deploy industrial agitation as a technique. Thus, the initial inability to gather enough to purchase a house leaves the poor exposed to inflation, bound to rental fluctuation, and thus less likely to gather enough in the future. The lucky ones above them who can secure mortgages are saddled with decades of debt. When coupled with the corresponding opportunities afforded the landlord and the way that capital reserves can be extended into political influence, we begin to see that there are ethical considerations that must be acknowledged around even a functioning real estate market.

This renders the protests in support of Quinn all the more bizarre. There is a sense that he was the victim of an orchestrated campaign by a resentful Anglo Irish Bank throughout the discourse, even though Anglo Irish Bank had ceased to exist more than a year earlier. The protestors reveled in their rural identities, some arriving at the marches in tractors, emphasizing their connection to their land and their distance from the urban elites in Dublin. Those who sided with Quinn embodied a pastoral view of Ireland, under threat from the cosmopolitan culture of the capital and the bankers and regulators based there.[152] That Quinn could not have taken the risks he took without being at the very center of the elite of Irish society faded into the background and was replaced by the presentation of the local boy made good. That the risks he took endangered the livelihoods of the marchers faded into the background as they concerned themselves with the endangerment he now faced. That the risks he took were intended to grant him control over the property speculation market, whose very forces were pushing basic shelter out of reach, was not a component of any speeches made that day. Quinn was a "job creator" and any systematic considerations of what that meant were not on the agenda.

---

151. Marx, *Economic and Philosophic Manuscripts of 1844*, 65.
152. Daly and Kehoe, *Citizen Quinn*, 270.

The Deep Relationality of Debt

The central cause of the 2008 crash, according to the official account, can be summed up in the *Taoiseach* Brian Cowen's catchphrase: "we all partied."[153] His successor, Enda Kenny, analyzed the situation, concluding in a similar fashion that, "people simply went mad, borrowing."[154] John Paul Getty famously quipped, "If you owe the bank $100, that's your problem. If you owe the bank $100 million, that's the bank's problem."[155] When the extent of Seán Quinn's position on Anglo Irish shares became evident, he very much became the bank's problem. The bank responded by offering loans to ten privileged clients to purchase those options and shares. They trusted this golden circle, which came to be known as the "Maple Ten." When the crowds marched in Ballyconnell, they were seeking, among other things, debt forgiveness for Quinn. They trusted Quinn. Debt inextricably binds us into relationship; debtor and creditor are drawn close by their financial arrangements.

It was hoped that the Irish government's banking guarantee would head off the need to bail out banks: when all deposits were guaranteed, capital flight would cease and the banks would stabilize. The problems in the Irish banking sector went deeper than could have been imagined, with Seán Quinn's "Maple Ten" being a characteristic example of the Byzantine arrangements that had been allowed to develop. Therefore, the guarantee, instead of preventing the need for bailouts, committed the Irish government to bailouts. Irish savers were assured that their deposits were safe, but they were not given any assistance with their debts. In effect, by bailing out the banks, without bailing out the people, Irish economic policy wrote a blank check for the lenders but a double check for the end borrowers. The marchers in Ballyconnell did not protest seeking debt forgiveness for themselves, shackled as they were to burdensome mortgages.

In characterizing the crash as the natural consequence after "we all partied" or the aftermath of 2008 as the hangover after "people simply went mad, borrowing," the ways in which debt and indebtedness were normalized and even thought of as inevitable is obscured. We see here why it is a profound mistake to imagine that neoliberalism seeks to shrink the State. The State acted decisively and powerfully to relocate the cost of risk away from the corporate realm and towards the communal realm.

153. Kerrigan, *The Big Lie*, 104.
154. Kerrigan, *The Big Lie*, 104.
155. Weiner, *The Shadow Market*, 21.

Economies built out of debt focus risk on the citizen.[156] The titans of Celtic Tiger industry were enabled to speculate, confident in the knowledge that the structure of political relations in Ireland would concentrate the costs, if their projects floundered, on the debtor of last resort—mortgage holders like those who marched in Ballyconnell. The banking guarantee transformed the private debt of speculators like Quinn and FitzPatrick into the public debt of the masses.

The dynamic by which the government's economic policy sides with those who control capital, at the expense of those who do not, has a shorthand descriptor. It is called austerity. The effect in Ireland has been devastating,[157] as the parts of the State that care for the marginalized are shrunk in the light of this commitment to care for the struggling corporate world.[158] When a government so arranges debt accrued in the private pursuit of profit so that it rests on the wider public in the form of sovereign liabilities and spending cuts, they have committed themselves to a course that discredits the rhetoric of democracy and justice. Nigel Dodd, in his *The Social Life of Money*, summarizes this well:

> Today, this mutually supportive relationship [of earlier eras] between public debt and democracy has been fundamentally weakened. The spectacle of pensioners, public sector workers, schoolchildren, and students bearing the brunt of the public debt burden that grew dramatically since the banking crisis began shed a new and disconcerting light on the ideals of public finance, its dependence upon the financial sector, and the relationship of both to the social production of money.[159]

This disconcerting light illuminates the logical gaps in this culture of debt. The collapse of Anglo Irish and other banks precipitated a recession that led to widespread, deep, and long-lasting hardship—unemployment, homelessness, emigration, childhood poverty—by all available metrics.[160] The economic and political leaders in a society can account for such costs as the unfortunate consequences of capitalist reality.[161] But how can we

156. Mian and Sufi, *House of Debt*, 12.

157. Heffernan, McHale, and Moore-Cherry, eds., *Debating Austerity in Ireland*.

158. Government spending as a proportion of GDP has reduced from 48 percent in 2008 to 27 percent in 2016 and is estimated to continue shrinking at least until 2022. OECD, "General government spending (Indicator)"

159. Dodd, *The Social Life of Money*, 179.

160. Rigney, "The Impact of Anti-Crisis Measures and the Social and Employment Situation."

161. Allen and O'Boyle share an illuminating speech made by the Minister for

account for the fact that the people who suffer the most also adopt this political perspective? Why did they view Quinn as a case worthy of sympathy and not ire?

What We Do, What We Think, What We Value

The Irish economic crash was a direct result of a property bubble. Almost by definition, a bubble can only be identified after it bursts, but once the crash comes, the pattern of market manias bears a striking set of family resemblances. In the definitive treatment of the phenomenon, Kindleberger and Aliber summarize the lead-up to the end of manias:

> Rational exuberance morphs into irrational exuberance, economic euphoria develops and investment spending and consumption spending increase. There is a pervasive sense that it is 'time to get on the train before it leaves the station' and the exceptionally profitable opportunities disappear. Asset prices increase further. An increasingly large share of the purchases of these assets is undertaken in anticipation of short-term capital gains and an exceptionally large share of these purchases is financed with credit.[162]

One of the remarkable aspects of public discourse in the years leading up to the crash was the absence of discussion of manias, panics, or bubbles.[163] Julien Mercille has demonstrated how representations of the construction sector and property market in the media played a crucial role in sustaining the property bubble. He records that "between 2000 and 2007, the *Irish Times* published more than 40,000 articles about the economy— but only 78 were about the property bubble."[164] There were voices of dissent. In one famous 2003 broadcast, the Irish economist David McWilliams announced, "The Irish housing market is a scam. It is an enormous financial

Trade and Employment, Richard Bruton, about the importance of lubricating the economy with capital as gasoline functions in an engine. It is an instructively mechanistic metaphor to describe the very human pressures effected by austerity. Allen and O'Boyle, *Austerity Ireland*, 6.

162. Kindleberger and Aliber, *Manias, Panics, and Crashes*, 12.

163. Michael Casey has demonstrated how this confidence was reinforced by the reports produced by trusted international bodies, which for the most part were proven to be profoundly in error. The OECD suggested Ireland was due a "soft landing" even though none of the forty-nine examples used in its historical study had experienced a soft landing. Casey, "Averting Crisis?," 553.

164. Mercille, *The Political Economy and Media Coverage of the European Economic Crisis*, 38.

swindle that could potentially confine an entire generation of young Irish workers to years of bad debt."[165] Such opinions were not favorably received. In response to a 2007 editorial penned by the economist Morgan Kelly, the *Taoiseach* of the time, Bertie Ahern, railed that "sitting on the side-lines or sitting on the fence, cribbing and moaning, is a lost opportunity. In fact, I don't know how people who engage in that don't commit suicide."[166]

The official message was that the fundamentals of the Irish economy were sound and that if the property market was to shrink, it would do so with a soft landing. The prominent economist and commentator Marc Coleman wrote that "Far from an economic storm—or a property shock—Ireland's economy is set to rock and roll into the century."[167] The columnist and television presenter Brendan O'Connor wrote in the summer of 2007 that "the smart, ballsy guys are buying up property right now."[168] These populist figures were joined by acknowledged experts from the industry and the academy, reassuring people that the fundamentals of the market were strong.

The positive editorial focus that prevailed during the boom extended into the bust. A systemic review of editorial opinion pieces showed 90 percent were in favor of austerity.[169] Mercille's research brings rigor to the instinctive sense that those immersed in an environment where the orthodoxies of Irish capitalism were so insistently reinforced are likely to be a people who see Seán Quinn as a victim. The structuring power of media means that public discourse can shape our private dispositions.[170]

What is at stake here is the scope of what can be imagined. Our understanding of what is reasonable or moderate or warranted and our decisions about how to act are influenced by the narratives to which we are daily exposed. As neoliberalism influences what we value, how we think, and how we act, so we can see the complex of forces that are played out in the shifting commitments that meant a Berlin-based bank would end up going bankrupt in Dublin, the leap into irrationality surrounding Anglo Irish, and the decision to protest in support of Quinn. As neoliberalism exerts its totalizing influence, the irrational economics of a property bubble and the extreme politics of austerity become coherent and even common sense (in

---

165. *Prime Time, October 16th, 2003.*

166. Donovan and Murphy, *The Fall of the Celtic Tiger*, 144.

167. Coleman, "We Need These Expert Scaremongers."

168. O'Connor, "The Smart, Ballsy Guys Are Buying up Property Right Now."

169. Mercille, *The Political Economy and Media Coverage of the European Economic Crisis*, 175.

170. McLuhan, *The Gutenberg Galaxy*, 216.

the literal sense of the phrase). An apocalyptic interruption is required to break the hermetic universe represented by received opinion. A theological analysis of these same issues will invariably challenge the scope of what can be imagined, broadening the boundaries of what is reasonable and what is warranted. The voices arguing for restraint in the property market met few welcome hearers. Opponents of austerity had to fight for time on the podium. There is a coherent explanation for the seams of apparent irrationality that ran through the Irish economy.

Quinn was a celebrated entrepreneur, a visionary of commerce who is given credit for transforming the economic fortunes of an entire region.[171] Yet this public presentation of the man, along with the public understanding of the property market, and the public perception of the economy's stability were unfinished to such a degree that they bordered on uncomprehending. If the crash came when it came because of turmoil in larger markets abroad, and if the crash came as it came because of fundamental failures within the Irish economy (especially its banks), then Quinn cannot be depicted as an unfortunate titan. His move to take control of Anglo Irish was not just another strategic bet on profit. It was an attempt to take control of a property market that was spiraling away from reality while simultaneously oppressing his workers, limiting their access to the basic human need of shelter. It did not simply betray a bad business sense, but a flawed relationship to the very people who were most loyal to him—his employees, his neighbors, and those people marching in Ballyconnell.

Conclusion

The 2008 crash punctured the delusions of a society collectively convinced that the Celtic Tiger would continue to roar. It is not clear that the puncturing process is complete. The deadends of the Celtic Tiger dream are still being pursued. At the time of writing, in summer 2018, a renewed property bubble is rapidly inflating in Dublin.[172] A decade of continuous austerity has ravaged the vulnerable and marginalized of society. Wealth inequality has

---

171. The esteemed Irish novelist Colm Tóibín interviewed Quinn in 1986, as part of a larger project about the despair in the border county region during the Northern Irish troubles. Daly and Kehoe report in their book that Tóibín found "Derrylin and Ballyconnell depressed and depressing. Young people were emigrating and the weather was so bad that farmers in the south were sending truckloads of hay north for farmers whose crops had been destroyed by the rain. The area was lucky in one respect, however: it had Seán Quinn." Daly and Kehoe, *Citizen Quinn*, 12–13.

172. Gerlach, "Is Ireland Setting Itself up for a Crash with New Housing Bubble?"

widened in a dramatic fashion.[173] Yet the underlying dynamic that we have
sought to expose is that an unconstrained drive for wealth was at work in
the collapse of the Irish economy and it has not been challenged in the years
since. It is not enough to lament that the rich are getting richer and the poor
are getting poorer. That is true and is to be lamented, but below that surface
appearance lies a deep drive to accumulate that is, at base, unjust, ungener-
ous, and unhealthy.

In this chapter we have sought to redescribe this reality. The longer
economic history of Ireland poses a puzzle—"why was Ireland so poor for
so long"?[174] It is within this broader picture that we locate the recent economic history of Ireland, which is a story of a rapid expansion, with an
unusual stamina, and then a quite remarkable collapse in 2008.

Ireland may be an island geographically but it is immersed in a globalized, neoliberal capitalism. In chapter 1 we sketched how neoliberalism
promises globalization, legality, and an efficiency born of markets. In this
chapter we have seen concrete expressions of how these promises are delivered. The crash began with turmoil in New York and the story of Depfa
sought to unpick some of the threads of that. Globalization means connection. The turmoil in Manhattan became tragedy in Dublin. In an intercon-
nected economy, where do we locate Depfa? Depfa raises questions about
what it is we value and globalization raises questions of sovereignty.

When the crash did arrive, it did so rapidly and found an unbalanced
economy in the grip of a banking-construction nexus that was highly dys-
functional. The extent to which this was news to Irish people, who widely
believed that the economy was on a sound footing, was investigated by reference to the interrogation of Anglo Irish Bank and the curious borrowing
and investment habits of its chief executive. Neoliberalism promises a stable
and trustworthy legal structure but the concentration of power in the hands
of a small elite means that different law is applied to the rich than to the
poor. Sean FitzPatrick was committed to irrational beliefs that the market
encouraged and the neoliberal legal structures in which he operated press
upon us questions of corruption.

The recession bit deeply and in subsequent years unemployment almost quadrupled as small firms and major conglomerates went out of business. It is at this point in the story, already after years of austerity and in
the aftermath of the 2010 Troika bailout, that we encounter the marches in
support of Seán Quinn. Unrestricted markets are a critical component of

173. McWilliams, "Ireland's Great Wealth Divide"; O'Connor and Staunton, *Cherishing All Equally.*

174. The subtitle of Tom Garvin's *Preventing The Future.*

the neoliberal package. Yet the lack of action from regulators allowed Quinn to build up his position in Anglo and then turned a blind eye as Anglo manufactured a compromise solution. All the while, the property market was being stoked by the media. The story Irish people were telling was about success and more success to come. The apparently bizarre action of protest in defense of a billionaire makes sense when we consider how what we do is informed by how we think and what we value. Neoliberalism forms our subjectivity and in so doing wins our allegiance. Neoliberalism's logic re-describes the human labor of the Quinn Group employees as a side effect of a particular individual's potent productivity.

These stories thus chart the path whereby boom turned to bust. The goal has been to integrate econometric, social scientific, and journalistic accounts in a creative fashion that simultaneously does justice to the history and focuses attention on the complicated themes that sit below the headlines or the statistics. By approaching matters in this way, the embeddedness of the market can be more clearly detected. Economic tools such as GNP and GDP have their place, but the work of theological ethics requires a closer view. The totalized aspirations of neoliberalism are challenged by Jesus's parables of the kingdom and this plays out in unexpected ways as we look again at stories that we too easily think are settled, straightforward, and amenable to singular interpretations.

CHAPTER 4

Rich Worship and the Response to Wealth

Narrating the Future

INTRODUCTION

In the redescription of the 2008 Irish economic crash in chapter 3, it became clear that Irish political discourse seemed inarticulate in a situation
where protest might be expected. During the Celtic Tiger, any divergent
voices from the consensus about how economic growth is generated and
sustained were effectively marginalized.[1] After the economic crash came
the intervention of the Troika and a period of sustained austerity. There
were effectively two crises. The first was the collapse in the construction
industry prompted by a liquidity crisis in the banking sector and the second was a response to that fiscal trauma that took the form of a "doubling
down" in the intensity with which neoliberal philosophy was implemented. In both the range of political policy responses considered feasible and
in the range of political protest options considered coherent, Ireland was
remarkably quiet.[2]

---

1. Mercille, *The Political Economy and Media Coverage of the European Economic
Crisis*.

2. There are exceptions, of course. Alongside the Quinn protests detailed in
chapter 3, the residents of the small parish of Ballyhea, Co. Cork, maintained a weekly
protest that followed the end of 11 am mass. The "Ballyhea Says No" movement issued
a manifesto, reproduced in Gene Kerrigan's *The Big Lie*. Kerrigan, *The Big Lie*, 208–215.
Protests against the commodification of water supply led to the protests against the
formation of the Irish Water company. These were the largest protests of the period.
Barrett, "Irish General Election 2016 Report," 421–22. Popular movements in Irish
politics after the crash notably took the form of referenda disputes about equal marriage and abortion, both of which were, on both sides, well-funded, highly branded,
deeply coordinated modern political campaigns operating fully in line with the prevailing logics of neoliberalism.

Alasdair Roberts has argued that the successful suppression of protest is a component of neoliberalism. His threefold explanation for how this is achieved begins with neoliberalism's liberalization of labor law, which weakens trade unions, and in turn, hinders mass protest.[3] In the absence of strong trade unions, new vehicles for popular unrest were bound to emerge, but the non-hierarchical forms that such initiatives took, famously disrupting G8 and G20 meetings in the first decade of the century, are intrinsically limited. Their commitment to anarchic principles means they lack leaders who can focus energy. Furthermore, their reliance on Internet technology makes them eminently trackable.[4] This surveillance potential was a critical component of the third factor identified by Roberts, which explains the reduced rate of protest in the UK and the USA (and a similar case can be made for Ireland), even in times of profound economic distress. Policing tactics adapted to the "more fluid forms of disruption" associated with the non-hierarchical, network-based social agitation movements.[5] If we think about how difficult it is to generate and sustain mass protest movements, we begin to see from yet another angle how the political arena is disciplined and re-formed under the neoliberal impulse. During the age of neoliberalism, crowds are encouraged to gather as paying customers at a sporting event or a U2 concert. Yet at the same time, "the angry crowd, by contrast, was never more tightly policed. It was becoming extinct because crowds wield influence through disruption, and the neoliberal age has made us more allergic to disruption than ever before."[6]

Alongside the suppressive effect on protest, there is another factor at play in the relative lack of disruption in the Irish public square after the crash. The apparent quietism of the Irish citizenry is an outworking of neoliberal capitalism's hegemonic hold over our shared imagination. People do not protest because they have no hope for economic alternatives. The peculiar stories Jesus told take on fresh significance in contrast to the closed loop of calculative logic. Ireland's dilemma, after the Celtic Tiger and after the 2008 crash, is how to go on being wealthy. The dilemma of Irish Christians can be phrased the same way—how to go on being wealthy—but for Christians that should mean something very different.

The problem for wider society is how to re-establish economic stability and secure future economic growth so that the nation's place in the prosperous world is not threatened. The perceived solution to that problem is

3. Roberts, *The End of Protest*, 66–72.
4. Roberts, *The End of Protest*, 72–77.
5. Roberts, *The End of Protest*, 84.
6. Roberts, *The End of Protest*, 103–4.

renewed commitment to neoliberalism. The problem for Irish Christians is how to be faithful to Jesus as wealthy people, when he has so thoroughly questioned that possibility. The solution to this problem involves recognizing neoliberal wealth as a temptation to idolatry and to commit ourselves to a stance of resistance. Neoliberalism's unfulfilled promises of justice and prosperity, exposed in chapter 3, have no reason to claim our allegiance. Living in the apparent age of neoliberalism, in the parables we encounter the claim of the King and the kingdom, whose authority summons our lives in a complicated and tense fashion. With apocalyptic force, the parables of the Ten Virgins, the Talents, and the Sheep and the Goats shatter the supposed dominance of capitalism in our lives. Like the virgins, we are called to vigil, to literally keep watch for the signs of the kingdom in our midst. Like the investors given talents, we are called to anticipate the return of our Master who wants to usher us into friendship and share with us the spoils of his distinctive economics. Immersed as Christians are in the marketplace of Mammon, they stand alongside others not knowing—and never being able to know—who is among the sheep and who is among the goats. The stance of resistance is determined by these stories; keeping watch, planning for the advent of transformation, and responding in concrete action when the insistent Lord presents himself to us, hungry or thirsty, naked or imprisoned, in whatever form he comes. What we value, how we think, and what we do looks differently depending on whether we are in the apparent age of neoliberalism or counting time according to the returning King.

In this chapter, we will propose a response to this problem of wealth. The church is the community with time and space for vigil, for friendship with God, for provisionally representing the distinctive economics of the kingdom and the entailing concrete attention to the needs of others. The first step towards this is to explain why the obvious courses of action—an agenda of social activism that works towards reform of capitalism or a project of pious separatism that seeks to build righteous communities apart from the influence of Mammon—are to be avoided. The appropriate course of action, considering what we have learned about the apocalyptic potential of the parables in the apparent age of neoliberalism, is worship. The parables puncture capital's hegemonic hold over our imagination. It follows that the church, gathered around these and the other narratives that make up the Scriptures, should begin its response to neoliberalism in worship. Drawing on previous theologies of the political potency of worship, especially in the writings of William Cavanaugh, the ways in which worship is an appropriate and effective starting point from which to respond to the problem of wealth will be described.

Yet this presentation raises objections. Capitalism has a capacity to co-opt even the most firmly opposed foe. This flexibility in the face of challenge must be considered and countenanced. Worship is as prone to domestication under the seduction of wealth as any other human endeavor. In recognizing this threat, we must offer a response, and Karl Barth's critique of religion serves in just this capacity. His articulation of the danger posed to worship by religiosity underlines how the possible alternatives are dead ends, and charts a path by which we can conceive of worship in a fashion that guards against—if not fully protected from—capitalism's co-option.

The final move in this chapter involves extending Cavanaugh's model to give a prominent place to preaching as a mode of worship that can directly interrupt the hold that wealth exerts on our imaginations and desires. Worship allows us the possibility of reimagining narratives that appear set in stone under the reign of neoliberalism. With renewed vision, we encounter renewed opportunities for action.

At this stage then, our mature proposal can be articulated: worship can be an exercise of our liberation from Mammon's claim over our lives. This is not worship as a static, private, internal act of piety but a communal and political performance that invariably expresses itself in an unpredictable array of resistances against neoliberal capitalism, ranging from outright rebellion in fresh ways of conceiving trade and profit down to small, generous "micro-aggressions" against Mammon.[7] All of this adds up to a form of watchfulness that anticipates God's apocalyptic in-breaking on our lives, mired as they are in compromise and injustice. With men and women, it would be hopeless to oppose the systems of inequality generated by our wealth. But with God, all things are possible.

POSSIBLE ALTERNATIVES

Are Christians called to repudiate wealth entirely and seek non-economic ways of living together? Or are Christians called to a renewed courage to enter into the midst of the market, with all its potential for error, and engage bravely in a principled movement of transformation? Or is it the responsibility of Christians to develop some form of shadow economy that can stand as an alternative to neoliberalism?

---

7. Here we are following Ellul's suggestion that the primary path to the profaning of money is generosity. "There is one act par excellence which profanes money by going directly against the law of money, an act for which money is not made. This act is giving." Ellul, *Money and Power*, 110.

Christianity has indeed worked at generating alternatives. One historical example can be found among the Christian Socialists of Victorian Britain. In a culture where gross inequality was primarily alleviated by means of private charity, the Christian Socialists "went far beyond these palliatives and dared to contemplate, if not a transformed political structure, at any rate the vision of a humanity emancipated from the thrall of custom and the existing ties of social deference."[8] Rather than a formal political movement, the Christian Socialists were a loose association of figures whose political and theological commitments were located across a spectrum. What bound them together was context—their positions were a response to the decline of the Chartist movement in 1848—and their general conviction that the emerging socialist doctrines were an essential means by which Christians could oppose the brutal social consequences of the rapid industrialization of their society. This was a movement dedicated to "Christianizing" Socialism and not the other way around.[9]

Their attempt to craft an alternative vision of economic life was based around the empowerment of working men, through the formation of co-operatives, workers' associations, and what came to be known as the Working Men's College, which offered evening classes to working-class men who otherwise did not had access to any formal education. The Working Men's Colleges were experimental, drawing students around gifted teachers with the hope of affecting a change deeper than mere skills acquisition.[10] In response to the hardships and inequalities tolerated by Victorian Britain, the Christian Socialists sought to create institutions that would affirm the dignity and humanity of the economically and socially marginalized. One of the leading figures, J. M. Ludlow, recounts in his autobiography how laborers flocked to the classes hosted by the renowned artist and critic John Ruskin:

> There was always a steady attendance at the Mathematical classes, and Brewer's History and Geography classes soon came to be recognized as among the most interesting and instructive

8. Norman, *The Victorian Christian Socialists*, 2.

9. Norman, *The Victorian Christian Socialists*, 8.

10. "The Working Men's College was a successful experiment in non-instrumentalized education, and the art classes taught by Ruskin and Rossetti, which shunned the pursuit of practical applications in favor of the development of perception, most perfectly represent the college's departures from the utilitarian instruction offered at many other nineteenth-century educational institutions for working men." Mahoney, "Work, Lack, and Longing," 221.

of any . . . . But the drawing classes, so long as Ruskin presided over them, were the most popular of any.[11]

While their voices were disparate and never focused in such a way as to achieve concerted political change, what drove the Christian Socialists was a theological conviction about the injustice of the economic order of their day. In his book, *The End of Work*, John Hughes considers John Ruskin and William Morris, two members of the Christian Socialist movement, and finds in them a theological source to their social action. Hughes writes that "Ruskin insists that the benign self-interest of the political economists is nothing more than 'avarice', which they falsely presume to be more 'constant' in human nature than the merely 'accidental' virtues."[12] Ruskin rejected the utilitarian calculus that insisted that exchange was the goal of production. People do not craft things, in the first instance, to sell them but to use them; to enjoy them. It is as a result of this firm theological conviction that Ruskin would find himself giving over the prime of his career to teaching unschooled laborers how to draw. They were very unlikely to become professional artists. Teaching them to compose a still life did not even offer them hope of a promotion. It offered something else. It made real the theological truth that these impoverished urban Victorian men were more than units of labor.

The Christian Socialists, then, are one example of how Christians, having arrived at the verdict that an economic order is unjust, might endeavor to construct domains of human engagement not ordered by profit and efficiency. Their initiatives and writings had lingering influence into the twentieth century. Once people are liberated from the hermetic universe of their time, they are freed in many other ways besides.

While the Christian Socialists do not provide us with a panacea, they do offer us this critical insight. If the agreed-upon rules of the age are subverted at one point and on one issue, then that potentially has very wide knock-on effects in unexpected ways. Resistance requires liberation from calculative logic. Only then can formerly obscure goods and realities become visible and therefore orientate people's lives in new directions. The point is not that Ruskin's classes gave these working-class men a moment of relief from their life of back-breaking labor. This small experiment was something much more significant than a distraction. Canny bosses would welcome such initiatives since workers are probably more likely to be efficient if they have interests outside work! The point was that in the shared imagination of the Victorian era's strictly class-ordered society, Ruskin and

11. Ludlow, *John Ludlow*, 269–70.

12. Hughes, *The End of Work*, 102.

his co-conspirators were launching a silent attack on the anthropological conceits of the age. Drawing was no longer to be the preserve of those gifted elite whose works hang in private collections. It is a craft, a tangible, constructive human activity. When brutal nineteenth-century capitalism could view these men only as potential labor, Christian commitment demanded a response that engaged with them based on values other than their utility. The experiment matters not because it could be instrumentally useful, but because it would be valuable even if it was not useful.

The Guild Socialism movement and the related Distributist school (famously associated with G. K. Chesterton and Hilaire Belloc[13]) that arose in the second decade of the twentieth century both reflect the Victorian Christian Socialist commitment to resisting the dehumanizing effect on the laborer exerted by modern industrial economy.[14] Their Distributism aimed at reallocating capital so that the wage-earning laborer became a stakeholder.[15] This would be achieved through guilds of skilled workers aligning together and working for their common good. This economic subsidiarity was a theological response to injustices within the economic system of the day. Dorothy Sayers could be numbered among this group. She understood the task of Christian social justice to inherently imply a transformation of economic reality. The social action of the church must be primarily dedicated towards the love of neighbor, but for Sayers, that took a pointed form when it came to economics. She thought that Christians, faced with the deadening tedium of the modern factory, must reimagine work. As she put it, Christian social action "also calls for a no less truly Christian love of the work; and for a kind of work that shall be loveable by the Christian soul."[16] Eric Gill, one of the early leaders of the movement, judged industrial society to have separated craft from work. This represented a:

> fundamental change in the nature of work in the minds of men, producing a world in which the artist created solely to express himself, without relating to society, while the working man,

---

13. Boyd, "Chesterton and Distributism."

14. Peter Dominy notes how the influence of the Christian Socialists continued to exert a large influence in British Christianity. Alongside the movements discussed here, he notes that the Christian Social Union, founded in 1889, had "about two-thirds of all Oxford undergraduates" as members by the turn of the century and "fourteen out of the fifty-three bishops" were CSU members. Dominy, *Decoding Mammon*, 63–64.

15. It is worth nothing how this systematically differentiates the Distributism movement from the more paternalistic Christian Socialist drive of the Victorian era.

16. Sayers, *Mind of the Maker*, 177.

being dispossessed of the tools of production, was denied the only means by which he could express himself.[17]

The capitalism of their day was deeply troubling from a theological perspective, because it engaged the human as a tool, reducing her to bare utility. Gill's call to withdraw from the corrupt and corrupting factories and banks of industrial capitalism was not so much a retreat, as an attempt to create space where craft, trade, and the business of life could be conducted under a different logic. It continued the sentiment of the 1850s, but in a different form suited to the 1920s. He established semi-monastic communities in rural locations—Ditchling, Capel-y-ffin, and Piggotts—where those who shared his suspicions could inhabit a different way of life. Gill rejected both the capitalist and the communist options, and sought instead to develop an alternative account of work, of economy, of anthropology.

Experimenting with new social forms of production is one way to articulate a Christian distinctiveness in the face of an oppressive economic system. Occupying strategic points within that system with a view to reform is another. Such an approach is encountered in the Association of Christian Economists, an academic society formed in 1982, established to help Christian economists network and to explore the particular relationship that exists between their faith and their academic pursuit. Through the journal *Faith and Economics* and regular conferences, the association has developed a body of work that seeks to critically engage with contemporary capitalism while suggesting appropriate reform where possible.

Clive and Cara Beed might be taken as representative of this movement. Their essay collection, *Alternatives to Economics*, stands as an expression of academic economics inflected by the historical commitments of Christian belief. Thus, while broadly operating within the neoclassical economic tradition, their research charts an alternative path that more carefully acknowledges the historical contingencies of economic principles and explores the contemporary relevance of Christian (as well as Jewish and Islamic) doctrinal convictions so as to meaningfully inform economic policy discussions. For instance, they take up the idea of guilds and co-operatives that were so central in the thought of the Victorian Christian Socialists and suggest that many of the core objections that Christians raise against contemporary capitalism can be ameliorated today by the expansion of worker-ownership models.[18] Building their argument from both Catholic Social Teaching and contemporary evangelical thinking on the economy, they cite the examples of cooperatives such as Mondragón to demonstrate that there

---

17. Corrin, "The Formation of the Distributist Circle," 71.
18. Beed and Beed, "Christian Principles for the Organization of Employment."

are viable possibilities outside of the traditional joint stock company, which "does not accord with Biblical notions of personal responsibility in private property ownership or paid employment."[19]

There are paths available for Christians to pursue if, when faced with the injustices of neoliberalism, they decide they must reject certain aspects of economic culture. There are tracks available for Christians to tread if, when faced with the same injustices, they conclude differently, that they must be faithful voices of reform.[20] One approach steps out of the system and seeks thereby to repudiate its injustice, crafting something new and more equitable. The other approach aspires to reconcile the tensions of being part of a system it judges deficient but to dedicate their action towards reform. Both approaches can reasonably be pursued and both may indeed achieve their aim of rendering the wider economic life of a society more just. A renewed exploration of different ways of approaching making a living, in the spirit of the Christian Socialists, would be a thoroughly positive development. Similarly, the work of Christian economists and Christian business people who seek to soften the fatally sharp edges of globalized neoliberalism is not to be maligned.

Yet even if a range of alternative-generating responses were to arise and they were all to meet unexpected rapturous success such that society was transformed in a host of different ways, the problem of wealth for Christians remains.[21] While listening to the inventory of deficiencies that theologians can catalogue with neoliberalism, it is natural that the audience might be prompted to protest that it is easy to criticize something, but harder to build it. That understandable request for alternatives can be met, but it does not answer the question at the heart of this discussion. An economic approach that is not based on exploiting wage labor should be welcomed, but both the owners and the workers, however they are realigned in this new system, would still stand precariously before Jesus's teaching about wealth.

---

19. Beed and Beed, "Christian Principles for the Organization of Employment," 55.

20. The Christian Socialists might be construed in terms of Niebuhr's famous "Culture Transformers" response while the Association of Christian Economists and the Relational Approach contingent might be located in relation to James Davison Hunter's call to residual "faithful presence." Hunter, *To Change the World*, 237–86, and Niebuhr, *Christ and Culture*, 190–229.

21. The formal irony here deserves to be noted. I spend a large chunk of my working life with the Jesuit Centre for Faith and Justice marshalling arguments that the personal convictions of Christians ought to shape their politics. Here, I am arguing that our Christian politics must inform our personal lives. Wealth, in general, is not the problem. We need wealth to address poverty. *Our* wealth is the problem. Inverting a cliché, the parables of Jesus prompt us to recognize that the political is personal.

The instinct that wants to hear of alternatives, but does not want to hear about problems unless they also come pre-packaged with possible answers, is itself a capitalistic impulse. It is an instantiation of the ideology of choice.[22] If any given option does not work for us, the market must provide an alternative. But the desire to find a way to move immediately from the uncomfortable position of judgement to a position where the church can hope to construct for itself a justifying and justifiable position is illuminating in a deeper way. It speaks of a human impulse towards domesticating the ethical complexity of reality by presenting ourselves as good because we can construct a narrative whereby we are less bad than some others. It is not the goal of this book to provide answers to the problem of neoliberalism by means of offering alternatives that are ready-made and set to deploy wherever Christians become troubled by the words of Jesus in relation to wealth.[23] We need to shift the conversation from the problem/solution dynamic into a discourse between God and the church. Our search

22. These alternative accounts reinforce the very dynamics we are here opposing. On this topic, Alasdair MacIntyre is helpful in reminding us that the emergence of the academic discipline of economics is historically contingent on the rise to supremacy of both capitalism and a certain expressivist morality, which reduces the ethical life to the sum of choices made. When that story is fully told it becomes clear that apparent truisms such as "To be rational is to be a consistent maximizer of preference satisfaction" are products of a particular ethical formation. MacIntyre is even more helpful in offering his verdict of this kind of thinking: "For economists have largely assumed that the economy can be studied in abstraction from the political and social order of which it is a part, that its history can be studied in abstraction from the political, social, and psychological factors that shape it. It cannot." MacIntyre, *Ethics in the Conflicts of Modernity*, 102, 105.

23. It may be apposite at this juncture to quote again from Dorothy Sayers, who in this instance is discussing how writing detective novels had made her suspicious of calls for solutions to problems. The reader often "will lay hold of the artist and demand to be let into his secret. 'Here, you!' he will cry, 'you have some trick, some pass-word, some magic formula that unlocks the puzzle of the universe. Apply it for us. Give us the solution to the problems of civilization.' This, though excusable, is scarcely fair, since the artist does not see life as a problem to be solved, but as a medium for creation. He is asked to settle the common man's affairs for him; but he is well aware that creation settles nothing. . . . The desire of being persuaded that all human experience may be presented in terms of a problem having a predictable, final, complete and sole possible solution accounts, to a great extent, for the late extraordinary popularity of detective fiction. This, we feel, is the concept of life which we want the artist to show us. It is significant that readers should so often welcome the detective-story as a way of escape from the problems of existence. It 'takes their minds off their troubles'. Of course it does; for it softly persuades them that love and hatred, poverty and unemployment, finance and international politics, are problems, capable of being dealt with and solved in the same manner as the Death in the Library." Sayers, *Mind of the Maker*, 152.

for solutions is so often a quest to generate ever more complex problems.[24] An alternative to alternatives to capitalism must be imagined.

MAKING A MEAL AFTER THE PARABLES

Christian worship flows from revelation. Worship is the bearing witness to the action of God. The parables are paradigmatic expressions of how God's revelation punctures our neoliberal subjectivity. Worship (not economic engineering, social activism, or renewed entrepreneurship) is the appropriate response. Worship is not a state *prior* to action, a sort of reverential, preparatory, intermediate moment of pause that allows the activist congregation to begin engaging in their transformative task in a spirit of appropriately grounded mindfulness. Rather, worship is itself action, determinative because it is the response to the call of God, which is the only event capable of true transformation.[25] The hope for Christians who are wealthy lies in the transformation wrought by Jesus, the divine man, who shatters the false certainties of our world when he encounters us. Our response takes many forms but aims at harmonizing with the reconciling action of God.[26] Wealthy Christians who are called out by God to gather as the community called church arrive together in a state of perfidy and failure. To establish corrupted, fallible, unfaithful, and compromised human worship as the response to the dilemma of riches is not an invitation to pious withdrawal, or passive resignation, but instead is the form of action which flows from God's ongoing intervention in our cracked, stumbling, floundering, and prosperous lives. Just like the apostles who linger after the rich young ruler, Christians do not find themselves whisked away from corruption when they waken to how their wealth is compromised.

To seek liberation from the hold that Mammon has over us entails seeking out the fertile spaces left behind when solidarity with Christ has rendered old certainties stale. We cannot escape capitalism. We cannot

24. It is apt to note the influence here of Bonhoeffer: "The kind of thinking that starts out with human problems, and then looks for solutions from that vantage point has to be overcome—it is unbiblical. The way of Jesus Christ, and thus the way of all Christian thought, is not the way from the world to God but from God to the world." Bonhoeffer, *Ethics*, 356.

25. David Haddorff's summary of Barth's view of this double-sided, yet God-initiated shape for worship is instructive here, and it is worship in this meaning that will be followed in this chapter. "For Barth only in the 'double agency' of the divine-human encounter made real in Jesus Christ as 'true witness' is human agency set free to cooperate with God's agency in fulfilling the divine will and purpose." Haddorff, *Christian Ethics as Witness*, 265.

26. Haddorff, *Christian Ethics as Witness*, 265.

escape our riches.[27] We cannot escape the judgement that falls on us as a result of the injustices—systemic and personal, environmental and economic—required for us to have what we have. Yet hope persists because the Word of God intrudes on this apparent settled state of affairs and does that which would be impossible among mere mortals but is possible for God. God's good words shatter the hold that neoliberal capitalism falsely claims over our lives. To say that worship is the appropriate response is to say that we are responsible to bear witness to what God has done in our midst. To say that worship is the appropriate response is to say that our view of reality is brought into focus by encounter with God. To say that worship is the appropriate response is to say that the only way out of idolatry to Mammon is conversion to Jesus.[28] As Barth constantly reminds us, our invocation is hollow if it is merely *our* invocation.[29]

In §16 of *Church Dogmatics*, Barth grounds the possibility of our encountering God in the action of the Holy Spirit. The perception of God's beauty and goodness does not occur because of some quality in our being, "a vacuum for which we are not responsible and over which we have no control" but that is somehow activated by the Holy Spirit.[30] Rather, in every and all situations where God is revealed, which is a precondition for a worshipful response, "the subjective reality of revelation has the distinctive character of a miracle."[31] This understanding of worship is primarily ecclesial, since "to speak about the Holy Spirit and His work we must expound the biblical testimony to the revelation in Jesus Christ" and the church "is the one particular spot which corresponds to the particularly of the incarnation."[32] It is when the church gathers to worship that "that revela-

27. One thinks of the ostentatious philanthropy currently prevalent among the Western billionaire class, but the humble prosperity of Western suburbia is different in scale, not kind. Linsey McGoey's investigation of the Gates Foundation is helpful here because it exposes both how neoliberal the logic of such philanthropy is and how widely shared are the driving assumptions. McGoey, *No Such Thing as a Free Gift*, see especially chapter 4, 113–47.

28. Of course, *metanoia* is to have our minds changed. Christian accounts of conversion are always accounts of liberation, but it follows both logically and etymologically that they are accounts of seeing and understanding the world differently.

29. "The highly astonishing event that has to take place, and must continue to take place if there is to be invocation of God the Father by humans as his children, is that of the fruitful meeting and the living fellowship of the Holy Spirit with them and with their spirits: their experience, perception, contemplation and resolve." Barth, *The Christian Life*, 90.

30. Barth, *CD I/2*, 267.

31. Barth, *CD I/2*, 244.

32. Barth, *CD I/2*, 247.

tion is really subjective."[33] Yet it is always and in all instances the initiative of God that brings it about.[34]

Thus, the church gathered to worship the insistent Lord who uttered the parables is the church summoned to engage in an act that they are helpless on their own to achieve. Worship relies on revelation and revelation never relies on us. The shape of worship is not an instrumentalized act of pious self-help.[35] It is the action of communities that leads to the strange stories of the parables being received as divine words, sharp enough to pierce the apparent hegemony of neoliberal capitalism, and decisive enough to move us to trust in a Lord more faithful than Mammon.

God encounters us who are rich as those who have plenty when others have need, and in his grace, he does not leave us in that desperate

---

33. Barth, *CD* I/2, 247.

34. That revelation demands a response is made clear by Barth, and in a fashion that will resonate through this chapter. Our worshipful response will always fall short of the grace of God revealed to us. But what continues to matter is not our initiative, but God's. "And that means, of course, that as the people we are we have to participate in that work of the Word. Not as those who have to finish the work, to reach the goal, to bring in the results. In our very participation it is foreseen that we are men, and disobedient men, and therefore quite unsuitable for the work. Our participation does not depend upon our fitness for this work. It is a participation in spite of our unsuitability. It rests upon the forgiveness of sins. It is grace. It is a participation in fear and in love to the God who has mercy on us in that He calls us to it and permits it. That is just why it is not a participation which involves anxiety and worry whether we can really do what we are required to do. Of course we cannot do it. That is the presupposition of our participation. Only one thing is required of us. As those who cannot do it of ourselves, and never could, we have to participate when the Word does it. It is a matter of the receiving and adopting of man into participation in the Word of God." Barth, *CD* I/2, 275.

35. This risk of worship receding into pious performance is a concern that warrants continued vigilance. One of Barth's most penetrating considerations of this temptation comes in IV.1 when he considers the incident of the Golden Calf in Exodus 32. He does not read this as an act of rebellious idolatry so much as sincere, but deeply distorted religiosity. "When they could no longer see and hear Moses" the Israelites found themselves in a situation where "all that remained now was they themselves . . . listening and looking in the void with empty ears and empty eyes." With deep pastoral and exegetical sensitivity, Barth asks, "Is it not obvious that in these empty hearts, in the place which was left empty and was now shown to be empty, there had to rise up in this snorting and stamping and tail-threshing bull, the picture of their own vital and creative power as a people when left to themselves and controlling their own life?" The golden calf is an expression of their religious best practice, their finest technological choreography to cope with their desperate, barren, desert situation. It would be dangerous to note that very often Christian attempts to reform or retreat from capitalism can look a lot like Aaron's efforts without also underlining how a call to "worship as a response to wealth" bears an even stronger relationship. For this reason, it is of critical importance that Barth's robust account of worship as a God-initiated possibility must be firmly established. Barth, *Church Dogmatics* IV/1, 423–32, especially 430–31.

situation. To worship from that place, as compromised congregations, is to take the one solid course of action available to the wealthy. Having heard the good news, "in prayer, the Church is given the freedom to ask God 'what are we to do?' and the openness to receive the guidance of the Holy Spirit in each new moment."[36] In different times and in different places, the faithful responses to wealth will demand different courses of action. By plotting those responses in terms of worship, the Spirit—and not casuistic systems or moderated principles—determines the appropriate action of a congregation. To some Jesus said, "Sell everything." To all he said, "Follow me." Some, like Peter, followed but kept their fishing boats. There is no set path lined out for the Christian community as it seeks to disentangle the injustice of wealth. Worship is the means of exploring what that path looks like in each particular setting. When the church gathers in prayer, it is "an unavoidably and fundamentally political event."[37] The worshippers are engaged in a "life of 'revolt' against all that exercises power in harmfully dominating, oppressive and 'lordless' ways."[38] Prayer is the beginning of our uprising against wealth. It is always "a supremely social matter, publicly social, not to say political and even cosmic."[39] It is never passive, but the congregation in prayer is "empowered, instructed, and summoned to fight against human unrighteousness."[40] As Ashley Cocksworth explains it, Barth's account of worship is a "rejection of versions of eschatology that wait passively for the arrival of the future."[41]

Yet that fight takes the form of a patience that resists jumping straight to concrete action against a vast complex of injustice, waiting instead on the Spirit. Such waiting is determinative action, especially when considered under the urgency and love of innovation cultivated through neoliberalism. This "theological anarchism" is simultaneously in revolt against "the prevalent world order" while also being "endlessly uncomfortable with the way things

---

36. Cocksworth, *Karl Barth on Prayer*, 149.

37. Cocksworth, *Karl Barth on Prayer*, 150.

38. Cocksworth, *Karl Barth on Prayer*, 150.

39. Barth, *The Christian Life*, 95.

40. Barth, *The Christian Life*, 266.

41. An example of which is the neoliberal conception of time we discussed in chapter 2 vis-à-vis the liturgical meal. Honoring debt is an economic action that projects the present into the future. The future has been established by the commitments we made in the past when we took up lines of credit. Sharing Eucharist is a liturgical practice which stands radically opposed to this. It keeps the past alive ("Do this in memory of me . . .") but it is also a point in time when the future consummation of all things breaks in on the present. This temporally rich, eschatological experience ruptures the empty, passive time of neoliberalism. Cocksworth, *Karl Barth on Prayer*, 153.

are and intolerant of playing by the rules of the status quo," because it is, at base, a stance "totally ordered by its obedience to God's command."[42]

Arguing that worship is the counter-practice by which Christians can address the deep problem of wealth does not involve forging an entirely new path. James K. A. Smith, for example, begins his Cultural Liturgies series with an anthropological exploration of the shopping mall as a modern-day site for religious formation. "While other religions are promising salvation through the thin, dry media of books and messages," Smith notes that consumerism's "new global religion is offering embodied pictures of the redeemed that invite us to imagine ourselves in their shoes—to imagine ourselves otherwise, and thus to willingly submit to the disciplines that produce the saints evoked in the icons."[43] Our affections are excited by the righteousness of The Body Shop and the glory of Tommy Hilfiger. Smith is explicit that his phenomenological tour of the suburban shopping center is neither tongue-in-cheek, nor merely metaphorical.[44] It is intended "to be apocalyptic, in a sense, unveiling the real character of what presents itself as benign."[45] What is required, argues Smith, in the face of this liturgical indoctrination into the ways of Mammon are sites of counter-formation, alternative spaces and times in the midst of those immersed in neoliberalism, which are ordered around different narratives than those that structure our consumerism. The Christian church, gathered in worship, is that center for counter-formation. The congregation that gathers on Sunday mornings needs its desires confronted, healed, and reformed so it can escape the gravitational pull of Mammon's globalized consumerism. The parables read and preached are a particularly distinct aspect of this alternative school of desire, set among the rich tapestry of texts, prayers, and practices available to the churches. This "education of desire requires a project that aims below the head; it requires the pedagogical formation of our imagination, which, we might say, lies closer to our gut (*kardia*) than our head."[46]

The contention being made here is that the path of reforming economic systems misses the basic objection that Jesus continues to pose to wealth

42. Cocksworth, *Karl Barth on Prayer*, 161. Cocksworth explains further, arguing that "Barth's ethics nevertheless always assumes that the ethical agent must await divine speech in particular political situations and space must be made to hear the unexpected interruptions of the Word of God" (163).

43. Smith, *Desiring the Kingdom*, 21.

44. In a curious oversight, Smith does not connect his work explicitly to Walter Benjamin's Arcades project that walked similar paths a century before him. Benjamin, *Arcades Project*.

45. Smith, *Desiring the Kingdom*, 23.

46. Smith, *Desiring the Kingdom*, 26.

and the path of retreating to alternative communities of the righteous misses the basic objection that Mammon continues to pose to worship. By following this third trail, what is being argued is grounded on the confidence that the Spirit is at work.[47] Our various efforts to save the world (through reform of the economy) or save ourselves (through the retreat to purity) are wasted efforts, not just because they fail but because they are redundant. God is intervening in the midst of our exploitative economic practices and our corrupt worship services. The task of being liberated from our wealth begins with a renewed attention to this pneumatic work. We must be given eyes to see the Spirit. Only through worshipping the true God, who meets us while we are still far off, can we be liberated from our false worship of Mammon, with all its fatal empty promises.[48]

The theologian who has perhaps most intently wrestled with the possibility of worship as a political response to injustice is William T. Cavanaugh. Across his work, Cavanaugh has consistently focused on the ethical significance of the sacramental practices of the church.[49] In *Torture and Eucharist*, Cavanaugh explored how the sacramental devotion of Chilean Catholics informed, influenced, and even came to express the resistance to the neoliberal dictatorship of Pinochet and his torture regime.[50] In *Theopolitical Imagination* he showed how the space represented by the pilgrimaging Catholic church is at odds with that occupied by the surveilled territories of globalized capitalism.[51] In *Being Consumed*, he explored how the consum-

47. "Worship makes possible the time Christians have to be with the poor. Put even more strongly, in and by worship Christians can imagine being poor." Hauerwas, *The Work of Theology*, 225.

48. As will be explored further in the conclusion, the most likely key in which this worship will be conducted, considering the frailty and compromise embedded in its performance, is lament.

49. Cavanaugh's first three works will be our focus here because they share a direct preoccupation with the ways in which worship is potentially ethically incendiary. His three subsequent works should be noted however. In *The Myth of Religious Violence* he attempts to revise the common trope that religious commitment tends to cause war. In *Migrations of the Holy* he charts the ways in which the nation state can replace the church in the affections of the modern citizen. In his latest work, *Field Hospital*, which is a collection of essays, four deal directly with questions of the economy. Since neoliberalism is not merely an economic proposition, but a complex nexus of many factors—of which politics plays a central role—these books would be valuably considered, if only there were space to do so. Cavanaugh, *The Myth of Religious Violence*; Cavanaugh, *Migrations of the Holy*; Cavanaugh, *Field Hospital*.

50. Cavanaugh extensively discusses how public liturgies represented direct challenges to the apparent totalized system of Pinochet's torture regime. The protest that began over the arrest of Juan Antonio Aguirre is especially affecting: Cavanaugh, *Torture and Eucharist*, 274–75.

51. Cavanaugh explicitly draws out the economic implications. "When Christians

eristic drive to possess more and more is predicated on the inevitability of constant discarding. In contrast to this, the church is formed by the practice of consuming that which has already been discarded: the flesh of Jesus.[52]

Cavanaugh's work represents one of the most sustained engagements with how the worship of the church is an effective affective response to the temptations of neoliberal capitalism. His writing is also notable for explicating through illustration what it might mean to begin to live out this "theopolitical imagination." From *Torture and Eucharist*, if we learn that Eucharist is so politically potent that it destabilizes dictatorships, then we can expect that our worship will spill out into the streets of the *agora*.[53] The church in Chile primes us to be ready with peaceful acts of interruption in the face of organized violence.[54] Similarly, in *Theopolitical Imagination* we find that taking the church seriously as a "space" not controlled by the logic of the globalized markets means that experiments in how to live outside the competitive imagination of capitalism should be routine.[55] Cavanaugh gives the example of church supported community agriculture schemes that "in a significant and material way" short-circuit the logic of provider and consumer by giving "priority to personal friendships, community re-

---

approach the creation and use of material goods, for example, we have been trained to think in terms of 'economic policy,' by which is meant the conversation in civil society and state among banks, the Federal Reserve, corporations, labor unions, Congress and other concerned parties over how the state ought to manage or not manage the flow of money, taxes, tariffs, etc. When framed in these terms, the only responsible reaction seems to be lobbying. Under certain circumstances lobbying, or, better, 'witnessing' may be helpful. The most fruitful way to dialogue with those outside of the Church, however, is through concrete practices that do not need translation into some putatively 'neutral' language to be understood. A significant response would be creating spaces in which alternative stories about material goods are told, and alternative forms of economics are made possible." Cavanaugh, *Theopolitical Imagination*, 94.

52. As the church is gathered, "instead of simply consuming the body of Christ, we are consumed by it" such that "the very distinction between what is mine and what is yours breaks down in the body of Christ." Cavanaugh, *Being Consumed*, 54, 56.

53. In such worship, "the future Kingdom of God is brought into the present to bring the world's time under the rule of Divine Providence, and thus create spaces of resistance where bodies belong to God, not the state." Cavanaugh, *Torture and Eucharist*, 275.

54. Cavanaugh clarifies that "to say that the Eucharist does in fact realize the body of Christ is not in any way to idealize the church as institution or those who hold authority in it. . . . the church militant is always flawed and sinful. . . . In the Eucharist the church is always called to become what it eschatologically is." Cavanaugh, *Torture and Eucharist*, 206.

55. "To speak of the Church as a public space means, then, that Christians perform stories which transform the way space is configured." Cavanaugh, *Theopolitical Imagination*, 93.

sponsibility, a livable income for farmers, and a direct stewardship of the land from which our food comes."[56] In *Being Consumed*, a host of examples are offered that point to the ways in which our allegiance to the kingdom expresses itself as distinct from the claims of the market.[57] Our baptisms represent a very different form of branding from the example he shares of a Nebraskan college student who sold his forehead as advertising space.[58] The worship of the outcast child, born among farm animals and crucified between thieves forms us to see the world not in terms of opportunity to be exploited, or threats to be avoided, but through a commitment to the other in solidarity with the suffering and easily overlooked Christ. If neoliberalism is informed by a complex web of economic, political, and historical factors, then Christian worship will counteract it in a complex cluster of ways. The diversity of examples that Cavanaugh offers reminds us that we cannot account for the outcome of worship as a response to wealth in advance. The desire to track projected outcomes is inherently of a part with the neoliberal imagination. The Spirit will call us to different tasks depending on the contingent factors we face. Yet Cavanaugh is clear: worship will press us out of the sanctuary and into the world.

Cavanaugh presents sacramental worship as a profoundly potent political act that both stands as a prophetic judgement against the injustices of the world, but also invites in, transforms, and sends out Christians to imagine a different way of being. Worship is the engine room of reality. The worship that stands as a response to wealth is this muscular, robust account of worship as an intrinsically political practice that is at play. "In the Eucharist," Cavanaugh avers, "God breaks in and disrupts the tragic despair of human history with a message of hope and a demand for justice. The hungry cannot wait; the heavenly feast is now."[59] In praise, the wealthy can hope to encounter their poverty. In worship, the rich can anticipate the liberating unveiling of their desperate starvation. From that moment of conversion,

---

56. Cavanaugh, *Theopolitical Imagination*, 94–95.

57. Against the scarcity that drives the market, Cavanaugh argues "the Eucharist tells another story about hunger and consumption. It does not begin with scarcity, but with the one who came that we might have life, and have it abundantly (John 10:10). "Jesus said to them, 'I am the bread of life. Whoever comes to me will never be hungry'" (John 6:35). The insatiability of human desire is absorbed by the abundance of God's grace in the gift of the body and blood of Christ. "Those who eat my flesh and drink my blood have eternal life" (6:54); they are raised above mere temporal longing for novelty. And the body and blood of Christ are not scarce commodities; the host and the cup are multiplied daily at thousands of eucharistic celebrations throughout the world." Cavanaugh, *Being Consumed*, 94.

58. Cavanaugh, *Being Consumed*, 33.

59. Cavanaugh, *Being Consumed*, 98.

analogically similar to the moments of epiphany when the sheep and the goats are confronted by the Master, a flourishing response can flow. That response will differ from person to person, community to community, place to place, time to time. But it will be funded by the reality that God is at work and is directing us to work in ways that cannot be anticipated in advance, cannot be predicted based on principles, but that can respond in surprising, appropriate, concretely specific ways.

Neoliberalism is a "cultural liturgy" that trains us to be worshipful consumers, in love with the ceaseless hunger for *more*. In such a context, worship is the appropriate place for Christians to begin their resistance against this captivity. God's present action is at the center of worship. It is there, in prayer and song, in listening to the Scriptures and in the sacraments, that we are confronted with God's lordship over even Mammon's markets. As we are consumed by the Eucharistic meal, our status as consumers is suspended and exposed as an illusion. It is in worship that we get to spy how we have ordered our lives around the worship of money. The starting point for turning our back on money is through turning our face to God. We cannot know in advance what he may then call us to, economically speaking. But only by waiting on his prior action in encountering us can we evade the religious temptation of making up our own counterfeit solutions.

The Co-opting Power of Capitalism

We can try to reform neoliberalism or incite a revolution to replace it, but the problem of our wealth persists. Even more troubling, neoliberalism has a capacity to co-opt critiques, domesticating them and turning them to profit. This makes the path of withdrawal, by which Christians might engage in an internal secession from the love of money by constructing a separatist worshipping community, even more attractive. But such an approach risks leaving the problem of poverty unaddressed as the sanctified few concern themselves with unburdening their prosperous consciences. If worship is the response to wealth, how do we avoid these counterfeit solutions and still avoid the co-opting capacity of neoliberal capitalism?

The potential of worship to serve as a school for desire, to reorientate our vision, so that we can perceive God's reality more clearly is fundamentally challenged by this ability of capitalism to absorb critique and transform it into stimulus. The teaching of Jesus is profoundly problematic for capitalism. Discounting the economic teaching of the Old Testament Law, or the jeremiads of the prophets, or the explicit New Testament dismissals of wealth, the parables alone unsettle easy participation in the cut and thrust of the neoliberal markets. Yet in many churches, this genuine protest potential is rendered almost mute. Regardless of how rich the biblical material is, and how committed to justice a congregation might be, how does a church deal with the co-opting capacity of neoliberal capitalism?

The most obvious expression of neoliberal capitalism's influence on Christianity is the "prosperity Gospel" tradition present within Pentecostalism, which inherently affirms "the basic economic structures on which individual enterprise stood."[60] The entrepreneur of the self that neoliberalism anticipates in the workplace becomes the entrepreneur of the soul in the sanctuary. One of the movement's leaders went so far as to describe Jesus as "a spiritreneur."[61] It is important to consider the ways in which the rhetoric of the prosperity churches integrates with the logic of neoliberal capitalism.[62] Yet the sheer excess on display in prosperity churches weakens it as an example of neoliberalism's infiltration of the church. The world of private jets and multimillion-dollar homes is remote to most wealthy Christians.[63] If one considers traditions that are not convinced by the "health and wealth" doctrines, where does this neoliberal co-option show up?

In the most mundane of Catholic, mainline Protestant, or evangelical Christian congregations, there is likely to be one glaring expression of the logic of capitalism at the heart of the community's practice: the music played as part of worship.[64] The capitalist logic enmeshes itself far below surface debates about electric guitars or archaic lyrics, in the mechanism by which music is generated. Whether it is Saturday evening folk mass in the local Catholic parish church, a form of Christian pop music in a megachurch

60. Bowler, *Blessed*, 226.

61. The writer in question is Laurie Beth Jones. Quoted in Bowler, *Blessed*, 228.

62. The bestselling book from one of the most prominent voices in the movement, Joel Osteen, promises to show the reader the seven steps to their best life, now. The extent to which this idea meshes with neoliberal capitalism's anthropological vision could not be exaggerated. Osteen, *Your Best Life Now*.

63. It is important to recognize that there is "health and wealth" for poor people that is often maligned, while there is "health and wealth" theology for rich people that is often *fêted*. A similar mind-set, in thrall to econometric efficiency and progress through personal diligence can be discovered in many of the projects backed by the Templeton Foundation, for example. This fund, established by the billionaire stock analyst John Templeton, seeks to bring the science of metrics to the study of religion. Entrepreneurial religiosity can thus be found in the corridors of the most elite universities, almost as easily as in the Midwestern megachurches. Koenig, *Spirituality in Patient Care*.

64. By referencing worship music, it is important to clarify that the question at hand has nothing to do with the reaction against contemporary musical styles which has come to be known as "the worship wars." For books engaged in that conversation, see: Ashton, Hughes, and Keller, *Worship by the Book*; Dawn, *Reaching Out without Dumbing Down*; Long, *Beyond the Worship Wars*.

on the outskirts of an American Midwestern city, or the austere orchestral music common at Redeemer Presbyterian Church in Manhattan, contemporary praise music across the denominational and theological spectrum is bound up with a capitalist notion of copyright.[65]

Worship music is now a large global market.[66] Albums released by the top "stars" sell millions of copies. While the industry, of a part with the wider musical scene, appears to be in decline, it still sold 17 million records in the US alone during 2014.[67] There is no legal difference between downloading (or, in a romantic nod to the past, purchasing a physical disc from a brick-and-mortar store) an old Rolling Stones album or a new contemporary Christian musical act's debut offering. Both are subject to standard copyright law in whatever jurisdiction in which they are sold. Yet the music sung by congregations on Sunday has also become the focus of licensing authorities.[68] The majority of these payments are made through Church Copyright License International (CCLI). It was established in its original form in 1985, after a small publishing house successfully litigated the Archdiocese of Chicago for distributing homemade photocopies of songs to choir members.[69] Based in Vancouver, Washington, CCLI is a for-profit company, which charges churches between $59 and $5,266 annually to play praise music at their worship services. Various "add-ons" must be purchased for "rehearsal" purposes, and if the songs will be made available

---

65. From the same §16 of *Church Dogmatics*, Barth opines that "the history of the hymn reveals to us the inner secularization which has taken place" in Protestantism. Barth, *Church Dogmatics* I/2, 257.

66. This industry is thoroughly embedded within the larger infrastructure of marketing. The Christian music "genre" is an important component of many advertising programs run by corporations that intend to associate with a perception of "family values." The industry overview breathlessly reports that "Major brands are recognizing the huge potential of the Christian/Gospel marketplace" and goes on to detail how Cracker Barrel "signed on as official sponsor of Michael W. Smith's 'The Spirit of Christmas Tour'" and that the megachurch pastor T. D. Jakes had enlisted the support of McDonald's, Wells Fargo, Coca Cola, Starbucks, and others as "corporate partners" in his outreach efforts. Gospel Music Association, and Christian Music Trade Association, "The Sound of Impact" 8.

67. Huckabee, "Who Killed the Contemporary Christian Music Industry?"

68. Journalists Mike Hertenstein and Jon Trott wrote an exposé of a popular Christian comedian named Mike Warnke, who claimed to have once been a chief priest within a Satanist cult. Warnke's acts were recorded and sold on cassette around North America and so, indirectly, their exploration of his fanciful and fantastic biography, ends up being a fascinating account of the modern evolution of the Christian music scene. Hertenstein and Trott, *Selling Satan*, 195–211.

69. Beaujon, *Body Piercing Saved My Life*, 229.

to house-bound church members.[70] Today, 240,000 churches around the world take up these services.[71]

While copyright laws tend to have exemptions for the performance of religious works, the licensing industry is established on a loophole interpretation that means that the song can be sung in total liberty, but the holding of a copy of the song in the form of a file on a computer, or a sheet music app on a phone, or a photocopied page, constitutes copyright infringement. The risk of punitive fines motivates churches to participate in this scheme. Thus, the weekly gathering of Christians in the smallest of house churches and in the largest of cathedrals is subject to an interpretation of intellectual property imported directly from the world of secular music, an industry shaped by the 1960s co-option of youth culture for the sake of profit.[72] The artists who write the songs tend to be employees of churches, but their salaries are supplemented by the revenue generated through this licensing process. The associated celebrity culture that arises to support and market the output of the bestselling songwriters is a further expression of a neoliberal capitalist logic at play. A consequence of this dynamic is an increased homogeneity in worship music. Globalization does not bring the music of the world to the local parishes, but spreads the music of the worship superstars to the ends of the Earth.[73]

There are many other angles from which the influence of capitalism can be considered in the church. We could consider the phenomenon of branding churches for the sake of marketing impact.[74] We could analyze the

70. https://us.ccli.com/copyright-license/#pricing.

71. http://uk.ccli.com/about/. These figures are accurate as of spring 2017.

72. There has been little theological critique of the modern worship music industry from an economic or systemic perspective. Pete Ward is one of the few theologians to address the issue at all, but his critique terminates at the level of individual morality. "Largely unacknowledged are the problems that have arisen from the economic and business side of the worship scene. Thus the roles of record companies, music publishers and festival organizations have not really been examined in any detail. In particular, the weaknesses and failings of individuals, organizations and companies, whilst evident to many, are very often glossed over by the need to appear successful, or Christian, or morally correct." Ward, *Selling Worship*, 180–81.

73. My wife visited with Christians in South Africa and was amazed to find that in the white and mixed-race churches on Sunday mornings they were singing the same songs sung in the Irish Republic. Aided by neoliberal globalization, a dozen or so artists have achieved a catholicity of liturgy within Protestantism that few would have thought possible!

74. "In order for a religious institution to be noticed by people, it has to find a way to 'stick out in the clutter,' that is, be heard above all the other noise of the culture. That's what branding does. But taking on the mantle of branding means also taking on the mantel of marketing." Einstein, *Brands of Faith*, 94.

focus on "leadership" and its implicit importation of corporate models and practices into church leadership.[75] We could examine the preponderance of multi-site churches[76] or strictly commodified evangelism resources[77] or the sale of sermons.[78] The material influence of neoliberal capitalism can be approached from many perspectives, all of which testify to the under-the-surface, deep manipulation of Christian assumptions and intentions.

What we have considered here is yet one more aspect of the hegemonic hold that neoliberal capitalism intends to extend over the imagination of its citizen consumers. Mammon's power can convert an iconic image of the Argentinian Socialist revolutionary Che Guevara into one of the most easily recognized symbols of commodification in global culture.[79] It can subvert sincere, naïve Christian efforts to bring about change. Capitalism's reach is merciless in this way. Ernesto Guevara "fought and died resisting capitalist material excess and yet his image is emblazoned on T-shirts, transformed into pop art and irreverently integrated into the global capitalist market."[80] Christianity cannot and has not avoided the same colonizing potency, as the ubiquity of crosses as a decorative fashion accessory makes obvious.

75. The now disgraced megachurch pastor Bill Hybels is a major figure in this movement. In his appeal for leadership development within the church, he explicitly calls on pastors to recognize how their practices fall behind the cutting edge of the American business world. "In my interviewing and speaking with top corporate leaders around the country, I've been surprised to learn how much of their time is devoted to leadership development." Hybels, *Courageous Leadership*, 133. His church, Willow Creek, runs an annual "Global Leadership Summit" that is attended by hundreds of thousands of people via multimedia link-ups and introduces church leaders to the wisdom of the corporate world. The 2016 event featured as speakers: the former president of the Ritz-Carlton hotel group, the former CEO of Ford, six leading business consultants, and Melinda Gates. http://willowcreek.org.uk/events/gls/gls-speakers/. A bracing critique of this broader movement is found in Anglican theologian Justin Lewis-Anthony's 2013 book. Lewis-Anthony, *You Are the Messiah and I Should Know*.

76. That the economic aspect is at the fore in many of these ecclesiological innovations can be plainly discerned in the literature. "The multi-site approach at Allison Church saved huge amounts of money." Surratt, Ligon, and Bird, *A Multi-Site Church Roadtrip*, 13.

77. "We consider anyone using the Alpha brand identity to be a brand guardian. You are responsible for protecting the integrity of Alpha through brand application, as laid out in these guidelines." Alpha International, "Alpha Brand Guidelines," 3.

78. One thinks here of the prominent (and previously mentioned) Redeemer Presbyterian Church of Manhattan but other renowned churches charge to listen to sermons, such as the North Point megachurch led by the celebrity pastor Andy Stanley.

79. The original image by the photographer Alberto Korda and the stylized representation by the Irish artist Jim Fitzpatrick first became a symbol of the 1968 student revolts and has now "become ubiquitous, a brand spectacle." Odih, *Advertising and Cultural Politics in Global Times*, 89.

80. Odih, *Advertising and Cultural Politics in Global Times*, 89.

THE CRITIQUE OF RELIGION

This is a problem. It is all well and good to propose worship as a response to wealth, but how do we handle the fact that our worship can be co-opted by capitalism? To even consider worship as a "potential" as this book has is already running this risk of turning the work of the people into a resource for an institution. It might strain credulity to imagine that sharing Eucharist is the beginning of an uprising against the disorder of the world, but how much moreso if capitalism positions liturgy as the next hip thing, a lifestyle choice that will mark a contemporary Western consumer in with the fashions? Even without capitalism directly co-opting the praise of the church in the future, here in the present our worship is compromised by being collectively structured around ideas of ownership and property that do not find an easy fit in the memory of the church, but click snugly into place with the neoliberal imagination. If worship is our response to our idolatrous temptation to wealth, how do we respond when our worship becomes compromised by the same idolatry?

In chapter 1, we discussed how our neoliberal subjectivity encourages an idolatrous commitment to wealth. Idolatry, following Luther, is looking not to the Creator but to a creature or a created thing as the one from whom we can expect "all good and to which we are to take refuge in distress."[81] This describes the devotion of large swathes of the Western nations towards the prosperity provided by the markets. We can accuse neoliberal capitalism of idolatry, but what are we to make of the Christians who inhabit, direct, and submit to the discipline of this false god? At the conclusion of this book, we are proposing that the response to finding neoliberal capitalism to be profoundly troubling on a theological level is not to dedicate ourselves to developing a less vicious alternative, but to consider our Christianity in the light of this infidelity.

Following after Barth, as he read the parables, allowed us to see the ways in which the kingdom of God stands opposed to the totalized ambitions of neoliberalism. In the face of capitalism's apparent hegemony after "the end of history," we discover in Jesus's divine yarns that another world is already being born, is taking shape in and around us. The kingdom of God is coming and is already here, and it operates on a logic separate from that which drives a profit and loss account or calculates GDP. Barth returns at this point as our collaborator because his critique of religion allows us to think about how Christians, who spend their working lives immersed in service to the aims of Mammon, can ever hope to praise God without being

81. Luther, "The Large Catechism," 565.

co-opted by neoliberalism. Barth's uncompromising words offer hope to compromised Christians. His criticism of religion exposes how worship—if it is not delusion—relies on the prior action of God.

This is of central importance because as we propose worship as the response to wealth, we run the risk of licensing a toxic and self-delusional religiosity. Convinced by the sort of argument extended here, religious communities could carefully and self-consciously adapt their words and liturgies on Sunday to precisely articulate a protest against the brutalities of the economy, and thereby license themselves to collude in such brutalities in a myriad of ways on the other days of the week.[82] Barth was unrelenting in his exposure of the self-conceit involved in performing a religious duty to atone for the ways the world is unjust, such that one need not address the injustice.[83] We discover, via Barth, what we mean by worship. It is not the human effort to assemble scripts and rituals that can serve as an engine for some other endeavor. It is a human response to the confrontation with God that summons the community known as the church to praise.

The critique of religion is not a side interest in Barth's work. From the very start, *Church Dogmatics* is an ecclesial and liturgical project.[84] In I/1, we read the famous lines that God "may speak to us through Russian Communism, a flute concerto, a blossoming shrub, or a dead dog. We do well to listen to Him if He really does."[85] God may speak to us through these diverse media but our proclamation about God is much more limited. God may take up and speak through anything but the church is left with the particular commission to preach and administer the sacraments.[86] That is to say, our worship follows God's speech.[87] Among the first moves that

82. From this perspective, the best outcome we could dare to hope for is that we would be peddling some variety of pie-in-the-sky-when-you-die religion, but likely doing something far worse. Instead, what is proposed in this political worship, is something better captured by the Irish poet Aidan Mathews in his lines: "The world I want is what lies about me, What crops up where you least expect it, In a surplus bigger than barns can harvest." Mathews, "Adam's Enlightenment," 119.

83. The critique of religion begins, for Barth, after Schleiermacher, who he describes in the following terms: "By birth and upbringing in its innermost sanctuary his theology is cultural theology: in religion itself which is the true object of his theology." Barth, *Protestant Thought from Rousseau to Ritschl*, 316.

84. Think even of what was at play when Barth abandoned his *Christian Dogmatics* in favor of pursuing a Church *Dogmatics*.

85. Barth, *CD* I/1, 55.

86. "In attempting to interpret what we have described in this way, our primary task must be to make it clear that, when man cannot regard himself as the one who gives the commission but only as the one who is commissioned." Barth, *CD* I/1, 56.

87. A few pages earlier, in the same line of argument, Barth baldly states that worship is the response to the Word of God heard. "If God exists for man, as the Church's

Barth makes in *Church Dogmatics* is this insistence on the nature and order of dialogue between God and man.

The urge to save ourselves from judgement that can be discerned behind our instinctive plea for less unjust economic alternatives is seen in this light to be fundamentally religious. The religious instinct replaces the immanent revelation of God with the far more domesticated wisdom of humankind. It presents humanity as responsible for the saving of the world, which begins to render plausible the idea that it is reckless or irresponsible to query the desire to serve prepackaged alternatives. Waiting on God to speak first can be an exercise in exasperation and desperation. Barth's entire theological project arises from reading Scripture "with the urgency, perplexity and helplessness of the preacher."[88] Left to their own devices, they have nothing to say. The possibility of worship necessitates the speech of God.

What this means is that worship is, at base, a listening act before it is a speech act. The community gathered in worship can trust that God speaks, but they cannot take that for granted, or behave as if they have become familiar enough with the content of that speech that they can somehow replicate or extend it for themselves. For this reason, a critique of religion was always a component of Barth's account of revelation.

If finding a way to preach is a primary factor that agitates Barth's theological project, this critique of religion is one of the first definitive steps towards that goal. In *Dogmatics*, Barth begins "by stating that religion is unbelief" but this mature position is reflected in his earliest work.[89] In the *Romans* commentary, he interrogates the meaning of religion and finds that it is the triumph *and* the downfall of civilization. It is both "the supreme possibility of all human possibilities" and it "is the supremacy of human arrogance stretching itself even to God."[90] Our religions, with their moral codes, cultic practices, holy scriptures, sacred architecture, and so on, are remarkable cultural products of humanity that stand very much on the terrestrial side of the vast gulf that separates earth from heaven. Yet in part because they

---

prayer, praise and confession declare in answer to the proclamation heard, then this man as the man for whom God exists must also exist for his fellow-men with whom alone he is real man. Yet the special utterance about God which consists in the action of this man is primarily and properly directed to God and not to men. It can neither try to enter into quite superfluous competition with society's necessary efforts at self-help in its straits, nor can it seek, as the demonstration of distinctively Christian action, to proclaim how God helps." Barth, *CD* I/1, 50.

88. Webster, *Barth*, 33.

89. Barth, *CD* I/2, 300.

90. Barth, *The Epistle to the Romans*, 241.

are so impressive, they are cultural products invested with such import as to present themselves as other from what they are. There is no prepackaged way for us to avoid the risk of slipping into mistaking our very human constructions as divine mandates. Whether through the form of noble renunciations or solemn commitments to reform, it does not matter how we might insist that we will avoid the temptation, since "the apparent radicalism of all these simplifications is pseudo-radicalism."[91]

In §17 of *Church Dogmatics*, Barth presents an extended exploration of how God's revelation abolishes religion. The question of how "God does and can come to man in His revelation," both in theory and in practice, relies on "the being and action only of God, and especially of God the Holy Spirit."[92] Humans and their creative effort are clearly at play in every worship act, but for the hope that it is anything but an act of communal self-delusion to be realized, we must remember that the congregation who listens and the presider who leads wait first and fundamentally on the God who speaks. When it is construed as a joint endeavor such that God and man meet and collaborate, it is destructively delusional.

For Barth, this critique is not to be levied against other religions, as a sort of apologetic in favor of Christianity. This argument is not of the variety that holds that the *Vedas* or the *Tripitaka*, or we might even dare to add *Dianetics*, are mere psychological projections while biblical Christianity is the *real* thing. The necessity of God's revelation, which is required for all worship, means that engagement with the question of religion "must be characterized primarily by the great cautiousness and charity of its assessment and judgements."[93] It is not that "the Christian religion is the true religion, fundamentally superior to all religions,"[94] but that the dreadful temptation to confuse human culture for divine revelation "above all" affects the "adherents of the Christian religion."[95] Barth recounts the common response of Christian evangelists after a widespread conversion in a population. Old temples were leveled, idols were smashed, and altars were destroyed. In such settings, "irony usually had it that Christian churches were built on the very sites of these temples and with materials taken from their pillars and furnishings."[96] The conversion of, say, the Pantheon in Rome, goes to show that "the devaluation and negation of what is human may occasionally have a practical and

---

91. Barth, *The Epistle to the Romans*, 241.
92. Barth, *CD* I/2, 280.
93. Barth, *CD* I/2, 297.
94. Barth, *CD* I/2, 298.
95. Barth, *CD* I/2, 300.
96. Barth, *CD* I/2, 300.

symbolical significance in detail," but Christianity can never set itself apart from the religious tendency to build temples to our culture, raise idols to our heroes, and construct altars to our sources of well-being.[97] The reality of God's revelation in Jesus does not render Christians immune to such impulses, but rather makes the instinct all the more deathly.[98]

The critique of religion present in *Romans* is sharpened in the *Church Dogmatics*, as Barth emphasizes the extent to which the religious impulse to find righteousness in our own actions is inherently a refusal to accept the righteousness that Christ offers us.[99] The problem religion poses is that it confuses a universal human cultural product for a particular action of God. Revelation drives straight through this confusion. It contradicts religion. "It displaces it," filling with substance what had previously been occupied by empty space dressed up as knowledge of pious truths.[100] Barth does not intend to smugly present Christianity as the "true religion." "Religion," he argues, "is never true in itself and as such. The revelation of God denies that any religion is true."[101] This holds for Christianity even more than other traditions. True religion is a different proposition entirely. It is always and everywhere the religion of the "justified sinner."[102] Only when worship flows as a response to the "outpouring of the Holy Spirit" which is both "the judging but also reconciling presence of God in the world of human religion" can something true be said to have occurred.[103] Barth will never allow us to equate Christianity straightforwardly with true religion, "because Christianity is a religion in response to God's revelation in Jesus Christ who *is* the abolition of religion."[104]

In our age, when our shopping malls are modelled as cathedrals,[105] our finance officials are treated as priests,[106] and our communal life is struc-

---

97. Barth, *CD* I/2, 300.

98. "Idolatry must be analyzed, then, not as an inadequate attempt to reach God who remains unknown, but as the rejection of God who is known." Since Christians are the people invited to gather around the God who has made himself known, the idolatry of religion is "firstly a problem for the church, not for others; it is the test of whether its religion is dependent on the revelation." Clough, "Karl Barth on Religious and Irreligious Idolatry," 226.

99. Greggs, *Theology Against Religion*, 25; Boulton, *God Against Religion*, 58.

100. Barth, *CD* I/2, 303.

101. Barth, *CD* I/2, 325.

102. Barth, *CD* I/2, 325.

103. Barth, *CD* I/2, 280.

104. Greggs, *Theology Against Religion*, 29.

105. Backes, "Reading the Shopping Mall City," 7.

106. Juliet Johnson's account of how the community of western central bankers,

tured around the sacrifices required to sustain prosperity,[107] the religious impulse is bound up with the market.[108] Barth's critique of religion primes us to expect not just that the liturgical gatherings of Christians will often be inflected by the demands of the market, but that we will also find reactions against this situation that amount to simplifications posing as "pseudo-radicalism." If the plan to construct an alternative economic system that saves us from implication is a road with little hope, the option to withdraw into a pristine world of worship is a positive dead end.[109] As Matthew Myer Boulton powerfully argues in his discussion of Barth's critique of religion, "a Christian worship service is not a hiatus from corruption, but rather an epitome of it."[110]

Barth's critique of religion assumes that the human actors engaged in preaching and praying are compromised, and yet still God uses them. The logic and imagination of neoliberal capitalism can invade and infiltrate the church in countless different ways and yet the Christian can still resolutely hope that God will encounter them in worship. That encounter, should it occur, occurs on the same terms that have always prevailed, through the action of God and independent of the merit or demerit of the congregation gathered to praise. Worship is possible even in our infidelity and our betrayal because God deigns to meet us in the word preached and in the bread broken.[111]

---

sharing a common language and creed, offered a sort of evangelizing hospitality to the economic leaders of the former Communist states to build a catholic understanding of how economies should function is a notable recent contribution to this form of analysis. Johnson, *Priests of Prosperity*.

107. Cf. the discussion of Ireland's austerity regime in chapter 3.

108. "Wherever the qualitative distinction between man and the final Omega is overlooked or misunderstood, that fetishism is bound to appear in which God is experienced in 'birds and fourfooted things' and finally, in the likeness of corruptible man — Personality, the Child, the Woman—and in the Half-spiritual, half-material creations, exhibitions, and representations of His creative ability—Family, Nation, State, Church, Fatherland. And so the 'No God' is set up, idols are erected, and God, who dwells beyond all this and that, is 'given up.'" Technologized, neoliberal capitalist prosperity is surely at home when added to the list of the "half-spiritual, half-material creations" of human creativity. Barth, *The Epistle to the Romans*, 50.

109. One is reminded of Stanley Hauerwas's oft-made witticism that he would not mind withdrawing, but there is no place to which we can retreat. "How can the church possibly withdraw when it, by necessity, must always find itself surrounded?" Barth's critique is deeper than this. The religious impulse means that among the front-line infantry, the essential logistical support, and (especially) among the top generals, the church militant has been thoroughly infiltrated by the opposition. Hauerwas, *After Christendom*, 18.

110. Boulton, *God Against Religion*, 202.

111. "He grants to us over and above existence no less a gift than Himself, fellowship

In Barth's critique of religion, we perceive Christianity as intrinsically prone to idolatry. Christians are the capitalists engaged in idolatry. Their infidelity is embedded in the practices that make up the very business of worship. Yet, the worshipping congregation, embroiled in unfaithfulness it struggles to even describe, is still the worshipping congregation that waits on the Lord. Christian capitulation to capitalism makes the hope of a sectarian withdrawal to a pristine communal life that is untouched by the brutalities of the market impossible. Yet this same Christian capitulation does not bring worship to an end. The assumption that this is the way it is bound to be is embedded in the graciousness of God's reaching out to us in revelation. Our capitalist unfaithfulness is not a worship conversation-stopper. Quite the opposite. The Word of God always starts the worship conversation.[112]

Christians who are wealthy, which from some perspectives is bound to include the vast majority of Christians in the Western world, find themselves in a predicament in following Jesus. He has no words of comfort for those who are rich. He grants no honor to self-sufficiency,[113] pays no heed to wage-rate inflation,[114] and is utterly dismissive in the face of the importance of circumspect business practices.[115] We who are rich are found to fall short. We have seen that the possible alternatives can ameliorate the

---

and intercourse with Himself. What does this mean? It means that in His revelation Jesus Christ the Word of God does not need to get from some other source the authority to address and claim us; He already has it antecedently in Himself. It is not a question of whether we want to respond to Him or not. We are already responsible to Him and in different ways our whole being is response to Him. In relation to Him there is no possibility of appealing or withdrawing to some domain of our own where we were once alone and where He does not yet reach us or does so no longer, to a neutral human existence, as it were, where it is first up to us to place ourselves or not under the judgment and the grace that He declares to us, and from which we might comfortably come to an understanding with Him. In fact we do not know anything about our human existence except through the Word which declares to us judgment and grace. In declaring this, it tells us that it is itself the ground of our being as men; on this ground alone are we men, and not otherwise. It comes to us because it already applies to us even before it comes. It is the hand that already holds us even as it grasps us. It is the ruling act of the king who was already a king before and who has both the might and the right to perform this act. It encompasses us on every side (Ps. 139:5). It is the Word which has power, the Word of the Lord. And it is the Word of the Lord because it is the Word of the Reconciler who is also the Creator." Barth, *Church Dogmatics I/1*, 444–45.

112. This thought is inspired by the wording of Derek Alan Woodard-Lehman, "Barth's theology of revelation is not a theological conversation-stopper." Woodard-Lehman, "Reason After Revelation," 24.

113. He himself existed off the charity of women who travelled with him (Luke 8:3).

114. Paying a day's wage to men who worked only an hour! (Matthew 20:9–10).

115. Casting men who simply want to tend to recently purchased fields as fools in his stories (Matthew 22:5, Luke 14:19).

environmental and human brutalities of neoliberal capitalism, but they do not address the fundamental disjunction that the riches we carry slow us down as we seek to follow Jesus. With the option of reforming capitalism largely closed off, we further considered how there is no possibility of withdrawing into an immaculate worshipping community. We are, after all, dismissed at the end of worship back into the compromises of the marketplace, but the logic of that marketplace had already infiltrated the practice of worship prior to our gathering.

This is where Barth's critique of religion becomes load-bearing for our argument. Our wealth does not annihilate the possibility of worship. But our worship is essentially compromised. In the ironic kingdom, it has nothing to its name. It is, to use a financial image, utterly bankrupt. In the face of this desperate unveiling of religious ineptitude, Barth insists that there is still hope. Discussing Barth's religious critique, Matthew Myer Boulton argues that "Christ transforms the catastrophe of worship by entering it, assuming it, and providing it with a new basis, a new direction, and a new purpose."[116] Through this transformation—Barth talks about it as *Aufhebung*[117]—Christ "carries out our work with us and for us, not destroying the human work of prayer but rather assuming it, undertaking it in God's name, and thus making it God's own."[118] As it is with prayer, it is with our singing and sacraments, our preaching and processing. While there is no utopian economic system waiting to be discovered and there is no exquisite worshipping community waiting to be established, there is hope in compromised congregations of Christians gathering to worship. God speaks, even to the rich, and his word is revealed, through human voices, in shaky pulpits or gilded baptismal fonts.[119]

PREACHING THAT MAKES THE WORLD NEW

With his strong emphasis on sacrament as an event of God, Cavanaugh's theology of worship intersects fruitfully with Barth's critique of religion.[120] It is an example of an account of liturgy that escapes the risk of thinking

116. Boulton, *God Against Religion*, 170.

117. A German word meaning "to pick up," which has particular philosophical resonance after Hegel, who used it to mean something like the *aha!* moment when the penny drops and you finally understand something that was previously obscure.

118. Boulton, *God Against Religion*, 170.

119. But Jesus looked at them and said, "For mortals it is impossible, but for God all things are possible" (Matthew 19:26).

120. Which is not to claim that Cavanaugh's sacramental theology could be straightforwardly aligned with Barth's "low" sacramentality.

that religious activity has some merit of its own, even to the extent of causing the reader to question the utility of the concept "religion" at all in the light of historical reality.[121] Yet it expectantly awaits the action of God in worship that would constitute the disparate individuals—citizens, employees, consumers—into a community around the tortured and crucified body of Christ. The people called to sit and eat at that table are consumed into the narrative of reality that stands over and against the hollow narratives of neoliberal capitalism.

When worship is understood as an engagement distinguished from religion by the prior action of God, it is the first response for the Christian finding themselves in the tricky spot of being wealthy and following Jesus. For Barth, "the decisive action of their revolt against disorder . . . is their calling upon God."[122] In discussing this claim, Ashley Cocksworth argues that "the very act of petitioning for our daily bread, for example, counterculturally revolts against any myth of human self-sufficiency."[123] Worship "overflows into a complete rearrangement and reimagining of all other relations, including reconfiguring the ways in which we relate to the now dedemonized mammon."[124]

While our argument began by questioning the various efforts that might be made to "Christianize" neoliberal capitalism through reform, this proposal is not an invitation to quietism. It explicitly rejects the option of separatist retreat as impossible on the practical level and dubious on the theological level. Instead, we worship and recognize that this is potent in the political sphere.[125] Sketching out how that "overflow" might function is the final step required in this book.

The refusal to lay out a developed manifesto for living as Christians who are rich is a theological response to the risk of co-option and to the temptation to use such solutions to evade the command of God. It is also a pragmatic response, a healthy skepticism that any such plan would address

121. Cavanaugh is presumably amenable to some formulation similar to this. Consider one of the fundamental moves in *The Myth of Religious Violence*: "There is nothing close to agreement among scholars on what defines religion." Cavanaugh, *The Myth of Religious Violence*, 2009, 57.

122. Barth, *The Christian Life*, 212.

123. Cocksworth, *Karl Barth on Prayer*, 160–61.

124. Cocksworth, *Karl Barth on Prayer*, 161.

125. Examples abound to demonstrate this point. Famously we can think of the American civil rights movement, or the East German prayer meetings centered on Dresden that played such a critical role in the collapse of the Iron Curtain, or the role that church communities played in the South African opposition to apartheid. In these and countless other examples, worship spilled out of the sanctuary into the public square, with effects that could not have been calculated or predicted in advance.

the countless challenges that Christians face as they seek to be faithful in the midst of their wealth in their particular times and places. Such an approach can be positioned as a rejection of strategy, in favor of tactics. Strategies "seek to create places in conformity with abstract models."[126] Tactics seek to exploit those tabulations, those formulations, those analyses towards ends for which they were never intended.[127] We cannot escape the consumptive patterns of capitalism, but we can redirect the trajectories implicit in neoliberalism towards goals that more closely align with the kingdom. Economic interventions that "flow over" in this fashion arise out of the action communities engaged in tiny and seemingly inconsequential acts of rebellion against the logic of Mammon. Through these micro-aggressions, born of worship, the church will find itself increasingly committed in unexpected and unpredictable ways in a host of resistance movements that stand as a counter-testimony to the hegemony of the markets.[128]

The age that we apparently live in is the reign of neoliberal capitalism. Time is segmented by quarterly profit reports. Space is obscured by global supply chains. In the parables of Jesus we find enigmatic stories that test, probe, and puncture the totalized imagination of this economic system. For all its valorization of competition, the language and thought-world of neoliberal capitalism aspires to monopolistic status. It presents itself as the true account of things, the only realistic way to think about trade, prosperity, and development.

Yet the register in which Jesus speaks is radically different. To modern eyes, he appears to have an alarming lack of aptitude for business. The characters in the parables act in a way that disregards the common sense of our era. As we read them under the guidance of Barth we found that they represent an in-breaking apocalyptic word that reorientates our sight towards a different reality and our hearts toward different affections. This insight prompted us to turn to a particular place at a specific time and to

126. de Certeau, *The Practice of Everyday Life*, 29.

127. de Certeau, *The Practice of Everyday Life*, 30.

128. Some readers may be troubled by my reticence to endorse, promote, or join any particular movement that aims to bring down the oppressive machine of neoliberalism. They may find comfort in Srnicek and Williams's work, who agree that neoliberalism is effectively hegemonic but would staunchly disagree with my refusal to therefore sign up to some pre-existing resistance movement. The argument presented here would be read by them as an exercise in "horizontalism," the desire to change the world without taking power. It is, however, the exact opposite. It is the refutation of that great myth of progress expressed in the desire "to change the world" because power is in the hands of Jesus, and it is there securely. Not even Mammon can take it away. If our doctrine of God is aright, then we can live unruffled under that authority. Indeed, that is the only way of life open to us. Srnicek and Williams, *Inventing the Future*, 51, 26.

retell an economic story without reference to the econometric language and profit-loss logic of the age. In Ireland, at the end of the Celtic Tiger, we found that if we hope to understand the human toil of economic turmoil, it must be investigated through thicker language than a balance sheet can provide. Without for a moment licensing a disregard of the serious utility of economic science, we found that the details of locality, history, and contingency are at least as determinative for ethical reflection as the drop in GDP or the rise in public debt. The Christian gaze, when it comes to think Christianly about wealth (and by extension, poverty), must be retrained to search for and pay heed to the scale upon which the parables function—the scale of human lives as they are lived.

The place where the retraining begins is worship. This is where we encounter the parables and the stories like them in the Bible and where we are encountered by them as God's word. Our discussion has relied on Barth, whose critique of religion serves to guard our proposal from collapsing into a form of pious self-help. This call to worship is not an invitation to craft an inner peace in the face of economic inequality. But neither is it a call to straightforward outward activism. The confrontation with the apocalyptic Word of God which is external to us demands a corresponding public response, but one aimed primarily towards faithfulness, and only then concerned with efficiency. The provocation that saves us from piety is also a discipline that restrains us from confusing our agendas with a divine word. In its roundabout way, worship is the most direct response available to us.[129]

The church is that community called out to be together in their love of God. We are gathered as people who have split allegiances. In our zealous moments we yearn for the kingdom but we are convinced by and committed to many other traditions and institutions that seek our affections. In eliciting this drama within us, Christianity trains us to question why the commonsense understanding of things should be taken as true. In worship, we spy the absurdity of a world ordered toward profit. If the parables smash through the totalized narrative of neoliberalism, then the Christian who encounters them as Scripture will be driven to interrogate the endless need for more that is stirred up through constant marketing, the merciless pursuit of lower costs for the sake of the shareholder, or the environmental violence that must be conducted hour after hour to sustain our levels of comfort. The response to wealth that worship represents will involve this searing critique of neoliberal capitalism and the things it teaches us to take

---

129. My thinking here is heavily indebted to Jacques Ellul, who conceived of Christian ethics as always being about problematizing ("de-institutionalization" and "destructuralization") our relationship to the social structures and institutions around us. Ellul, *The Ethics of Freedom*, 471.

for granted. Figuring out what it means to be citizens of the kingdom of God must be "accompanied by vigilant and constant criticism of the false meanings which, whether we like it or not, are continually growing up around us."[130] That criticism will invariably involve contestation of how our social reality is described and that vigilance will entail renarration of the economic order in which we live, as was attempted in chapter 3.

At the heart of this conflict is the grip that wealth and its promises of security hold over us. When mired in the problem of wealth, we too easily assume that with sufficient technique, we can find a way out of our dilemma with our riches intact. It takes discipline to resist the various plans on offer that promise responsible stewardship and canny management of finances with a Christian gloss. But the critique would also extend to charitable proposals that simplify the problem down to a simple compulsion to relinquish your assets.[131] Off-the-shelf solutions promise much, but will deliver only deeper captivity. It is only as we are led by the Spirit, from our worship, that we can hope to engage in substantial subversion of the power of money. Too much of our endeavor in this area is a complicated attempt to avoid coming face to face with the many-tentacled entity that is Mammon and the realization of how deep is his hold over us. To effectively engage in a critique of the "abstraction and bureaucratization" of capital, we are compelled to countenance "sabotage in the sense of considered action at the weakest and most sensitive point with a view to restoring authenticity of life where now there is only repetition and bureaucratic vacuity."[132] We are called to micro-aggressions against the logic of neoliberal capitalism. Even if all the church's efforts amount to nothing more than displaying "how stupid the machine is," unveiling the truth of things is no small achievement.[133] Even if these steps appear tiny, having renarrated the shape of the economy in the light of the parables, we are given renewed vision to see how such small measures can have immense significance. In the economy of the kingdom, contributions that come easily from abundance often do not amount to much.[134]

Calling worship the response to our wealth is not an invitation to inducing warm, pious feelings as an antidote to existential angst in the face of economic injustice. It is a call to take seriously the plight of the marginalized

130. Ellul, *The Ethics of Freedom*, 470.

131. Such proposals are to be especially critiqued when they emerge from the comfortable academic halls of a theological faculty or from the office at the top of a building housing a Jesuit social center!

132. Ellul, *The Ethics of Freedom*, 472–73.

133. Ellul, *The Ethics of Freedom*, 474.

134. Mark 12:41–44.

and oppressed and to take seriously our inability to extract ourselves from the complex of causes that sustains this systemic financial violence. Through worship, our vision is sharpened to see this apparently hopeless panorama and to yet hope that the Lord can make possible new things. It is for this reason that our discussion has followed Cavanaugh and Barth and their different accounts of the potency of praise as a political performance.

Yet for our purposes, Cavanaugh's work demands extension. His account of worship is explicitly sacramental, tending always to the eucharistic. While his work may not especially invite capitalism's co-opting invasion (and indeed, his robust sacramentology may be able to resist it based on its deep roots in the action of God), it does lack a striking element. Throughout his work, Cavanaugh offers no account of preaching. In all his writing on liturgy, the homily is consistently overlooked. The absence of the sermon in his work is notable.[135] As a historical fact, the ministry of the word may be easily co-opted.[136] Yet the sacrament is absolutely naked without the ministry of the word. Simply placing bread and wine on the table and having people eat, even reverentially, does not Eucharist make. The words are central to its institution.[137]

This lacuna may not be a weakness intrinsic to Cavanaugh's work, since this conception of the theopolitical imagination flowing from the

135. There are, of course, references here and there to preaching or sermons or homilies in Cavanaugh's work. In *Torture and Eucharist* there are discussions of various homilies preached by Chilean priests and discussion of what it might mean for preaching to be authentic in the light of the operative ecclesiology at play. Cavanaugh, *Torture and Eucharist*, 83–84, 91, 115–16, 164, 190. In *Theopolitical Imagination*, there is a discussion of a sermon by Oscar Romero and a brief reference to Luther's view on preaching. Cavanaugh, *Theopolitical Imagination*, 23, 88. There are no explicit engagements with the task of preaching in *Being Consumed*.

136. In his essay, "The Need and Promise of Christian Preaching," Barth describes the fraught dilemma of preaching, knowing full well that the air of expectancy with which the congregation gathers can so easily be met by culturally conditioned, lukewarm words, the paltry best the minister could manage. "I sought to find my way between the problem of human life on the one hand and the content of the Bible on the other. As a minister I wanted to speak to the people in the infinite contradiction of their life, but to speak the no less infinite message of the Bible, which was as much of a riddle as life. Often enough these two magnitudes, life and the Bible, have risen before me (and still rise!) like Scylla and Charybdis: if these are the whence and whither of Christian preaching, who shall, who can, be a minister and preach?" Barth, *The Word of God and the Word of Man*, 100.

137. John H. McKenna's investigation of twentieth-century accounts of the epiclesis is helpful here for showing how inseparable is the liturgy of the sacrament from the liturgy of the word. He writes that the epiclesis "is a prayer and not a formula. Even those who maintain that it is consecratory, generally do not regard it alone as consecratory. They tend rather to see it as forming an indivisible consecratory unit with the institution narrative." McKenna, *The Eucharistic Epiclesis*, 150–51.

communion table implicitly assumes the homily as part of the regular acts of worship, but it needs to be addressed when considering the particular problem of wealth. Since the decisive effect of the parables—which are portions of Scripture which must be preached—involves a rupturing of the totalized imagination of neoliberal capitalism, it follows that the sermon as an event of verbal proclamation, of persuasive rhetoric, must be anticipated as a central component in helping the rich see their poverty in the light of God's kingdom. Cavanaugh lacks an account of preaching that illuminates the reading of Scripture and its exposition as a primary means of interruption. When preached, the Scriptures are heard by a community in a specific, local time and space. The preacher and the congregation gather to hear from God in this particular time and place.[138] The sermon is a potential moment of gospel apocalypse in the communal worship of God, and it is no accident that it is temporally prior to the liturgy of the Eucharist. In the word preached, the congregation is confronted. In the bread broken, the congregation is comforted. Taken together, such worship is the antidote to Mammon's formation of us as entrepreneurs of self, as consumers, as subjects of neoliberal capitalism.[139] But a central ingredient in that antidote is the preaching of the Bible, especially those strange tales Jesus tells, or the enigmatic prophetic confrontations with wealth and comfort, or the direct protestations of Paul or James in the face of wealthy and privileged Christians avoiding inequality. The preached word and the lection read is the most direct way in which the false gospel of neoliberal capitalism is shown to be hollow, and as such, it must be part of the beginning of an answer to the theological problem of wealth.

It is important to supplement the sacramental focus on worship with the centrality of homiletics, but the extent to which worship serves as the

---

138. "Preaching aims at the people of a specific time to tell them that their lives have their basis and hope in Jesus Christ. . . . The sermon does not take place in a vacuum. It has a human counterpart at which its proclamation is directed, i.e., specific people in a very specific type of present, in a specific place at a specific time." Barth, *Homiletics*, 89.

139. This position seeks to extend rather than correct Cavanaugh by articulating an argument congruent with but distinct from his work. It closely follows Martin Luther's account of Eucharist from the Marburg Colloquoy with Zwingli. That that conversation was held as part of a plan to create a Protestant federation highlights how worship is a politically potent force. But Luther's argument throughout is what is most significant for our purposes. In the "Report by Hedio," it is recorded that Luther agrees with Oecolampadius's summary statement that "the word brings the body of Christ into the bread" (18). On the same topic, in the "Report by Anonymous," we read him declare that the Eucharist rests on "the power of God's word" (42). This view is a repeated theme in Luther's writing on these issues, for example: "When God adds his word and sign to something it becomes a totally spiritual food and drink." Luther, *Luther's Works: Word and Sacrament IV*, 38:12, 19, 42, 18.

therapy of our disordered desire for more can be considered from other angles. As our response to wealth differs from place to place and time to time, it is to be expected that different church cultures with diverse operating theologies will find that there are aspects of their shared worshipful acts that agitate them in unexpected ways towards economic conversion.[140] A Pentecostal engagement with worship as a response to wealth might align the speaking of tongues and prophetic speech alongside sacrament and preaching. A Quaker community might expect to find in their collective silence a voice that breaks in on them with words of liberation. A Methodist community might discover a new direction in the midst of song.[141]

This conception of worship follows Cavanaugh, but represents a sort of geographical reimagining of his account of worship. For Cavanaugh, Eucharist is the center, a pivot point around which everything else turns. In advocating for a similarly central place for the pulpit, what is being proposed here is, instead, a spectrum, defined by the tension and mutual illumination provided by the interaction between sermon and sacrament. Yet flowing out of these two central poles will come all the distinctive emphases of worshipping congregations with their different traditions and contrasting practices. The collective worship of the church catholic, which is the center of our counter-formation in the face of Mammon, thus becomes a shifting, mobile, multi-nodal event, resistant to co-option through its diversity and its flexibility. Eucharist remains the root of the church's action, but it is not separated from preaching, and it is complemented by a vast array of local, contingent responses that Christian communities have developed as acts of praise in their time and place. Remembering Barth's discussion of the parables, we come to see that our ecclesiology is the ground for our humanitarianism. The worshipping community prays and preaches, it breaks bread together and serves its neighbors as an act of praise to God. But what, if anything, can be said about the particular response to wealth that flows from this?

As the parables reveal to us that another world truly exists, and that neoliberal capitalism does not have the last word on what is realistic, we have been reminded of the importance of paying attention to the specific

---

140. Within the Irish theological conversation, there is a point of contact, perhaps in contra-distinction from, the rich work of Siobhán Garrigan. Her insistence that tradition is the foundation for liturgical celebration, fostering "an endlessly vibrant trust about the presence it simultaneously creates and envisages in the world" is fascinatingly similar to and very different from what is argued here. Garrigan, *Beyond Ritual*, 199–202.

141. Some of their most famous hymns are already laden with capitalist notions awaiting subversion, "And can it be, that I should gain, an *interest* in the Savior's love . . ."

and the concrete. In our retelling of recent Irish economic history, we saw how there are levels of analysis beyond the econometric required to nourish our ethical attention. By resisting the desire to try to solve the problems of the world—either by reforming capitalism or refining our pristine praise—and instead turning to worship as the site of encounter with the Spirit, we become alert to the concrete needs that confront us in our own place and time. God *is* at work in the midst of human structures of sin. God *does* meet with the individual human communities trapped in their own self-referential compromise under the idolatry of Mammon. And in worship, God *will* direct us to the people and tasks that demand our attention where and when we are.

Neoliberal capitalism aspires to a globalized, uniform business culture; to a legal framework that establishes social stability; to unregulated markets that guarantee personal freedom; and to the efficient distribution of scarce resources. Yet as we read the parables alongside Barth we find in Jesus's unruffled authority a subversive spirit, which is not merely happy to oppose solitary injustices but searches for paths of liberation that transcend the liberal/conservative dichotomy. The kingdom of God is not a tinkering with otherwise laudatory socially progressive political goals, nor is it a progressive reform of some conservative political agenda which on the whole is meritorious. It is an overturning deeper than revolution, which refuses the categories offered by any spirit of the age. The parables shatter our common sense and leave us dependent on the Spirit to show us the way.

We began to see what this means when we retell economic stories without econometric abstraction. As we considered Depfa, we found ourselves up close to one of neoliberalism's central agendas: globalization. The collapse of Depfa exposed how the borderless freedom of capital to roam entails a transformation of what we value. If globalized neoliberalism can be characterized as a sort of recapitulation of imperialism, one of the likely out-workings of worship will be a recommitment to the resident alien status of Christians. Thus, the response to wealth will involve a distancing from the identifiers that neoliberalism promotes, both that of globalized cosmopolitanism and of nation-state nationality. A keen attention to specific locality will be a component of our various micro-aggressions against Mammon. In an age of mobility, when capital traverses the world in the blink of an eye and labor gets moved across the planet like a chessboard pawn, being fixed in one place and identified as such becomes a revolutionary proposition.

Furthermore, we considered the case of Sean FitzPatrick and his bizarre, self-defeating loans. Neoliberalism promises legality, but the corruption present during the Celtic Tiger and its aftermath remind us that even the most robust institutional frameworks will not assure stability. Regardless of political rhetoric, a clear injustice is revealed by relative incarceration rates depending on whether the offender is poor or rich. The corruption of the Irish elites looked like a self-protecting community. The rich and the powerful looked out for each other, as friends do. The collapse of Anglo Irish Bank as a result of irrational exuberance exposes how neoliberal subjectivity entails a transformation in how we think. In such a setting, the Christian church can stand as a counter-witness to the injustices of such a system by welcoming those who are not like them. Basic Christian hospitality takes on a revolutionary tone when it is performed in such a context. For if we welcome only those who welcome us, what reward can we expect? Do not even corrupt bankers and dodgy politicians do the same? Under the lights of neoliberal capitalism, it looks like a wise investment to spend your wealth helping friends. In the kingdom, wisdom is expressed when we turn our wealth to the betterment of strangers and even enemies. Thinking along kingdom lines generates a range of actions that oppose the prevailing culture of clientism and corruption.

The strange story of Seán Quinn and the mass protests in support of him in the midst of his bankruptcy are an example of the attempt to establish markets free from regulation. In neoliberal Ireland, Quinn found his reckless agenda could be pursued without challenge. He sought to take control of Anglo Irish Bank, in part because of the vast profits that it was generating from Ireland's booming property construction industry. The people who marched in support of the billionaire who caused their job losses sought a comfort that only the truth can offer. What we do is shaped by what we value and how we think, so of course neoliberalism will generate these moments of paradoxical absurdity. By committing to telling the truth—which is to say valuing things rightly and thinking clearly—the church automatically takes a profound political stance. Vivid, articulate preaching of the gospel is a decisive aspect of the church's response to the problems of its wealth and the injustices of neoliberalism. The speech-act of the sermon is what we do to show what we value and how we think. The embarrassing parables which pin us uncomfortably, the New Testament writings that leave us feeling inadequate, and the terrifying prophetic jeremiads that hold us in their targets are among the passages of Scripture to which we should run. God's Word convicts us, but the one certain way to deepen our problem is to avoid that verdict.

A fixed commitment to place, a solid determination towards hospitality, and a renewed vision for preaching represent a sort of boundary to the field upon which we can play out these micro-aggressions. All this flows first from the patient, communal act of worship.

In establishing worship as our response, we thus open up the possibility of a theological ethics that accounts for specificity (in keeping with chapter 3) and assumes that the interruptive word of the Lord (in keeping with chapter 2) is the primary way in this time (in keeping with chapter 1) to practice faithfulness. In some places this will lead to developed social justice initiatives. In other places it will take the form of what we have called micro-aggressions against Mammon. The critical point is that it will be a refusal to look away from the problematic space in which we, rich Christians, have placed ourselves in our prosperity.

Conclusion: The Hope of the Life of the World to Come

After 1989, we have been told we are living after the end of history. The hegemonic power of neoliberal capitalism means that a political arrangement built around the free market, global trade, and unfettered movement of capital is the only option available to us. Significant differences persist between Dublin and Dusseldorf, no less than between Cork and Cincinnati. Significant political disputes rage on. Yet the field on which they play out is firmly set by the commitments of neoliberalism. That totalized hold is justified by the prosperity provided by contemporary capitalism. We cannot imagine another world, but in this world of choice that does not actually matter so much, since the world we have is projected as the best of all possible, so long as we are being economically realistic.

To be wealthy in any age poses a problem for the Christian. But to be wealthy in this age demands a recovery of sight, an overcoming of this complicated set of blinders represented by the reigning economic, political, and cultural powers. The parables convey a Damascene Road light that, just as with Saul-who-became-Paul, cures us of a blindness we did not even recognize. Yet the parables are encountered in worship. They are heard when read publicly in community. They are understood when preached by our pastors. The worship of the church is the (beginning of the) treatment of our wealth. There may be need for reform, retreat, or revolution, but before everything there is revelation.

To have those blinders removed is to have sight restored, but there must be some formation, born of worship and encounter with God, that follows. The blinders of capitalism are the practices that situate us in the delusion of scarcity, in the fantasy of needing more, in the illusion of imminent threat. The church is a community and so a natural expression of this restored sight will find Christians engaging together with pre-existing groups walking a similar path, away from the prevailing logic of neoliberal capitalism. Hence, local credit union co-operatives which reorientate the business of credit in sustainable ways towards those who most need it will warrant our attention.[142] Local churches can learn from the example of "Economy of Communion" initiatives that have successful started or reformed enterprises all over the globe.[143] Transition town projects, which push back against urban planning that assumes private motor car ownership and ongoing environmental degradation, will be exciting places for Christians awoken to the violence implicit in how we order our shared life.[144] These movements, and others like them, reject scarcity as a starting point. The ancient Christian practices of fasting will have their place in strengthening the acuity of our sight, weakened from under-use. Joining in initiatives like "Neighborly Covenants,"[145] "Buy Nothing Day,"[146] "Advent Conspiracy,"[147] or "The Restart Project"[148] are possible first steps in inhabiting "enough." Practices of hospitality are critical for resisting the culture of fear and threat that motivates so much of our defensive allegiance with the ways of Mammon.[149] There are countless ways, depending on location and prevailing political problems, by which the church can open its doors in ways which trace the parabolic arc of Jesus's kingdom, against the hard, straight bar graphs of neoliberal capitalism's abstractions. His unruffled authority means that the church cannot set a course in advance for how to react to neoliberalism. The insistent Lord will not, however, leave us short of inspiration. Flowing from our reflection on the Scriptures and our par-

142. Especially well established in Ireland, credit unions are a primary bulwark against the growing influence of predatory lenders: http://www.creditunion.ie/

143. Gold, *New Financial Horizons*, 103–16.

144. A movement of communities established to sustainably prepare towns for a world of increasing environmental volatility: https://transitionnetwork.org/

145. A proposal recently advocated by Peter Block, Walter Brueggemann, and John McKnight that looks to reorientate the church's life towards community development in directions that are counter to consumer culture. Block, Brueggemann, and McKnight, *An Other Kingdom*.

146. A response to the phenomenon of Black Friday: http://www.buynothingday.co.uk/

147. A response to the commercialization of Christmas: http://www.adventconspiracy.org/

148. A response to the planned obsolescence that drives the consumer electronics market: https://therestartproject.org/

149. The homeless initiative, Good Works, Inc., working in rural Appalachia since 1981 might be a notable example here. Seeking to go beyond "emergency response, it works to foster longer-term relationships to help people recover a place in community." http://good-works.net/; Pohl, *Making Room*, 192.

ticipation in the sacrament, we may be prompted in one place to join with Sanctuary cities,[150] in another to console the homeless,[151] and in a third to joining in political action to change the law around specific topics.[152] We may be prompted to do all three together.

Compiling such a series can all too easily lead to a soulless, bureaucratic operation, a menu for witness, ethics by checklist. Tick all these suggestions and everything will be okay. Wealthy people have the material and cultural resources to contribute to all of these initiatives and more. This does not amount to a recipe for justice, but instead is intended to give some concrete examples of what it might mean to *begin* to resist the blinders that neoliberalism places on our imagination. Practices that keep in step with the ways of the kingdom are necessary for keeping our vision sharp, but they are not sufficient. Only the Spirit can liberate us from the bondage of Mammon's false gospel. Capitalism's pragmatism—"It works, doesn't it?"—trains us to expect an examination of the problem of wealth to produce a course of action, or at least a set of principles that will chart a course of action to resolve the problem. What worship refuses to do is become a technology instrumentalized to fix an issue.[153] To propose worship as a response in this mode is always to run the risk of falling back into that dreadful pit of human creativity gone awry which Barth calls "religion."

Instead, by considering worship primarily as an action of God, a waiting on his encounter, a hopeful anticipation of a liberation that only he can provide, the response to wealth that we offer here is inherently ambiguous. It cannot be predicted. It does not rest on our competency.[154] It will look wildly

150. A geographic network established to provide refuge for those who need it across the UK and Ireland: https://cityofsanctuary.org/

151. Any number of movements could be cited, but the principal voice in the UK is Housing Justice: http://www.housingjustice.org.uk/

152. In Ireland, "Ruhama" is an NGO with Christian roots and widespread support in churches which has played an influential role in the reform of Irish legislation around prostitution: www.ruhama.ie.

153. This is a point that cannot be emphasized enough. The potency of worship which is here discussed is not a utility of worship. Worship has political potential because worship has no practical point. It is good in and of itself. It is clear ground in the midst of our busy lives where we have built towers on every other minute and hour. God's beauty draws out our praise, his grace calls out our gratitude and in that "royal waste of time," we find the neoliberal urge towards productive self-production is exposed as the lamest squandering of our lives possible. It is in that interruptive moment, the Spirit can plant a new thing.

154. It rests on the reality of what Hans Ulrich has called God's "apocalyptic-messianic" presence, in which God "directly confronts every so-called 'history' that claims to be transforming our world age. God's faithfulness is to bring his story into this world age to provoke what we may call true history." Neoliberalism's hollow reign runs out of

different across the churches, across the globe, through time, and in the lives of individuals. Just as Jesus asked some to sell all and give the proceeds to the poor, while leaving others with their assets intact, in some places the response to Mammon in our age might be straightforwardly ascetic, or deeply immersed in new economic initiatives, or dedicated to a subversive hospitality to strangers. It may erupt in organized political protests in one place, and quiet, careful, behind-the-scenes policy crafting in others, but in all, it will insist neoliberalism does not get to determine the boundaries of what is feasible. The form liberation takes from one community to the next can no more be predicted than could be Zacchaeus's decision to reimburse everyone he defrauded fourfold (Luke 19:8). Whether the infamous tax collector awoke that fateful day aware of how he was captive to wealth cannot be known. But what is certain is that when he was confronted with Jesus, his freedom was bought at a price that represented amazing value. The price, fundamentally, was paid in advance by God in his commitment to be *for us*.

And so this worshipful response is born out of a particular confidence in telling the time. Living in the reign of the already, but not fully here kingdom requires disciplined patience, because it will often appear as if we do indeed live in the age of neoliberalism. The worshipful response involves a waiting on the Lord. In this sense, it is wholly in line with the parable of the Ten Virgins. They were called to stand *vigil*, Latin for awake. They stood watching. Then they slumped asleep. They were thoroughly compromised in the task set to them. After waiting and waiting, the groom did indeed show up and he was received by those on watch who moments earlier had been deep in slumber. The wise virgins were floundering failures at their job. They could not escape their sleepiness. The groom met them all the same.

Barth argues that the parable looks to the hope that "the Church of the interim will stand at His [Jesus'] side, with its testimony to the whole world."[155] It is tiring work to stand vigil, to stay awake, when the comforts of prosperity so tantalizingly invite respite. In the age of neoliberal capitalism, the tragic risk is that we become like virgins who "having kept their lamps alight for a long time" ultimately have kept them lit "apparently to no purpose" since at the critical moment they "had no reserves of oil and could not therefore meet and escort the bridegroom."[156]

---

time in the face of this revelation. He goes on to say that for Barth, "the Christian ethos is the liturgical existence and worshipping activity of the community as it witnesses to God's ongoing actions, which is to say, the actual living God." Ulrich, "The Messianic Contours of Evangelical Ethics," 45, 52.

155. Barth, *CD III/2*, 505.

156. Barth, *CD III/2*, 505.

When we understand this worshipful stance as a waiting on the Lord, we begin to see how much good, hard work is involved in the superficially simple task of keeping watch. Keeping watch, planning for the moment of encounter, and responding in concrete action to the good news that God brings is what we are primed for when our worshipful attention is attuned by the parables. Continuing to believe in the logic of the kingdom that is here and not yet, in the face of the market that appears to be absolutely everywhere, can be an exhausting task. The regular gathering of Christians in corporate worship becomes ever more essential for keeping going on this narrow path.

As Christians gather they often say the creed, a document as politically potent as any manifesto or bill of rights. In its conclusion, the community declares that they "look for the resurrection of the dead, and the life of the world to come." Such a commitment goes beyond the secular suggestion that another world is possible in its conviction that a certain, concrete, particular other world is imminent. It is here and it is on its way. Those who are at home in it are rich in ways that balance sheets and profit statements cannot track. It is the hope of that life of that world which is almost here which motivates Christians to squander their wealth on the kingdom, in exchange for the kind of abundance found in the parables. Such hope is awoken in the sermon, nourished in Eucharist, and expressed in service to neighbor and stranger. Such hope cannot but praise.

Afterword

WHAT THE MAP EXCLUDES

In "That the Science of Cartography is Limited," Irish poet Eavan Boland reflects on a path she finds while walking with her husband through a coppice in western Ireland. They find themselves on what is known as a "famine road," a throughway to nowhere, built so that the starving Irish could have the benefit of hard work, lest emergency charity dull their human hunger for toil:

> I looked down at ivy and the scotch grass
> rough-cast stone had
> disappeared into as you told me
> in the second winter of their ordeal, in
>
> 1847, when the crop had failed twice,
> Relief Committees gave
> the starving Irish such roads to build.
>
> Where they died, there the road ended[1]

She reflects on how the agony of those who laid these stones went unremembered in the history books and how their pointless exertion is not even noted on maps:

> and ends still and when I take down
> the map of this island, it is never so
> I can say here is the masterful, the apt rendering of
>
> the spherical as flat, nor
> an ingenious design which persuades a curve

---

1. Boland, *In a Time of Violence*, 7.

into a plane
but to tell myself again that

the line which says woodland and cries hunger
and gives out among sweet pine and cypress,
and finds no horizon

will not be there.[2]

There was a time, a long time, when a theology of wealth written with Irish Christians in mind would have occupied a niche within a niche. Irish Christians, for many centuries, identified more naturally with Lazarus than the rich man.

This is no longer the case.[3]

Yet the official stories that we tell about the Ireland of the Celtic Tiger and its aftermath is deficient in just the same way that Boland finds even masterful cartography limited. The Ordinance Survey maps cannot account for the historic hunger cries of those who died laying futile stone. The charts of growing GDP and recovering GNP cannot account for the specific loneliness of Dublin's homeless, or the particular pains of the middle-aged man, laid off years ago and facing into a future of under-employment, if not unemployment. Economic descriptions of reality demand augmentation to even begin an ethical analysis.

This book has sought to do something other than account theologically for the problem of poverty. It has tried to describe the problem of prosperity, a problem unknown and unimaginable to those who suffered the black harvest of 1847. To describe prosperity as a problem appears to be a shocking claim, almost an insult to those who died laying famine roads centuries ago or those who will sleep rough on Dublin's bridges tonight. Yet this shock is created by our habituation in the shared imagination of neoliberal capitalism. Through competition and unregulated market forces, we are promised prosperity and the many sacrifices that must be made— of the social security net, of the environmental equilibrium, of the social

---

2. Boland, *In a Time of Violence*, 7–8.

3. The warning about the days of surplus in Deuteronomy 8:10–14 have recent and profound relevance for the Irish church: "When you have eaten and are satisfied, praise the Lord your God for the good land he has given you. Be careful that you do not forget the Lord your God, failing to observe his commands, his laws and his decrees that I am giving you this day. Otherwise, when you eat and are satisfied, when you build fine houses and settle down, and when your herds and flocks grow large and your silver and gold increase and all you have is multiplied, then your heart will become proud and you will forget the Lord your God, who brought you out of Egypt, out of the land of slavery."

fabric—are justified because the path neoliberalism has beaten out will lead to prosperity. Prosperity will resolve our problems.

Jesus disagrees. He presents "the kingdom as the only goal worthy of human pursuit."[4] In his teaching generally, but in his parables specifically, we have encountered a perspective on wealth that is diametrically opposed to our commonsense assumption that more is better and the more *we* have is better again. The path this book takes flows from this realization. Boland reminds us that the science of cartography is limited. All can agree that the science of economics is limited. Yet, by considering the problem of wealth, we have identified theologically compelling reasons to argue that ethical reflection for Christians requires maps that economics cannot draw on its own.

In reading the parables after Barth, we encountered a sharp rebuke to neoliberalism's totalizing claims. Barth emboldened us to declare *"Nein!"* in response to the totalizing claims of neoliberalism. Time remains God's. We will spend our days repudiating this fact if we do not pay heed to the challenge that breaks in on us through Jesus's teaching. The parables confront us with the logic of God's kingdom, which is not congruent or compatible with the logic of our age. When we take those bundled insights and reconsider contemporary economic history in their light, we find that the stories we are drawn to take on a different shape. In considering the years since the Irish economic crash, we found that the settled narratives of the credit crunch and the global financial crisis are everywhere complicated by the details of local stories and personal testimonies.

The response, then, in the face of this contestation between different ways of representing reality and our inevitable compromise with the competing claims of Mammon, is a turn to worship. Worship is what we do in God's time. It rests on God's encounter with us. It reorientates our vision to see life in terms of abundance and not scarcity. It retrains our affections to question the false promises of consumerism. It encourages a commitment to our locality, a dedication to hospitality, a hopefulness for the role of preaching and an openness to radical and risky economic ventures that seek a benefit other than the bottom line. Communal worship, consisting of the ministry of the word and the sacrament, along with the many other distinctive elements that are critical in different traditions of the church, is the beginning of the response to our wealth. It is the politically potent starting point from which the church can begin to disentangle itself from the false master, Mammon.

---

4. Wheeler, *Wealth as Peril and Obligation*, 70.

A Final Word on Lament as the Key of Worship

Our wealth is a synonym for comfort. Our comfort is supported by unholy inequality across the globe that means that in some places people die of thirst and hunger, while in others, people are crushed competing for bargains at the supermarket.[5] To find ourselves wealthy, whether in absolute or relative terms, is to find ourselves in the dock.[6]

There is no easy formula to secure our release. There is certainly no principle to follow that will guarantee that we will be found innocent. Aside from the mercy of God, there is no hope for the rich. Our wealth is spent on luxuries while millions die awaiting necessities.[7] Our wealth comes at the cost of environmental degradation while multitudes see their livelihoods washed away.[8] Our wealth rests on the violence of slavery, the conquests of colonialism, and the rampages of world wars.[9] Whatever way we slice it, we remain inextricably tied up by the rope of wealth.

In chapter 1 I suggested that neoliberal subjectivity is like an industrial forest, imposing a grid that sees profit as the primary goal and a certain kind of rational resource allocation as the method of life. There are reform movements that seek to diversify forestry monocultures. There are environmentalist movements that advocate for a human retreat from forests, arguing that we should create refuges free from human interference. We can imagine some self-proclaimed techno-utopian Silicon Valley billionaire

5. Pérez and Esposito, "The Global Addiction and Human Rights," 87.

6. Tiemstra is helpfully clear about the red herring that is sometimes found around this absolute/relative poverty distinction. "Poverty is always defined in the context of a particular society. The best definition I know of poverty is 'the lack of opportunity to fulfill God's callings.'" Tiemstra, *Stories Economists Tell*, 82.

7. This line of thinking should not be taken as an invitation to conceive of nations outside the West as "shithole countries." Wealth inequality goes all the way down, such that even in "the poorest countries in the world," there are social issues that are traditionally understood to be the effect of neoliberal affluence. Emily Yates-Doerr's remarkable anthropology of overweightness in Guatemala is a fascinating study of such dynamics. Guatemala is poor. Yet, statistically it faces a public health issue around obesity. She concludes that the straightforward accounting of the bare facts is distorting. Instead: "The Guatemalans I worked and lived among continued to find pleasure in fat, satisfaction in the commensality of the feast, and health in abundance. Joyfully gathered around carefully crafted meals, they were busy transforming, in ways that were as understated as they were radical, the terms of power. The pressure to possess the body was strong, but so too was a form of richness that refused possession." (It also noteworthy that obesity, tied as it is to calculations of BMI, was historically a product of actuarial science, not biomedical research. Neoliberal subjectivity—you are not imagining it!) Yates-Doerr, *The Weight of Obesity*, 185.

8. Wheeler and von Braun, "Climate Change Impacts on Global Food Security."

9. See, for example, Baptist, *The Half Has Never Been Told*.

who declares in the not-too-distant future that the thing we have to do is cut down all the forests and replace them with his cybernetic adaptable CO_2 machines. These are analogous to the standard Christian responses (reform, retreat, revolution) to the vagaries of neoliberal economics. But hidden within the diversity of the forest, unacknowledged by the urban accountants that track the efficiency of forestry concerns, lies a life-form that illuminates the peculiar position for the church as a worshipping community inextricably bound up with neoliberalism, and yet distinct.

As mentioned in chapter 1, Anna Lowenhaupt-Tsing's research has tracked the decline of carbon capitalism through an appreciation of the *Matsusake* mushroom. Mushrooms are the fruiting bodies of a fungus. As an acorn is to an oak, so is the little white button that you use to make risotto on a busy Thursday night to a sprawling, subterranean organism. Fungi, of course, are found all over the Earth; on the surface of cheese left too long in the fridge, among the currents of the ocean, and under your toenails. But the fungi we are discussing here live within the soil, where thread-like filaments that are termed *hyphae* fan out, digesting rocks and wrapping coils around other roots, generating an organic network of mutual exchange between all the different agents within the eco-system. Lowenhaupt-Tsing invites us on a journey:

> If you could make the soil liquid and transparent and walk into the ground, you would find yourself surrounded by nets of fungal hyphae. Follow fungi into that underground city, and you will find the strange and varied pleasures of interspecies life. Many people think fungi are plants, but they are actually closer to animals. Fungi do not make their food from sunlight, as plants do. Like animals, fungi must find something to eat. Yet fungal eating is often generous: It makes worlds for others.[10]

These vast webs—*mycelia* or *shiro*—are entangled in the life of the forest, both in the expressions that industrial investors care about and in the messy gray-zone of fecundity that defies calculative valuation.[11] It is largely a subterranean network, made of overlapping entities that share a remarkable genetic similarity while being complexly distinct. It fruits here and there, in season, and out, sometimes deliciously. But as everyone familiar with forests knows, the fruit can often be toxic, or have mind-bending effects.[12] The *mycelium* is invisible to many, but essential for the life of the forest. It is an

10. Lowenhaupt-Tsing, *The Mushroom at the End of the World*, 137.

11. I am grateful to my colleague Catherine Devitt for helping me to understand how under-appreciated these fungal networks are.

12. This analogy for the life of the church is a little too close for comfort!

apt image for the church described in these pages.[13] Inextricably entangled in the life of the markets such that it is meaningless to imagine it existing apart from the world in which it is immersed, but it is too different from that world to overhaul it. The soil upon which we live is literally made by the digestive effect of *hyphae* as they encounter the obstacles of rocks. Fertile ground is made from the dogged opposition to barrenness. The church has a vocation to worship that is both compromised by and separate from the hectic activity of neoliberalism. To conceive of our response to wealth as worship is not to hide from the challenge of confronting structural evil, but to go underground, to attack the roots of the system, especially where our affections and its machinations have entwined.[14] The cry that springs forth from recognizing that is bound to be lament.

Jesus depicts wealth as a problem because it is an obstacle to faithfulness. Worship is the response to wealth because worship is the definitive action of faithfulness.[15] Worship will give rise to economic actions—the buying of oil, confident investing, the sharing of food with the hungry and water with the thirsty—but the problem of wealth cannot be aligned with any pre-established activisms without replicating the mistake of the rich young ruler, who wanted to calculate the shortest path to eternal life.[16] As the climate debts of fossil capitalism accumulate, as we lurch into the Anthropocene, the likely primary lament of our wealth will take the form of anguish over the environmental poverty created for our excess. *Mycelia* can thrive amid devastation and gen-

13. Those who join the harvest "do not waste much time looking up into trees. Our gaze is directed below, where the mushrooms rise through the heaving earth. Some pickers mention that they pay attention to the dirt, favoring areas where the soil looks right." Lowenhaupt-Tsing, *The Mushroom at the End of the World*, 242.

14. Those who seek the Matsusake recognize that the vibrant organism does not always fruit in a predictable fashion. Some groups toil in making the soil ready, knowing that their entire lives could pass without a harvest of the mushroom they seek. "They hope their actions might stimulate a latent commons, that is, an eruption of shared assembly, even as they know they can't actually make a commons." So it is with this foregrounding of worship. It is not a pious form of strategic activism, nor is it a rejection of such activism, but rather is an insistence that there are categories of action that neoliberal capitalism cannot conceive and that we, therefore, too easily can pass over. Lowenhaupt-Tsing, *The Mushroom at the End of the World*, 258.

15. Thomas's "My Lord and my God!" can be read as both the narrative climax of John's gospel and the hallmark expression of Christian faithfulness (John 20:28).

16. My thinking here, about how the life of the church cannot be disentangled from the activity of neoliberalism is mirrored by Jason W. Moore when he discusses the negative consequences of imagining nature and human activity as distinct zones. As "the separation of humanity and nature has encouraged a way of thinking about history that privileges what humanity does to nature," the separation of capitalism as a zone apart from the church obscures the way in which the exchange goes both ways. Moore, *Capitalism in the Web of Life*, 5.

erate new possibilities for other life. Worship is a means to make disruption our home, for the sake of others' peace.

Before worship might blossom into various economic transformations—for example around fixity of place, hospitality, preaching, and radical investment in kingdom of God initiatives—it must begin in lamentation. To recover from our captivity to Mammon is to find ourselves dislocated. If it is a homecoming, it is also a long journey into doubt, vulnerability, and insecurity. Before he arrived home, the younger son of Luke 15 had to cross the far country. The path out of his land of dissolution must have stretched his hope. The experience of coming home must for us, similarly, first be an exile. In an age where the totalized grasp of neoliberal capitalism is almost all-pervasive, the Christian congregations who wrestle with how wealth implicates them in injustice will find themselves disorientated and alienated. It will be a place analogous to the faithful who gather in Lamentations 3:40–42 to repent of the sinfulness that saw them carried off into exile:

> Let us test and examine our ways,
>> and return to the Lord.
> Let us lift up our hearts as well as our hands
>> to God in heaven.
> We have transgressed and rebelled
>> and you have not forgiven.

To realize we are captive to our wealth is also to realize how our wealth holds the poor in captivity. That state of sin demands repentance and the mode of worship that is appropriate to such a crisis is lament. The hope for the renewal of practice that might flow from our worship is tied up in lamentation and repentance. As Soong-Chan Rah puts it, "spiritual renewal emerges as God's people engage in a corporate confession of sin, and sincere repentance moves the community toward a changed and renewed life."[17]

This is not an optional extra for some Christian communities who happen to feel themselves called to a particular focus on economic justice. The consequences of our commitment to the "*More!*" of neoliberal capitalism cry out from the ground, both in the form of the millions dead from hunger, thirst, and overwork and quite literally in the decreasing richness of our ecosystem. Jesus wept over Jerusalem because of his compatriots' commitment to hollow dreams of revolution against the Romans. Their determination to follow that path to the end was bound to be their end.[18] The call to lament and

---

17. Rah, *Prophetic Lament*, 130.

18. Luke 19:41–44

repent is similarly urgent in our day, as the ice caps melt, the climate changes, and a growing proportion of the world realizes that in neoliberal capitalism, only the elite super-yachts will sail over these rising tides.

This book is an apocalyptic intervention, but these last paragraphs aside, that is not meant as a license to doom-laden prophecy. Lamentations 3:42 leaves the question of forgiveness uncertain, which is not the situation that prevails for the Christians of the West. In rest and repentance, the rich will find their salvation. Resting from the constant seeking for more and repenting of the desire to make ourselves safe through such dead-end means will constitute a certain liberation. The prophecy that this book is meant to license is that there is no reason why Christians cannot again reclaim the hope of Acts 2:43–47 and 4:32–37. These are not mere idealizations; there was once a time when the idea that Christians held all that they owned in common was considered laudable. That time can come again.[19] The extent to which we do not even aspire to live up to this ideal shows the gulf between our vision and Jesus's articulation of the kingdom of God. The practices of worship, which will begin in lament, can then flourish into an array of creative initiatives and projects, practices and actions that will witness to the other world that is coming and is already here.

Such a vision is unlikely to have the G8 leaders gathering in huddled groups to whisper their concerns to one another. It will not cure hunger, slow climate change, or undo the gross damages of slavery, imperialism, and war. It is a resistance movement that seeks other goals. The parables train us to work on a scale unfamiliar in the corridors of power. In the face of hunger, the church can bring food to hungry people. In the face of climate change, the church can house the homeless. In the face of systemic violence, the church can offer hospitality across conceptual fences, hypothetical walls and notional borders, to befriend actual strangers and enemies. This resistance movement may not overcome the evil it confronts, but neither will it make peace with it.

Worship as a resistance movement appears to be unambitious only if examined by the logic of neoliberal capitalism. In the logic of the kingdom, as revealed in the parables, in giving food to the hungry and water to the thirsty, we can end up caring for God.[20] No human activity can compare with that.

19. The Bruderhof Community is a prophetic expression of this, demonstrating clearly that the sharing all things in common aspect of the *ekklesia* is not a utopian dream. For readers unfamiliar with their work, subscription to their publication, the Plough Quarterly (www.plough.com) is strongly recommended.

20. I am grateful to my wife, Claire, a prison chaplain, for directing me to resources that seek to explore the same insight in that particular context: "The fact is that Matthew

In *The Christian Life*, Barth talks about resistance movements that seek to stand firm in their witnessing to the goodness of God in the face of injustice. "Zeal," he says, "for the honor of God means holy and resolute marching off in that direction. It means revolt."[21] But this revolt has unusual aims. Barth says, "the overthrow of the regime cannot be an affair of our action. That God himself will overthrow it is what we pray for."[22] Embedded in the eschatological horizon to which our action is directed is the hope that one day—and soon—God might topple the titans of capital. But for us, in the in-between times, "to rise up in rebellion against the regime—this is what we want to emphasize—is something that is humanly possible, that we can do."[23] Even if local churches worshipping in lament at their own deep compromise cannot inflict even a bruise on Mammon, their resistance has profound significance. Even in apparent failure, the Christians who witness against systems like neoliberal capitalism can "question it in practice at various points, bring to light its limits, strengthen nonconformity over against it, issue an impressive warning against collaboration, and keep alive the hope of liberation."[24] Barth cites the example of a Huguenot woman held captive for her opposition to the Vichy regime. Alone in her cell, she scratched the word "*Résistez*" on to the windowpane. Confronting us with this tiny gesture, Barth reminds us that "the angels read this inscription and its message" and even if ours is only a "very relative and modest resistance" that may be received only by the angels, "this should be a great comfort to us." After all, "what is certain is that we cannot possibly fail to offer it, but must offer it with courage."[25]

Lament is born of the humility that comes from encounter with the insistent Lord. The protest that follows will be similarly expressed in humility—monkfish given away for free, music published without copyright, community gardens feeding homeless shelters—but it will be decisively potent because its origin is praise. In worship, the Spirit of God will give us courage to reject the false master Mammon and show us how to faithfully follow the only true Lord, Jesus.

25:31–46 remains and will remain next to the injustices of the system, within earshot of the cries of the imprisoned. And the invitation, the 'command,' not just the 'counsel'—as Luther would put it—to visit Jesus in jail also remains. Would not that be a most privileged opportunity? To 'see' Jesus in this intimate way? How is it that most Christian congregations bypass that holy invitation?" Vargas, "Who Ministers to Whom," 133.

21. Barth, *The Christian Life*, 174.

22. Barth, *The Christian Life*, 174.

23. Barth, *The Christian Life*, 174.

24. Barth, *The Christian Life*, 174.

25. Barth, *The Christian Life*, 174.

Bibliography

Allen, Kieran, and Brian O'Boyle. *Austerity Ireland: The Failure of Irish Capitalism.* Dublin: Pluto, 2013.

Alpha International. "Alpha Brand Guidelines." London: Alpha International, 2014. https://23kx692dmhij48mpfk2gm467-wpengine.netdna-ssl.com/wp-content /uploads/2012/07/Alpha-Brand-Guidelines-2014-2.0.pdf.

Amin, Samir. "Capitalism, Imperialism, Globalization." In *The Political Economy of Imperialism,* edited by Ronald M. Chilcote, 157–68. New York: Sprinter Science and Business Media, 1999.

Anglo Irish Bank. "Annual Report and Accounts 2007." Dublin: Anglo Irish Bank, 2007. http://www.ibrc.ie/About_us/Financial_information/Archived_reports/Annual_ Report_2007.pdf.

Ashton, Mark, R. Kent Hughes, and Timothy Keller. *Worship by the Book.* Edited by D. A. Carson. Grand Rapids: Zondervan, 2002.

Aughney, Jim. "Final Spin for Fruit of the Loom in Donegal." *Irish Independent,* May 20, 2006.

Augustine of Hippo. *City of God.* Cambridge: Cambridge University Press, 1998.

———. *Confessions.* Oxford: Oxford University Press, 2008.

Backes, Nancy. "Reading the Shopping Mall City." *The Journal of Popular Culture* 31, no. 3 (December 1, 1997) 1–17.

Bailey, James L., and Lyle D. Vander Broek, eds. *Literary Forms in the New Testament—A Handbook.* Louisville: Westminster John Knox, 1992.

Bailey, Kenneth E. *Poet & Peasant and Through Peasant Eyes.* Grand Rapids: Eerdmans, 1983.

Baptist, Edward E. *The Half Has Never Been Told.* New York: Basic, 2014.

Barrett, David. "Irish General Election 2016 Report: Whither the Party System?" *Irish Political Studies* 31, no. 3 (July 2, 2016) 418–31.

Barry, Frank. "Foreign investment and the politics of export profits tax relief 1956." *Irish Economic and Social History* 38, no. 1 (2011) 54–73.

Barth, Karl. *The Christian Life.* London: T&T Clark, 2004.

———. *Church Dogmatics I/1.* Edinburgh: T&T Clark, 2009.

———. *Church Dogmatics I/2.* Edinburgh: T&T Clark, 2009.

———. *Church Dogmatics II/1.* Edinburgh: T&T Clark, 2009.

———. *Church Dogmatics II/2.* Edinburgh: T&T Clark, 2009.

———. *Church Dogmatics III/1.* Edinburgh: T&T Clark, 2009.

———. *Church Dogmatics III/2.* Edinburgh: T&T Clark, 2009.

————. *Church Dogmatics III/4*. Edinburgh: T&T Clark, 2009.

————. *Church Dogmatics IV/1*. Edinburgh: T&T Clark, 2009.

————. *Church Dogmatics IV/2*. Edinburgh: T&T Clark, 2009.

————. *Church Dogmatics IV/3*. Edinburgh: T&T Clark, 2009.

————. *Die Kirchliche Dogmatik IV/2*. Zurich: Theologischer Verlag Zurich Ag Tvz, 1993.

————. *The Epistle to the Romans*. 6th ed. Oxford: Oxford University Press, 1968.

————. *Ethics*. New York: Seabury, 1981.

————. *Homiletics*. Louisville: Westminster John Knox, 1991.

————. *Protestant Thought from Rousseau to Ritschl*. New York: Harper & Brothers, 1959.

————. *The Word of God and the Word of Man*. London: Hodder & Stoughton, 1968.

Beaujon, Andrew. *Body Piercing Saved My Life: Inside the Phenomenon of Christian Rock*. Cambridge, MA: Da Capo, 2006.

Beed, Clive, and Cara Beed. "Christian Principles for the Organization of Employment." In *Alternatives to Economics*, 25–55. Lanham, MD: University Press of America, 2006.

Beer, David. *Metric Power*. London: Palgrave Macmillan, 2016.

Beesley, Arthur. "Directors of Depfa Bank Get €34m Pay Package." *The Irish Times*, September 14, 2005.

Bell, Daniel M. *The Economy of Desire*. Grand Rapids: Baker Academic, 2012.

Benjamin, Walter. *Arcades Project*. Cambridge, MA: Belknap, 1999.

————. "Capitalism as Religion." In *Selected Writings Volume 1, 1913–1926*, edited by Marcus Bullock and Michael W. Jennings, 288–91. Cambridge, MA: Belknap, 2002.

Bielenberg, Andy, and Raymond Ryan. *An Economic History of Ireland Since Independence*. New York: Routledge, 2012.

Birch, Kean. *We Have Never Been Neoliberal*. London: Zero, 2015.

Blanchard, Kathryn D. *The Protestant Ethic or the Spirit of Capitalism*. Eugene, OR: Cascade, 2010.

Block, Fred, and Margaret R. Somers. *The Power of Market Fundamentalism*. Cambridge, MA: Harvard University Press, 2014.

Block, Peter, Walter Brueggemann, and John McKnight. *An Other Kingdom*. Hoboken, NJ: Wiley, 2016.

Bobbitt, Philip. *Terror and Consent*. London: Allen Lane, 2008.

————. *The Shield of Achilles*. New York: Anchor, 2003.

Boland, Eavan. *In a Time of Violence*. New York: W. W. Norton, 1995.

Boland, Vincent. "Dublin Ditches Double Irish to Save Low Tax Regime." *Financial Times*, October 14, 2014.

Bonhoeffer, Dietrich. *Ethics*. Minneapolis: Fortress, 2006.

Boulton, Matthew Myer. *God Against Religion*. Grand Rapids: Eerdmans, 2008.

Bowler, Kate. *Blessed: A History of the American Prosperity Gospel*. Oxford: Oxford University Press, 2013.

Boyd, Ian. "Chesterton and Distributism." *New Blackfriars* 55, no. 649 (1974) 265–72.

Braudel, Fernand. *The Structures of Everyday Life*. London: William Collins & Sons, 1985.

Brennan, Declan. "Sean FitzPatrick Acquitted on All Counts after Direction of Trial Judge." *Irish Independent*, May 23, 2017.

Brock, Brian. *Captive to Christ, Open to the World*. Edited by Kenneth Oakes. Eugene, OR: Cascade, 2014.

———. "Globalisation, Eden and the Myth of Original Markets." *Studies in Christian Ethics* 28, no. 4 (November 1, 2015) 402–18.

Brown, Wendy. *Undoing the Demos*. New York: Zone, 2015.

Burns, Margaret, P. J. Drudy, Rory Hearne, and Peter McVerry. "Rebuilding Ireland: A Flawed Philosophy—Analysis of the Action Plan for Housing and Homelessness." *Working Notes* 80, no. 1 (2017) 3–20.

Byrne, Elaine A. *Political Corruption in Ireland 1922–2010: A Crooked Harp?* Manchester: Manchester University Press, 2012.

Byrne, Michael, and Michelle Norris. "Procyclical Social Housing and the Crisis of Irish Housing Policy: Marketization, Social Housing, and the Property Boom and Bust." *Housing Policy Debate* 27, no. 1 (March 2017) 1–14.

Carswell, Simon. *Anglo Republic: Inside the Bank That Broke Ireland*. Dublin: Penguin, 2011.

———. *Something Rotten: Irish Banking Scandals*. Dublin: Gill & Macmillan, 2006.

Casey, Ciarán Michael. "Averting Crisis? Commentary from the International Institutions on the Irish Property Sector in the Years Before the Crash." *The Economic and Social Review* 45, no. 4 (2014) 537–57.

Cavanaugh, William T. *Being Consumed*. Grand Rapids: Eerdmans, 2008.

———. *Field Hospital*. Grand Rapids: Eerdmans, 2016.

———. *Migrations of the Holy*. Grand Rapids: Eerdmans, 2011.

———. *The Myth of Religious Violence*. Oxford: Oxford University Press, 2009.

———. *Theopolitical Imagination*. London: T&T Clark, 2002.

———. *Torture and Eucharist*. Oxford: Blackwell, 1998.

Central Statistics Office. "The Average Industrial Wage and the Irish Economy 1938–2015." Dublin: CSO, 2015. Online: https://www.cso.ie/en/releasesandpublications/ep/p-hes/hes2015/aiw/.

de Certeau, Michel. *The Practice of Everyday Life*. Berkeley, CA: University of California Press, 1988.

Chazdon, Robin L., Pedro H. S. Brancalion, Lars Laestadius, Aoife Bennett-Curry, Kathleen Buckingham, Chetan Kumar, Julian Moll-Rocek, Ima Célia Guimarães Vieira, and Sarah Jane Wilson. "When Is a Forest a Forest? Forest Concepts and Definitions in the Era of Forest and Landscape Restoration." *Ambio* 45, no. 5 (September 2016) 538–50.

Chiappori, Pierre-André, and Steven D. Levitt. "An Examination of the Influence of Theory and Individual Theorists on Empirical Research in Microeconomics." *The American Economic Review* 93, no. 2 (2003) 151–55.

Clifford, Michael, and Shane Coleman. *Bertie Ahern and the Drumcondra Mafia*. Dublin: Hachette, 2010.

Clinch, Peter, Frank Convery, and Brendan Walsh. *After the Celtic Tiger*. Dublin: O'Brien, 2002.

Clough, David. "Karl Barth on Religious and Irreligious Idolatry." In *Idolatry: False Worship in the Bible, Early Judaism, and Christianity*, edited by Stephen C. Barton, 213–27. New York: T&T Clark, 2007.

Cloutier, David. *The Vice of Luxury*. Washington, DC: Georgetown University Press, 2015.

Cocksworth, Ashley. *Karl Barth on Prayer*. London: T&T Clark, 2015.

Coleman, Marc. "We Need These Expert Scaremongers." *The Sunday Independent*, September 23, 2007.

Congdon, David W. "Following the Deacon Jesus in the Prophetic Diaconate." In *Karl Barth in Conversation*, edited by W. Travis McMacken and David W. Congdon, 143–51. Eugene, OR: Pickwick, 2014.

Coogan, Philip. *Guide to Hedge Funds*. Hoboken, NJ: Wiley, 2010.

Cooper, Matt. *How Ireland Really Went Bust*. Dublin: Penguin, 2011.

———. *Who Really Runs Ireland*. Dublin: Penguin, 2010.

Corbet, Shaen, and Cian Twomey. "How Have Contracts for Difference Affected Irish Equity Market Volatility?" *The Economic and Social Review* 45, no. 4 (Winter 2014) 559–77.

Corrin, Jay P. "The Formation of the Distributist Circle." *The Chesterton Review* 1, no. 2 (1975) 52–83.

Costello, Francis J. "The Role of Propaganda in the Anglo-Irish War 1919–1921." *The Canadian Journal of Irish Studies* 14, no. 2 (1989) 5–24.

Cowan, David. *Economic Parables*. Milton Keynes: Paternoster, 2006.

Crossan, John Dominic. *Cliffs of Fall*. New York: Seabury, 1980.

Crouch, Colin. "From Markets versus States to Corporations versus Civil Society?" In *Politics in the Age of Austerity*, edited by Armin Schafer and Wolfgang Streeck, 219–38. Cambridge: Polity, 2013.

———. *The Strange Non-Death of Neoliberalism*. Cambridge: Polity, 2011.

Cudden, Jamie. "Dublin." In *Cities as Engines of Sustainable Competitiveness*, edited by Leo Van Den Berg, Jan Van Der Meer, and Luis Carvalho, 157–74. Farnham: Ashgate, 2014.

Cunningham, Darryl. *The Age of Selfishness*. New York: Abrams, 2015.

Daalen, David H. van. *The Kingdom of God Is Like This*. London: Epworth, 1976.

Daly, Gavin, and Ian Kehoe. *Citizen Quinn*. Dublin: Penguin, 2013.

Daly, Mary E. *Industrial Development and Irish National Identity 1922–1939*. Syracuse, NY: Syracuse University Press, 1992.

Davies, William. *The Limits of Neoliberalism*. London: Sage, 2017.

Dawn, Marva. *Reaching Out without Dumbing Down*. Grand Rapids: Eerdmans, 1995.

Department for Communities and Local Government. "Live Tables on House Building—Statistical Data Sets—GOV.UK." https://www.gov.uk/government/statistical-data-sets/live-tables-on-house-building.

Department of the Environment, Heritage and Local Government. "Annual Housing Statistics Bulletin 2008." http://www.environ.ie/en/Publications/StatisticsandRegularPublications/HousingStatistics/FileDownLoad,20957,en.pdf.

Dickens, Charles. *A Tale of Two Cities*. Delhi, IN: Global Media, 2006.

———. *The Christmas Books*. London: Penguin, 1994.

Dodd, Nigel. *The Social Life of Money*. Princeton, NJ: Princeton University Press, 2014.

Dominy, Peter. *Decoding Mammon*. Eugene, OR: Wipf and Stock, 2012.

Donovan, Donal, and Antoin E. Murphy. *The Fall of the Celtic Tiger: Ireland and the Euro Debt Crisis*. Oxford: Oxford University Press, 2013.

Downey, Dáithí D. "The Financialisation of Irish Homeownership and the Impact of the Global Financial Crisis." In *Neoliberal Urban Policy and the Transformation of the City*, edited by Andrew MacLaran and Sinéad Kelly, 120–38. Basingstoke: Palgrave Macmillan, 2014.

Drane, John. *The McDonaldization of the Church*. London: Darton, Longman and Todd, 2000.

Duhigg, Charles. *Smarter Faster Better: The Secrets of Being Productive in Life and Business*. London: Random House, 2016.

Duhigg, Charles, and Carter Dougherty. "From Midwest to M.T.A., Pain From Global Gamble." *The New York Times*, November 2, 2008.

Duménil, Gérard, and Dominique Lévy. *The Crisis of Neoliberalism*. Cambridge, MA: Harvard University Press, 2011.

Einstein, Mara. *Brands of Faith: Marketing Religion in a Commercial Age*. London: Routledge, 2008.

Eliot, T. S. *Collected Poems 1909–1962*. New York: Harcourt, Brace & World, 1963.

Ellul, Jacques. *Money and Power*. Eugene, OR: Wipf and Stock, 2009.

———. *The Ethics of Freedom*. London: Mowbrays, 1976.

Enright, Anne. *The Forgotten Waltz*. Toronto: McClelland & Stewart, 2011.

Espache, Antonio, and Danny Leipziger, eds. *Stuck in the Middle*. Washington DC: Brookings Institution, 2009.

Ewing, Jack. "Which Banks Hold Europe's Troubled Loans?" *The New York Times*, June 5, 2010.

Felton, Adam, Urban Nilsson, Johan Sonesson, Annika M. Felton, Jean-Michel Roberge, Thomas Ranius, Martin Ahlström, et al. "Replacing Monocultures with Mixed-Species Stands: Ecosystem Service Implications of Two Production Forest Alternatives in Sweden." *Ambio* 45, no. Suppl 2 (February 2016) 124–39.

Finn, Daniel. *The Moral Ecology of Markets*. Cambridge: Cambridge University Press, 2006.

Fisher, Mark. *Capitalist Realism*. Ropley: O Books, 2009.

Fleming, Peter. *The Mythology of Work*. London: Pluto, 2015.

Foucault, Michel. *The Birth of Biopolitics*. Edited by Michel Senellart. Basingstoke: Palgrave Macmillan, 2008.

Fourcade, Marion, and Kieran Healy. "Seeing like a Market." *Socio-Economic Review* 15, no. 1 (2017) 9–29.

Frank, Robert H. *The Economic Naturalist*. London: Virgin, 2008.

Friedman, Milton. "Neo-Liberalism and Its Prospects." *Farmand*, February 17, 1951.

Friedman, Thomas. *The World Is Flat*. New York: Farrar, Straus, and Giroux, 2006.

Fulcher, James. *Capitalism: A Very Short Introduction*. Oxford: Oxford University Press, 2009.

Furlong, Brendan. "No Catch as Fish given Away Free." *Irish Independent*. October 5, 2012.

Ganti, Tejaswini. "Neoliberalism." *Annual Review of Anthropology* 43, no. 1 (2014) 89–104.

Gardiner, Kevin. "The Irish Economy: A Celtic Tiger in Ireland, Challenging for Promotion." *Euroletter by Morgan Stanley*, August 31, 1994, 9–21.

Garfield, Simon. *Timekeepers: How the World Became Obsessed with Time*. Edinburgh: Canongate, 2016.

Garrigan, Siobhán. *Beyond Ritual*. Aldershot: Ashgate, 2004.

Garvin, Tom. *Preventing the Future*. Dublin: Gill & Macmillan, 2004.

Gerlach, Stefan. "Is Ireland Setting Itself up for a Crash with New Housing Bubble?" *Irish Examiner*, August 16, 2016.

Glaper, Jeffry. "The Speenhamland Scales: Political Social, or Economic Disaster?" *Social Service Review* 44, no. 1 (1970) 54–62.

Gleick, James. *Faster: Our Race Against Time*. London: Abacus, 2002.

Glyn, Andrew. *Capitalism Unleashed*. Oxford: Oxford University Press, 2006.

Gold, Lorna. *New Financial Horizons*. Hyde Park, NY: New City, 2010.

Goldblatt, David. *The Game of Our Lives*. London: Viking, 2014.

Goodchild, Philip. *Capitalism and Religion*. Abingdon: Routledge, 2002.

———. *Theology of Money*. London: SCM, 2007.

Gospel Music Association, and Christian Music Trade Association. "The Sound of Impact: Christian and Gospel Music 2014 Industry Overview." Nashville: Gospel Music Association 2014.

Gowler, David B. *The Parables after Jesus: Their Imaginative Receptions across Two Millennia*. Grand Rapids: Baker Academic, 2017.

Graeber, David. *Debt: The First 5,000 Years*. Brooklyn, NY: Melville House, 2011.

———. *Utopia of Rules*. Brooklyn, NY: Melville House, 2015.

Graetz, Michael J., and Rachael Doud. "Technological Innovation, International Competition, and the Challenges of International Income Taxation." *Columbia Law Review* 113, no. 2 (March 1, 2013) 347–445.

Grau, Marion. *Of Divine Economy*. New York: T&T Clark, 2004.

Greggs, Tom. *Theology Against Religion*. London: T&T Clark, 2011.

Gregory, Brad. *The Unintended Reformation*. Cambridge, MA: Belknap, 2012.

Gribbon, John. *The Time Illusion*. Seattle: Kindle Single, 2016.

Gruber, Diemut, and John Heinrich von Stein. "Privatisation in the German Banking Sector." In *Banking Privatisation in Europe*, edited by Roberto Ruozi and Luisa Anderloni, 269–94. Berlin: Springer, 1999.

Gustafson, Scott W. *At the Altar of Wall Street*. Grand Rapids: Eerdmans, 2015.

Haddorff, David. *Christian Ethics as Witness*. Cambridge: James Clarke, 2010.

Harford, Tim. *The Undercover Economist*. Oxford: Oxford University Press, 2006.

Harink, Douglas. *Paul Among the Postliberals*. Eugene, OR: Wipf and Stock, 2003.

Harker, Michael, and Catherine Waddams Price. "Introducing Competition and Deregulating the British Domestic Energy Markets: A Legal and Economic Discussion." Working Paper. Norwich: University of East Anglia, 2006.

Harries, Richard. *Is There a Gospel for the Rich?* London: Mowbray, 1992.

Harvey, David. *A Brief History of Neoliberalism*. Oxford: Oxford University Press, 2005.

Hauerwas, Stanley. *After Christendom*. Nashville, TN: Abingdon, 1999.

———. *The Hauerwas Reader*. Edited by John Berkman and Michael Cartwright. Durham, NC: Duke University Press, 2001.

———. *The State of the University*. Oxford: Blackwell, 2007.

———. *The Work of Theology*. Grand Rapids: Eerdmans, 2015.

———. *Wilderness Wanderings*. Boulder, CO: Westview, 1997.

———. *With the Grain of the Universe*. Grand Rapids: Brazos, 2001.

Haughton, Jonathan. "Historical Background." In *The Economy of Ireland*, edited by John O'Hagan and Carol Newman, 11th Edition, 2–28. Dublin: Gill & Macmillan, 2011.

Hayek, Friedrich. *The Road to Serfdom*. London: Routledge, 2001.

Heffernan, Emma, John McHale, and Niamh Moore-Cherry, eds. *Debating Austerity in Ireland: Crisis, Experience and Recovery*. Dublin: Royal Irish Academy, 2017.

Hertenstein, Mike, and Jon Trott. *Selling Satan*. Chicago: Cornerstone, 1993.

Herzog, William R., II. *Parables as Subversive Speech.* Louisville: Westminster John Knox, 1994.

Higgs, Kerryn. *Collision Course: Endless Growth on a Finite Planet.* Cambridge, MA: MIT Press, 2014.

Hinson-Hasty, Elizabeth L. *The Problem of Wealth.* Maryknoll, NY: Orbis, 2017.

Hodgson, Geoffrey M. "Conceptualizing Capitalism: A Summary." *Competition & Change* 20, no. 1 (February 1, 2016) 37–52.

———. *Conceptualizing Capitalism: Institutions, Evolution, Future.* Chicago: University of Chicago Press, 2015.

Holmes, Christopher R .J. "Karl Barth on the Economy: In Dialogue with Kathryn Tanner." In *Commanding Grace: Studies in Karl Barth's Ethics,* edited by Daniel L. Migliore, 198–215. Grand Rapids: Eerdmans, 2010.

Horsley, Richard A. *Jesus and Empire.* Minneapolis: Fortress, 2003.

Huckabee, Tyler. "Who Killed the Contemporary Christian Music Industry?" *The Week,* June 1, 2015. http://theweek.com/articles/555603/who-killed-contemporary-christian-music-industry.

Hughes, John. *The End of Work.* Oxford: Blackwell, 2007.

Hultgren, Arland J. *The Parables of Jesus: A Commentary.* Grand Rapids: Eerdmans, 2000.

Hunsinger, George. *Disruptive Grace.* Grand Rapids: Eerdmans, 2000.

Hunter, A. M. *Interpreting the Parables.* London: SCM, 1960.

Hunter, James Davison. *To Change the World.* Oxford: Oxford University Press, 2010.

Hutchinson, John. *Dynamics of Cultural Nationalism: The Gaelic Revival and the Creation of the Irish Nation State.* London: Taylor & Francis Routledge, 1987.

Hybels, Bill. *Courageous Leadership.* Grand Rapids: Zondervan, 2002.

Illich, Ivan, and David Cayley. *The Rivers North of the Future.* Toronto: Anansi, 2005.

Irish Prison Service. "Irish Prison Service Annual Report 2016." Longford: Irish Prison Service, 2016. Online: http://www.irishprisons.ie/wp-content/uploads/documents_pdf/12631-IPS-annualreport-2016_Web.pdf.

Jameson, Fredric. "Future City." *New Left Review* 21, no. 3 (2003) 65–79.

———. *Postmodernism, Or the Cultural Logic of Late Capitalism.* Durham, NC: Duke University Press, 1991.

Jennings, Willie James. "A Rich Disciple?" In *Reading the Gospels with Karl Barth,* edited by Daniel L. Migliore, 56–66. Grand Rapids: Eerdmans, 2017.

Jessop, Bob. "From Thatcherism to New Labour: Neo-Liberalism, Workfarism, and Labour Market Regulation." In *The Political Economy of European Employment: European Integration and the Transnationalization of the (Un)Employment Question,* edited by Henk Overbeek, RIPE Series in Global Political Economy, 137–153. London: Routledge, 2003.

———. "New Labour or the Normalization of Neo-Liberalism?" *British Politics* 2, no. 2 (July 2007) 282–88.

Johnson, Juliet. *Priests of Prosperity: How Central Bankers Transformed the Postcommunist World.* Ithaca, NY: Cornell University Press, 2016.

Johnson, Kelly S. *The Fear of Beggars.* Grand Rapids: Eerdmans, 2007.

Jones, C. I. "The Facts of Economic Growth." In *Handbook of Macroeconomics,* 2:3–69. Elsevier, 2016.

Jülicher, Adolf. *Die Gleichnisreden Jesu.* 2 vols. Darmstadt: Wissenschaftliche Buchgesellschaft, 1976.

Kafka, Franz. *The Complete Novels*. London: Vintage, 2008.

Keating, Paul, and Derry Desmond. *Culture and Capitalism in Contemporary Ireland*. Aldershot: Avebury, 1993.

Keen, Craig. *After Crucifixion*. Eugene, OR: Cascade, 2013.

Kelly, Simon. *Breakfast with Anglo*. Dublin: Penguin, 2010.

Kennedy, Anthony. *Citizens United v. Federal Election Commission*, No. 08–205 (US Supreme Court January 21, 2010).

Kerrigan, Gene. *The Big Lie*. London: Transworld Ireland, 2012.

Keynes, John Maynard. *The General Theory of Employment, Interest and Money*. New York: First Harvest, 1964.

Kilroy, Claire. *The Devil I Know*. London: Faber and Faber, 2012.

Kindleberger, Charles P., and Robert Z. Aliber. *Manias, Panics, and Crashes*. Hoboken, NJ: Wiley, 2005.

Kirby, Peadar. *Celtic Tiger in Collapse: Explaining the Weaknesses of the Irish Model*. Basingstoke: Palgrave Macmillan, 2010.

Kirkland, Mark. "Last Exit to Springfield." *The Simpsons*. Los Angeles: Fox, March 11, 1993.

Kitchin, Rob, Cian O'Callaghan, Mark Boyle, Justin Gleeson, and Karen Keaveney. "Placing Neoliberalism: The Rise and Fall of Ireland's Celtic Tiger." *Environment and Planning A* 6, no. 44 (2012) 1302–26.

Klein, Naomi. *No Logo*. New York: Picador, 2000.

Koenig, Harold G. *Spirituality in Patient Care: Why, How, When, and What*. Philadelphia: Templeton Foundation, 2002.

Kripal, Jeffrey J. *Esalen: America and the Religion of No Religion*. Chicago: University of Chicago Press, 2007.

Lambin, Jean Jacques. *Rethinking the Market Economy*. Basingstoke: Palgrave Macmillan, 2014.

Lazzarato, Maurizio. *Governing by Debt*. South Pasadena, CA: Semiotext(e) Intervention Series, 2013.

———. *The Making of the Indebted Man*. Translated by Joshua David Jordan. Amsterdam: Semiotext(e) Intervention Series, 2012.

Lear, Joseph M. *What Shall We Do?* Eugene, OR: Pickwick, 2018.

Leshem, Dotan. *The Origins of Neoliberalism*. New York: Columbia University Press, 2016.

Levitt, Steven D., and Stephen J. Dubner. *Freakonomics*. London: Harper Collins, 2009.

Lewis, Michael. *Boomerang*. London: Penguin, 2011.

Lewis-Anthony, Justin. *You Are the Messiah and I Should Know: Why Leadership Is a Myth (and Probably a Heresy)*. London: Bloomsbury, 2013.

Lischer, Richard. *Reading the Parables*. Louisville: Westminster John Knox, 2014.

Long, D. Stephen. *Divine Economy*. Abingdon: Routledge, 2000.

Long, Thomas G. *Beyond the Worship Wars*. Lanham, MD: Rowman & Littlefield, 2014.

Loomis, Stephen C. "The Double Irish Sandwich: Reforming Overseas Tax Havens Recent Development." *St. Mary's Law Journal* 43, no. 4 (2012) 825–54.

Lowe, Walter J. "Prospects for a Postmodern Christian Theology: Apocalyptic Without Reserve." *Modern Theology* 15, no. 1 (January 1, 1999) 17–24.

———. "Why We Need Apocalyptic." *Scottish Journal of Theology* 63, no. 01 (February 2010) 41–53.

Lowenhaupt-Tsing, Anna. *The Mushroom at the End of the World*. Princeton, NJ: Princeton University Press, 2015.

Ludlow, John. *John Ludlow: The Autobiography of a Christian Socialist*. Edited by A. D. Murray. London: Frank Cass, 1981.

Lupton, Deborah. *The Quantified Self*. Cambridge: Polity, 2016.

Lupton, Robert D. *Toxic Charity: How Churches and Charities Hurt Those They Help, And How to Reverse It*. New York: Harper One, 2012.

Luther, Martin. *Luther's Works: Word and Sacrament IV*. Vol. 38. Edited by Martin E. Lehmann. Philadelphia: Fortress, 1971.

———. "The Large Catechism." In *Triglot Concordia: The Symbolical Books of the Evangelical Lutheran Church*, 565–773. St. Louis: Concordia, 1921.

Lynch, David J. *When the Luck of the Irish Ran Out*. New York: Palgrave Macmillan, 2010.

Lyons, Tom, and Brian Carey. *The FitzPatrick Tapes*. Dublin: Penguin, 2011.

Mac Cormaic, Ruadhán. "Anglo Trial: Three Ex-Bankers Jailed over €7bn Fraud." *Irish Times*, July 29, 2016.

MacIntyre, Alasdair. *Ethics in the Conflicts of Modernity*. Cambridge: Cambridge University Press, 2016.

MacKinnon, Donald M. *The Problem of Metaphysics*. Cambridge: Cambridge University Press, 1974.

MacSharry, Ray, and Padraic White. *The Making of the Celtic Tiger*. Dublin: Mercier, 2000.

Mahoney, Kristin. "Work, Lack, and Longing: Rossetti's 'The Blessed Damozel' and the Working Men's College." *Victorian Studies* 52, no. 2 (Winter 2010) 219–48.

Marçal, Katrine. *Who Cooked Adam Smith's Dinner?* London: Portobello, 2015.

Martin, Patrick J. "Wealth." In *Eerdmans Dictionary of the Bible*, edited by David Noel Freedman, Allen C. Myers, and Astrid B. Beck, 1371. Grand Rapids: Eerdmans, 2000.

Marx, Karl. *Economic and Philosophic Manuscripts of 1844*. London: Lawrence & Wishart, 1970.

Mathews, Aidan. "Adam's Enlightenment." In *Strictly No Poetry*, 118–20. Dublin: Lilliput, 2018.

Mazzucato, Mariana. *The Entrepreneurial State*. London: Penguin, 2015.

———. *The Value of Everything*. London: Allen Lane, 2018.

McBride, William T. "Esther Passes: Chiasm, Lex Talio, and Money in the Book of Esther." In *Not in Heaven—Coherence and Complexity in Biblical Narrative*, edited by Jason P. Rosenblatt and Joseph C. Sitterson, Jr., 211–24. Bloomington, IN: Indiana University Press, 1991.

McCabe, Conor. *Sins of the Father: The Decisions That Shaped the Irish Economy*. 2nd ed. Dublin: The History Press Ireland, 2013.

McCreevy, Charlie. Central Bank Act 1971 (Approval of Scheme of Depfa Bank-Europe Plc and Depfa Bank Plc) Order 2002, 2002 S.I. No. 470 § (2002).

McDonagh, John Michael. *Calvary*. Drama. Fox Searchlight, 2014.

McDonald, Dearbhail. *Bust*. Dublin: Penguin, 2010.

McDonald, Frank, and Kathy Sheridan. *The Builders*. Dublin: Penguin, 2009.

McGoey, Linsey. *No Such Thing as a Free Gift*. London: Verso, 2015.

McKenna, John H. *The Eucharistic Epiclesis*. Chicago: Hillenbrand, 2009.

McLuhan, Marshall. *The Gutenberg Galaxy*. Toronto: The University of Toronto Press, 1962.

McMahon, Aine. "Skipper Defends Giving Away Free Fish." *Irish Times*, October 5, 2012.

McWilliams, David. *Follow The Money*. Dublin: Gill & Macmillan, 2009.

———. "Ireland's Great Wealth Divide." Dublin: Raidió Teilifís Éireann, September 21, 2015. http://www.rte.ie/tv/programmes/irelandsgreatwealthdivide.html.

Mentinis, Mihalis. *The Psyhcopolitics of Food: Culinary Rites of Passage in the Neoliberal Age*. Abingdon: Routledge, 2016.

Mercille, Julien. *The Political Economy and Media Coverage of the European Economic Crisis*. Abingdon: Routledge, 2015.

Mercille, Julien, and Enda Murphy. *Deepening Neoliberalism, Austerity, and Crisis: Europe's Treasure Ireland*. Basingstoke: Palgrave Macmillan, 2015.

Mian, Atif, and Amir Sufi. *House of Debt*. Chicago: University of Chicago Press, 2014.

Milanovic, Branko. *Global Inequality*. Cambridge, MA: Belknap, 2016.

Mirowski, Philip. *Never Let a Serious Crisis Go to Waste*. London: Verso, 2014.

———. "This Is Water (or Is It Neoliberalism?)." *Institute for New Economic Thinking: Neoliberalism Collection*, May 25, 2016. https://www.ineteconomics. org/perspectives/blog/this-is-water-or-is-it-neoliberalism.

Mirowski, Philip, and Dieter Plehwe, eds. *The Road from Mont Pèlerin: The Making of the Neoliberal Thought Collective*. Cambridge, MA: Harvard University Press, 2009.

Mitchell, William, and Thomas Fazi. "Everything You Know About Neoliberalism Is Wrong." *Social Europe*, October 20, 2017. https://www.socialeurope.eu/ everything-know-neoliberalism-wrong.

Moloney, Mark. "Fisherman Fight EU Dumping Disgrace." *An Phoblacht*, November 4, 2012.

Moore, Jason W. *Capitalism in the Web of Life*. London: Verso, 2015.

Moriarty, Michael. "Report of the Tribunal of Inquiry into Payments to Politicians and Related Matters, Volume II." Dublin: An Gúm, 2011.

Murphy, David, and Martina Devlin. *Banksters: How a Powerful Elite Squandered Ireland's Wealth*. Dublin: Hachette, 2009.

Nagel, Thomas. *The View from Nowhere*. New York: Oxford University Press, 1986.

Nelson, Robert H. *Economics as Religion*. University Park, PA: Pennsylvania State University Press, 2001.

Nesbitt, Louisa, and Ian Guider. "Dell Confirms Plans to Shed 1,900 Jobs in Limerick." *Irish Independent*, August 1, 2009.

Niebuhr, H. Richard. *Christ and Culture*. New York: Harper One, 2001.

Norman, Edward R. *The Victorian Christian Socialists*. Cambridge: Cambridge University Press, 1987.

O'Connor, Brendan. "The Smart, Ballsy Guys Are Buying up Property Right Now." *Sunday Independent*, July 29, 2007.

O'Connor, Flannery. *Wise Blood: A Novel*. New York: Farrar, Straus, and Giroux, 2001.

O'Connor, Nat, and Cormac Staunton. *Cherishing All Equally: Economic Inequality in Ireland*. Dublin: TASC, 2015.

Odih, Pamela. *Advertising and Cultural Politics in Global Times*. London: Routledge, 2016.

OECD. "General Government Spending (Indicator)." Paris: Organisation for Economic Co-operation and Development, 2018, doi: 10.1787/a31cbf4d-en.

———. "Gross Domestic Product (GDP) (Indicator)." Paris: Organisation for Economic Co-operation and Development, 2018, doi: 10.1787/dc2f7aec-en.

Ó'Gráda, Cormac. *A Rocky Road.* Manchester: Manchester University Press, 1997.

O'Hanlon, Gerry. *The Recession and God.* Dublin: Messenger, 2009.

O'Hearn, Denis. *Inside the Celtic Tiger.* London: Pluto, 1998.

O'Keefe, Cormac. "9,000 Jailed for Not Paying a Fine." *Irish Examiner*, February 14, 2015.

Ó'Riain, Seán. *The Rise and Fall of Ireland's Celtic Tiger.* Cambridge: Cambridge University Press, 2014.

Ormerod, Neil, Paul Oslington, and Robin Koning. "The Development of Catholic Social Teaching on Economics: Bernard Lonergan and Benedict XVI." *Theological Studies* 73, no. 2 (May 2012) 391–421.

Osteen, Joel. *Your Best Life Now.* New York: Time Warner, 2004.

O'Sullivan, Claire. "Nearly One in Five TDs Are Landlords, Registry Shows." *Irish Examiner*, May 17, 2016.

O'Toole, Fintan. *Enough Is Enough.* London: Faber and Faber, 2011.

———. *Ship of Fools.* London: Faber and Faber, 2009.

Ó'Túama, Pádraig. *Sorry for Your Troubles.* London: Canterbury, 2013.

Palley, Thomas I. *From Financial Crisis to Stagnation.* Cambridge: Cambridge University Press, 2012.

Pasquale, Frank. *The Black Box Society.* Cambridge, MA: Harvard University Press, 2015.

Paul, Mark. "UK Takes on Ireland with Lower Corporation Tax Regime." *The Irish Times*, May 5, 2014.

Payne, Christopher. *The Consumer, Credit and Neoliberalism: Governing the Modern Economy.* Abingdon: Routledge, 2012.

Pérez, Fernando, and Luigi Esposito. "The Global Addiction and Human Rights: Insatiable Consumerism, Neoliberalism, and Harm Reduction." *Perspectives on Global Development and Technology* 9, no. 1–2 (January 1, 2010) 84–100.

Piketty, Thomas. *Capital.* Cambridge, MA: Harvard University Press, 2014.

Pirie, Madsen. "The Neoliberal Mind." London: Adam Smith Institute, 2017.

Pohl, Christine D. *Making Room.* Grand Rapids: Eerdmans, 1999.

Polanyi, Karl. *The Great Transformation.* Boston: Beacon, 2001.

Pollock, Allyson M. *NHS Plc: The Privatisation of Our Health Care.* London: Verso, 2005.

Pope Francis. *Gaudete et Exsultate.* Vatican City: Vatican, 2018.

Prime Time, October 16th 2003. http://www.youtube.com/watch?v=6gWPmufcOTo&feature=youtube_gdata_player.

Quiggin, John. *Zombie Economics.* Princeton, NJ: Princeton University Press, 2010.

Rah, Soong-Chan. *Prophetic Lament.* Downers Grove, IL: InterVaristy, 2015.

Reilly, Gavan. "At Least 5,000 Attend Rally Supporting Quinn Family in Co Cavan." *TheJournal.ie*, October 14, 2012. http://www.thejournal.ie/ballyconnell-rally-quinn-family-635338-Oct2012/.

Republic of Ireland. *Bunreacht Na hÉireann.* Dublin: An Gúm, 2015.

Rigney, Peter. "The Impact of Anti-Crisis Measures and the Social and Employment Situation: Ireland." presented at the European Economic and Social Committee

Workers' Group, Brussels, February 28, 2012. http://www.ictu.ie/download/pdf/impact_of_austerity_on_ireland_eesc_paper.pdf.

Robbins, Lionel. *An Essay on the Nature and Significance of Economic Science*. London: Macmillan & Co., 1945.

Roberts, Alasdair. *The End of Protest*. Ithaca, NY: Cornell University Press, 2013.

Robertson, Korie, and Chrys Howard. *Faith Commander: Living Five Values from the Parables of Jesus*. Grand Rapids: Zondervan, 2014.

Robertson, Morgan. "Discovering Price in All the Wrong Places: The Work of Commodity Definition and Price under Neoliberal Environmental Policy." *Antipode* 39, no. 3 (June 1, 2007) 500–26.

Rodrik, Dani. "Rescuing Economics from Neoliberalism." *The Boston Review*, November 6, 2017. http://bostonreview.net/class-inequality/dani-rodrik-rescuing -economics-neoliberalism.

Ross, Shane. *The Bankers*. Dublin: Penguin, 2009.

Ruane, Frances, and Ali Ugur. "Trade and Foreign Direct Investment in Manufacturing and Services." In *The Economy of Ireland*, edited by John O'Hagan and Carol Newman, 9th Edition. Dublin: Gill & Macmillan, 2005.

Saigol, Lina, and Jamie Smyth. "The Men behind the Anglo Irish Scandal." *Financial Times*, June 25, 2013.

Sayers, Dorothy L. *Mind of the Maker*. London: Mowbray, 1994.

Scott, James C. *Seeing Like a State*. New Haven, CT: Yale University Press, 1998.

Selby, Peter. *Grace and Mortgage*. London: Darton, Longman and Todd, 1997.

Shaxson, Nicholas. *Treasure Islands*. Basingstoke: Palgrave Macmillan, 2011.

Shiva, Vandana. *Monocultures of the Mind*. London: Zed, 1997.

Slobodian, Quinn. *Globalists*. Cambridge: Harvard University Press, 2018.

Smith, Adam. *An Inquiry into the Nature and Causes of the Wealth of Nations*. Indianapolis: Liberty Classics, 1981.

Smith, Arthur A. "Neoliberal Institutionalism." In *The Oxford Handbook of International Relations*, edited by Christian Reus-Smit and Duncan Snidal, 201–21. Oxford: Oxford University Press, 2008.

Smith, James K. A. *Desiring the Kingdom*. Grand Rapids: Baker Academic, 2009.

Smythe, Shannon Nicole. *Forensic Apocalyptic Theology*. Minneapolis: Fortress, 2016.

Snodgrass, Klyne R. *Stories with Intent*. Grand Rapids: Eerdmans, 2008.

Spencer, Douglas. *The Architecture of Neoliberalism*. London: Bloomsbury Academic, 2016.

Srnicek, Nick, and Alex Williams. *Inventing the Future*. London: Verso, 2016.

St. Jerome. *St. Jerome's Commentary on Matthew*. Translated by Thomas P. Scheck. Vol. 117. The Fathers of the Church. Washington, DC: The Catholic University of America Press, 2008.

Staunton, Cormac. "The Distribution of Wealth in Ireland." Dublin: TASC, 2015.

Stiglitz, Joseph E. *The Price of Inequality*. New York: W. W. Norton & Company, 2013.

Streeck, Wolfgang. "The Politics of Public Debt: Neoliberalism, Capitalist Development and the Restructuring of the State." *German Economic Review* 15, no. 1 (February 1, 2014) 143–65.

Stringfellow, William. *Dissenter in a Great Society*. Eugene, OR: Wipf and Stock, 2005.

Sullivan, Teresa A., Elizabeth Warren, and Jay Lawrence Westbrook. *The Fragile Middle Class: Americans in Debt*. New Haven, CT: Yale University Press, 2000.

Surratt, Geoff, Greg Ligon, and Warren Bird. *A Multi-Site Church Roadtrip*. Grand Rapids: Zondervan, 2009.

Swinton, John. *Becoming Friends of Time*. Waco, TX: Baylor University Press, 2016.

Tanner, Kathryn. "Barth and the Economy of Grace." In *Commanding Grace: Studies in Karl Barth's Ethics*, edited by Daniel L. Migliore, 176–97. Grand Rapids: Eerdmans, 2010.

———. "Is Capitalism a Belief System?" *Anglican Theological Review* 92, no. 4 (2010) 617–35.

Taylor, Charles. *A Secular Age*. Cambridge, MA: Belknap, 2007.

———. *Modern Social Imaginaries*. Durham, NC: Duke University Press, 2004.

Ticciati, Susannah. *Job and the Disruption of Identity*. London: T&T Clark, 2005.

Tiemstra, John P. *Stories Economists Tell*. Eugene, OR: Pickwick, 2012.

Ulrich, Hans G. "The Messianic Contours of Evangelical Ethics." In *The Freedom of a Christian Ethicist*, edited by Michael Mawson and Brian Brock, 39–64. London: T&T Clark, 2016.

University of Aberdeen Directorate of Student Life. "Your Employability." *Aberdeen Graduate Attributes*, 2015. http://www.abdn.ac.uk/study/undergraduate/employability-1524.php.

Van Horn, Robert, and Philip Mirowski. "Neoliberalism and Chicago." In *The Elgar Companion to the Chicago School of Economics*, edited by Ross B. Emmet, 196–206. Cheltenham: Edward Elgar, 2010.

Vargas, Alicia. "Who Ministers to Whom: Matthew 25:31–46 and Prison Ministry." *Dialog: A Journal of Theology* 52, no. 2 (2013) 128–37.

Wagenfuhr, G. P. *Plundering Egypt*. Eugene, OR: Cascade, 2016.

Ward, Pete. *Selling Worship*. Milton Keynes: Paternoster, 2005.

Waters, Brent. *Just Capitalism*. Louisville: Westminster/John Knox, 2016.

Webster, John. *Barth*. London: Continuum, 2000.

———. *Barth's Moral Theology*. Edinburgh: T&T Clark, 1998.

Weiner, Eric J. *The Shadow Market*. New York: Scribner, 2010.

Wheeler, Sondra Ely. *Wealth as Peril and Obligation*. Grand Rapids: Eerdmans, 1995.

Wheeler, Tim, and Joachim von Braun. "Climate Change Impacts on Global Food Security." *Science* 341, no. 6145 (August 2, 2013) 508–13.

Whelan, Karl. "Ireland's Economic Crisis: The Good, the Bad and the Ugly." *UCD Centre for Economic Research Working Paper Series*, no. WP 13/06 (July 2013). http://www.ucd.ie/t4cms/WP13_06.pdf.

Whitaker, T. K. "From Protection to Free Trade—The Irish Experience." *Social Policy & Administration* 8, no. 2 (1974) 95–115.

White, Roger. "MacKinnon and the Parables." In *Christ, Ethics and Tragedy*, edited by Kenneth Surin, 49–70. Cambridge: Cambridge University Press, 1989.

Wilde, Oscar. *Lady Windermere's Fan*. London: Penguin, 1995.

Wilder, Amos N. *Jesus' Parables and the War of Myths*. Philadelphia: Fortress, 1983.

Woodard-Lehman, Derek Alan. "Reason After Revelation: Karl Barth on Divine Word and Human Words." *Modern Theology* 33, no. 1 (November 1, 2016) 1–24.

Wright, N.T. *Jesus and the Victory of God*. London: SPCK, 1996.

Wyman, Oliver. "10th Annual State of the Financial Services Industry 2007." New York: Mercer Oliver Wyman, 2007.

Yates-Doerr, Emily. *The Weight of Obesity*. Oakland, CA: University of California Press, 2015.

Young, Michael. *The Rise of the Meritocracy*. Harmondsworth: Penguin, 1961.

Ziegler, Philip G. *Militant Grace*. Grand Rapids: Baker Academic, 2018.

Index of Names

Index of Subjects

Index of Scriptural Passages